The Mystery of Reason

The Mystery of Reason

Paul Haffner

GRACEWING

First published in 2001
by

Gracewing
2 Southern Avenue,
Leominster
Herefordshire
HR6 0QF

© Paul Haffner 2001

ISBN 0 85244 538 5

Typeset by Action Publishing Technology Ltd,
Gloucester GL1 5SR

Printed in England by
MPG Books Ltd, Bodmin PL31 1EG

CONTENTS

PREFACE

This work is an attempt to describe the human approach to God through reason, and also how God communicates knowledge with us. It explores the relation between human reason and the various aspects of faith. The work involves a mixture of philosophical, theological and mystical reflections, and rather than being a systematic tract represents the personal approach of the author showing how human intelligence can connect with God and with other aspects of human religious experience. Here we propose to investigate the projection of faith upon the plane of reason, or in other words to examine the impact of the divine upon the human, of God upon the world of man and woman.

This book thus aspires to show how reason searches for God, namely how understanding seeks faith, to indicate how reason supports faith and how faith aids reason. It suggests how God seeks out the human mind, how faith seeks understanding, and also how true faith is reasonable. The work portrays how reason is open to faith, and how faith backs up and yet transcends reason. It proposes a pleasant harmony between faith and reason, not a dialectical opposition; nevertheless this is a harmony to be cultivated. The book also illustrates the relation between the mind and the heart in a search for God.

The starting point is analysis of the tools of reason, involving some of the basic definitions and acquisitions of philosophy, which will be part of the luggage taken on the excursion which this book proposes. Next, in chapter two, some of the basic encounters between faith and reason in the New Testament are explored. Afterwards, in chapter three, the development of reason in relation to Christian faith is explored in the Church Fathers. The fruition of reflection on the relations between faith and reason in the Middle Ages is portrayed in chapter four. How fragmentation in this relation came about in modern times is illustrated in chapter five. The particularly interesting challenge of scientific reason is presented in chapter six. In some senses, chapter seven is the centre of the book as it describes many ancient and modern rational demonstrations of the existence of God. Chapter eight seeks to draw some threads together and show how and why Christian faith is reasonable. Finally the last chapter indicates that love must enter into any discussion of the relations between faith and reason.

This book has been written primarily for philosophy and theology students, but not solely for this particular audience. It should be of service for anyone who is searching for rational illustrations of the existence of God, and also for those who are trying to bring Christian faith into closer contact with human experience. Thus I have relegated to the notes more difficult or intricate material, in the hope that the less academic reader may proceed without too many obstacles. I am grateful to many people for their help in the gestation of this volume. Discussions with students at various Roman universities sowed the seed for some of the ideas which it contains. Thanks are due to Rev. Dr. Michael Cullinan for his helpful comments and suggestions. I express my thanks to Thomas Longford the publisher who has helped bring the book to birth, and to Jo Ashworth. The book is dedicated to my mother.

Rome, 29th June 2001
Solemnity of the Apostles Peter and Paul

FOREWORD

by Fr Paul von Habsburg, LC

I warmly commend this book, *The Mystery of Reason*, as a very timely and much-needed publication, which responds well to the wishes of Pope John Paul II in his monumental encyclical *Fides et Ratio* on the mutual relations between faith and reason. In an increasingly complex and specialised world with all its strengths and weaknesses, more and more people are seeking answers to the most basic questions: What is the purpose of our lives? Who is behind the magnificent backdrop of the cosmos? Why does evil and suffering exist? Why believe in God? In short, men and women of today are seeking God through the world around them and especially through the people whom they meet. The first steps towards God are made easy upon the paths which the benevolent Creator Himself has imprinted upon this world.

Paul Haffner shows how Christians have always proposed that the human mind and heart are capable of finding God. The author illustrates how, despite the heady pride of Enlightenment thought and notwithstanding the despair of Kantian agnosticism, there were always truly realist thinkers who sought God in their philosophy. He demonstrates that the proofs of God's existence retain enduring validity, even more so than ever in this scientific and technological age.

This book clearly indicates that any intellectual enterprise is incomplete and impaired without an essential reference to God. At the same time, faith without reason can easily degenerate into fundamentalism or fanaticism. Finally, Christian faith not only needs the support of the mind but also of the heart. Paul Haffner makes this point most poignantly in his last chapter which is a fitting and beautiful conclusion to an incisive and penetrating study of the human quest for God. This work should be essential reading not only for students and academics, but also for all who desire to deepen their personal knowledge and love of God.

Father Paul von Habsburg, LC
Rome, 15th November 2001
Feast of St Albert the Great

ABBREVIATIONS

AAS =   *Acta Apostolicae Sedis. Commentarium officiale.*
Rome: Vatican Polyglot Press, 1909–?.

CCC =   *Cathechism of the Catholic Church*
Dublin: Veritas, 1994.

CCL =   *Corpus Christianorum series latina*
Tournai: Brepols, 1954-.

DP =   *Discourses of the Popes from Pius XI to John Paul II to the Pontifical Academy of Sciences. 1936–1986*
Vatican City: Pontifical Academy of Sciences, 1986.

DS =   H. Denzinger. *Enchiridion Symbolorum, Definitionum et Declarationum de rebus fidei et morum.* Bilingual edition edited by P. Hünermann.
Bologna: EDB, 1995.

IG =   *Insegnamenti di Giovanni Paolo II.*
Vatican City: Vatican Polyglot Press, 1978–?.

IP =   *Insegnamenti di Paolo VI*
Vatican City: Vatican Polyglot Press, 1963–1978.

ND =   J Neuner and J. Dupuis, *The Christian Faith in the Doctrinal Documents of the Catholic Church.* Sixth edition. New York: Alba House, 1996.

OR =   *L'Osservatore Romano,* daily Italian edition.

ORE =   *L'Osservatore Romano,* weekly English edition.

PG =   J.P. Migne. *Patrologiae cursus completus, series graeca.* 161 vols. Paris: 1857–1866.

PL =   J.P. Migne. *Patrologiae cursus completus, series latina.* 221 vols. Paris: 1844–1864.

The Scriptural quotations and abbreviations in this work are generally taken from the New Jerusalem Bible.

The Hebrew numbering of the psalms is employed.

CHAPTER 1

TOOLS OF REASON

To become a Catholic is not to leave off thinking, but to learn how to think.

G. K. Chesterton, *The Catholic Church and Conversion*

Although times change and knowledge increases, it is possible to discern a core of philosophical insight within the history of thought as a whole. Consider, for example, the principles of non-contradiction, finality and causality, as well as the concept of the person as a free and intelligent subject, with the capacity to know God, truth and goodness. Consider as well certain fundamental moral norms which are shared by all. These are among the indications that, beyond different schools of thought, there exists a body of knowledge which may be judged a kind of spiritual heritage of humanity. It is as if we had come upon an implicit philosophy, as a result of which all feel that they possess these principles, albeit in a general and unreflective way. Precisely because it is shared in some measure by all, this knowledge should serve as a kind of reference-point for the different philosophical schools. Once reason successfully intuits and formulates the first universal principles of being and correctly draws from them conclusions which are coherent both logically and ethically, then it may be called right reason or, as the ancients called it, orthós logos, recta ratio.

John Paul II, *Fides et Ratio* 4

The mystery of reason is at the heart of human culture and Christian life. Through reason man and woman reach out to know the world, and above all tend towards God. Through faith man and woman experience how God reaches towards them. Faith is therefore not irrational but above reason. God cannot be confined within the bounds of human reason, and yet, at the same time, He has chosen to reveal Himself in Christ, His Word, and using human categories which have a value for all time. The word mystery is employed here advisedly, because in the search for all knowledge, reason reveals and yet veils; understanding is therefore an ongoing process, leading to truth in all its variety and richness. Above all, the relationship of reason with faith is mysterious. This book explores the contribution of human reason to a search for God, from a Christian perspective. The position adopted here is that it is not possible, honest or desirable to suspend Christian faith in order to examine reason,[1] since faith transcends reason and makes a positive impact healing and perfecting it. First, it will be helpful to examine the background to some of the symbols, hieroglyphs and tools in this reasoning process.

Reason

The expression 'rational animal'[2] in classical thought was used to describe the human person as endowed with reason, which sets man apart, making him 'a little less than the angels' and superior to the animals. First of all it is important to understand what is meant by the expression *reason*, a term which is used in everyday life, in philosophy and in theology, but with varying shades of meaning. The word originates from the Latin noun *ratio*, and then through French forms comes into English. The Latin verb from which *ratio* derives is *reor*, which means 'I think', or I propose something (a *res*) to my mind, in a very concrete way.[3] *Ratio*, on the one hand denotes the mode or act of thinking and by extension describes the faculty of thinking, and on the other means the formal element of thought, such as a plan, or an account. This wide use of the word *reason* to indicate the cognitive faculty (especially when dealing with intrinsic evidence, as opposed to authority) is still the commonest. Already in Aristotle a clear distinction is encountered between intellect (*noûs*), as the intuitive faculty, and reason (*lógos*), as the discursive or inferential faculty. This distinction was maintained by the medieval Schoolmen. However, since Kant, the word *reason* has often been used as an umbrella to cover a vast and confusing array of ideas.[4] For Newman, reason is that faculty of the mind by means of which knowledge of things external to us, whether they are beings, facts, or events, is attained beyond the ambit of what we can acquire simply through the capacity of the senses. Reason 'ascertains for us not natural things only, or immaterial only, or present only, or past, or future.' Despite the fact that reason is limited in its power, it is unlimited in its range. 'It reaches to the ends of the universe, and to the throne of God beyond them; it brings us knowledge, whether clear or uncertain, still knowledge, in whatever degree of perfection, from every side; but, at the same time, with this characteristic, that it obtains it indirectly, not directly.'[5]

The reasoning process in the human person consists of many aspects: deduction and induction, intuition and searching for empirical evidence. Some thinkers, like St Augustine, saw a resemblance between the word in man and in the Blessed Trinity.[6] However, in this life our knowledge is composed of shreds and patches, laboriously woven from the threads of sense. It is only in heaven that God's existence will be completely self-evident and also as immediate as our present intuition of personal consciousness. Then we shall be on a level with the angels, who are simple intelligences and operate by pure intuition. Man is also rational in the sense that he is a being who arrives at conclusions from premises, through logical deduction. Our intellectual life is a process, a voyage of discovery; our knowledge is not a static ready-made whole; it is rather an organism filled with life and growth. In building the castle of knowledge, stone by stone, each new conclusion becomes the basis of further inference. In this enterprise, the expression 'reason' is applied to the building process as well as to the stones which make up the body of knowledge.

Reasoning cannot always be exactly formulated or crystallised into words. Language, after all, is the clothing of thought, which is convenient for logical analysis and for communicating with others. However do we not in ordinary life often express ourselves in pictures and reason in sounds? Does not our mind in its inferences leap far ahead of the sluggish machinery of language? And which of us has ever succeeded in fully analysing his most commonplace attitude or emotion? To explain much of human existence it is necessary to own a faculty in the reasoning process which is an intuitive controlling and directing principle in practical judgement whether we call it the illative sense, or the artistic reason, or implicit thought.[7] The main thing to observe is that it is not a special faculty. Rather, it is reason acting despite the inadequacies of language to encapsulate the concepts of thought.

Also to be considered is the relationship between the mind and the heart, between reasoning and willing. The medievals understood these faculties in unison. Only later did philosophers like Kant and Schleiermacher exaggerate the dualism between head and heart. It is true that reason works purposefully, that is, reason is selective of its subject-matter, but it is not creative or transforming. Nature is an ordered cosmos of which we form a part, so that every object in it has a 'practical' bearing on our lives, is connected with our rational, sensitive, or natural appetite. The known is never completely out of resonance with our volitions and emotions. To affirm anything, or to reason about a subject, is straight away to take up a position about it. This is especially true of moral and religious issues, and the emotional genesis of ethical convictions has often been urged as a proof of their irrationality.

However, it should not forgotten that the liability to be influenced by emotional causes is not confined to ethical or religious reasoning. When I draw a conclusion, I do not necessarily mean that I prefer it or am affected by it. As St Thomas urged against the pseudo-mystics and voluntarists of all ages, volition is possible only in so far as it includes cognition; and, one may add, emotion is a mode of experience only inasmuch as it presupposes knowledge.[8]

Knowledge

Reason then leads to knowledge, of which some characteristics are now considered. It will be useful first to consider briefly the current uses of the verb 'to know'. To say that I know a certain person may mean simply that I have met him or her, and recognise them when I meet them again. This implies the permanence of a mental image enabling me to discern this person from all others. Sometimes, also, more than the mere familiarity with external features is implied. To know a person may mean to know their character, their inner and deeper qualities, and hence to expect them to act in a certain way under certain circumstances. The man who asserts that he knows an occurrence to be a fact means that he is so certain of it as to have no doubt concerning its reality. A student knows his material when he has mastered it and is able to answer questions about it, and this requires either mere retention in memory, or also, in addition to this retention, the intellectual work of understanding. A science is known when its principles, methods, and conclusions are understood, and the various facts and laws referring to it co-ordinated and explained. These various meanings may be reduced to two classes, one referring chiefly to sense-knowledge and to the recognition of particular experiences, the other referring chiefly to the understanding of general laws and principles. The former class deals more with the concrete, the latter with the abstract. This distinction is expressed in many languages by the use of two different verbs: by *gnônai* and *eidénai*, in Greek; by *cognoscere* and *scire*, in Latin, by *connaître* and *savoir* in French and other parallels in other Latin languages; in German by *kennen* and *wissen*.

Knowledge is essentially the awareness of an object, namely of any thing, fact, or principle belonging to the physical, mental, or metaphysical order, that may in any manner be reached by the faculties of reason. An event, a material substance, a man, a mathematical theorem, a mental process, the immortality of the soul, the existence and nature of God, may thus be objects of knowledge. Knowledge involves the relation between a knowing subject and a known object. It always possesses an objective character and any process that may be conceived as merely subjective is not a cognitive process. Any attempt to reduce the object to a purely subjective experience could result only in destroying the fact itself of knowledge, which implies the object, or not-self, as clearly as it does the subject, or self.

Knowledge supposes a judgement, explicit or implicit. Apprehension, that is the mental conception of a simple present object, is generally numbered among the cognitive processes, yet, of itself, it is not in the strict sense knowledge, but only its starting-point. Properly speaking, we know only when we compare, identify, discriminate, connect; and these processes, equivalent to judgements, are found implicitly even in ordinary sense-perception. A few judgements are reached immediately, but by far the greater number require patient investigation. The mind is not merely passive in knowing, not a mirror or photographic plate, in which objects picture themselves; it is also active in looking for conditions and causes, and in building up science out of the materials which it receives from experience. Thus observation and thought are two essential factors in knowledge.

Truth and certitude are conditions of knowledge. A

person may mistake error for truth and give his unreserved assent to a false statement. He may then be under the irresistible illusion that he knows, and subjectively the process is the same as that of knowledge; but an essential condition is lacking, namely, conformity of thought with reality, so here lies only the appearance of knowledge. On the other hand, as long as any serious doubt remains in his mind, a man cannot say that he knows. 'I think so' is far from meaning 'I know it is so'; knowledge is not mere opinion or probable assent. The distinction between knowledge and belief is more difficult to draw, owing chiefly to the vague meaning of the latter term. Sometimes belief refers to assent without certitude, and denotes the attitude of the mind especially in regard to matters that are not governed by strict and uniform laws like those of the physical world, but depend on many complex factors and circumstances, as happens in human affairs. I know that water will freeze when it reaches a certain temperature; I believe that a man is fit to assume a given office, or that the programme endorsed by one political party will be more beneficial than that advocated by another. Sometimes, also, both belief and knowledge imply certitude, and denote states of mental assurance of the truth. However, in belief the evidence is more obscure and indistinct than in knowledge, either because the grounds on which the assent rests are not so clear, or because the evidence is not personal, but based on the testimony of witnesses, or again because, in addition to the objective evidence which draws the assent, there are subjective conditions that predispose to it. Belief seems to depend on a great many influences, emotions, interests, surroundings, besides the convincing reasons for which assent is given to truth. Faith is based on the testimony of someone else, God or man according as one speaks of Divine or of human faith. If the authority on which it rests has all the required guarantees, faith gives the certitude of the fact, the knowledge that it is true; but, of itself, it does not give the intrinsic evidence why it is so.

It is impossible that all the knowledge a man has acquired should be simultaneously present in consciousness. The greater part, with the exception of the few thoughts actually present in the mind, is stored up in the form of latent dispositions which enable the mind to access it when wanted. Hence we may distinguish actual from habitual knowledge. The latter extends to whatever is preserved in memory and is capable of being recalled at will. This capacity of being recalled may require several experiences; a science is not always known after it has been mastered once, for even then it may be forgotten. By habitual knowledge is meant knowledge in readiness to come back to consciousness, and it is clear that it may have different degrees of perfection.

According to the process by which it is acquired, knowledge is intuitive and immediate or discursive and mediate. The former comes from the direct sense perception, or the direct mental intuition of the truth of a proposition, based on its own merits. The latter consists in the recognition of the truth of a proposition by seeing its synthetic connection with another already known to be true. The self-evident proposition is of such a nature as to be immediately clear to the mind. No one who understands the terms can fail to know that two and two are four, or that the whole is greater than any one of its parts. However, most human knowledge is acquired progressively. Inductive knowledge starts from self-evident facts, and rises to laws and causes. Deductive knowledge proceeds from general self-evident propositions in order to discover their particular application. In both cases the process may be long, difficult, and intricate. One may have to be satisfied with negative conception and analogical evidence, and, as a result, knowledge will be less clear, less certain, and more liable to error.

In various sciences, a different viewpoint is taken as regards knowledge. Philosophical psychology considers knowledge as a mental fact whose elements, conditions, laws, and growth are to be determined. It endeavours to discover the behaviour of the mind in knowing, and the development of the cognitive process out of its elements. It supplies the other sciences with the data on which they must work. Among these data are found certain laws of thought which the mind must observe in order to avoid contradiction and to reach consistent knowledge. Formal logic also takes the subjective point of view; it deals with these laws of thought, and neglecting the objective side of knowledge (that is, its materials), studies only the formal elements necessary to consistency and valid proof. At the other extreme, science, physical or metaphysical, postulating the validity of knowledge, or at least leaving this problem out of consideration, studies only the different objects of knowledge, their nature and properties. As to the crucial questions, the validity of knowledge, its limitations, and the relations between the knowing subject and the known object, these belong to the province of epistemology.

Knowledge is essentially objective. Such names as the 'given' or the 'content' of knowledge may be substituted for that of 'object', but the plain fact remains that we know something external, which is not formed by, but offered to, the mind. This must not, however, cause us to overlook another fact equally evident. Different minds will frequently take different views of the same object. Moreover, even in the same mind, knowledge undergoes great changes in the course of time; judgements are constantly modified, enlarged or narrowed down, in accordance with newly discovered facts and ascertained truths. Sense-perception is influenced among other things by past processes, associations and contrasts. In rational knowledge a great diversity of assents is produced by different personal dispositions, innate or acquired. In a word, knowledge clearly depends on the mind as St Thomas pointed out: 'Cognition is brought about by the presence of the known object in the knowing mind. But the object is in the knower after the fashion of the knower. Hence, for any knower, knowledge is after the fashion of his own nature.'[9] Knowledge is necessarily proportioned or relative to the capacity of the mind and the manifestations of the object. Not all people have the same acuteness of vision or hearing, or the same intellectual abilities. Nor is the same reality equally bright from all angles from which it may be viewed. Moreover, superhuman eyes might perceive rays beyond the red and the violet of the spectrum; higher intellects might unravel many mysteries of nature, know more and better, with greater facility, certainty, and clarity. This presence of the object in the subject is not a physical presence; not even in the form of a picture, a duplicate, or a copy. It cannot be defined by any comparison with the physical world, but it is in a class of its own and may be termed a cognitive likeness.

When knowledge, either of concrete realities or of abstract propositions, is said to consist in the presence of an object in the mind, this object is not isolated from the mind, for we cannot think outside our own thought, and the mind cannot know what is not somehow present within it. However, knowledge is not purely subjective, as in the idealist perspective. If the object of an assent or experience cannot be absolute reality, it does not follow that to an assent or experience there is no corresponding reality; and the fact that an object is reached through the conception of it does not justify the conclusion that the mental conception is the whole of the object's reality. To say that knowledge is a conscious process is true, but it is only a part of the truth. The subjectivist has his eyes wide open to the difficulty of explaining the transition from external reality to the mind, a difficulty which, after all, is but the mystery of consciousness itself. He keeps them obstinately closed to the utter impossibility of explaining the building up by the mind of an external reality out of mere conscious processes. Human experience shows that in the knowing process the mind is not merely active, but also passive; that it must conform, not simply to its own laws, but to external reality as well; that it does not create facts and laws, but discovers them; and that the right of truth to recognition persists even when it is actually ignored or violated. The mind, it is true, contributes its share to the knowing process, but, as St Augustine remarked, the generation of knowledge requires another cause: 'Whatever object we know is a co-factor in the generation of the knowledge of it. For knowledge is begotten both by the knowing subject and the known object.'[10]

All knowledge begins with concrete experience, but requires other factors, not given in experience, in order to reach its perfection. It needs reason interpreting the data of observation, abstracting the contents of experience from the conditions which locate them in space and time, removing, as it were, the outer envelope of the concrete, and going to the core of reality. Thus knowledge is not, as in the Kantian perspective, a fusion of two elements, one external, the other depending only on the nature of the mind; not the filling up of empty shells, *a priori* mental forms or categories, with the unknown and unknowable reality. Even abstract knowledge reveals reality, although its object cannot exist outside the mind, without conditions of which the mind in the act of knowing divests it.

The fact that we do not know everything, and that all our knowledge is incomplete, does not invalidate the knowledge which we possess, any more than the horizon which bounds our view prevents us from perceiving more or less distinctly the various objects within its limits. Reality manifests itself to the mind in different ways and with varying degrees of clarity. Some objects are bright in themselves and are perceived immediately. Others are known indirectly by throwing on them light borrowed from elsewhere, indicating by way of causality, similarity, and analogy their connection with what we already know. Scientific progress essentially consists in finding connections between various objects, to proceed from the known to the unknown. As we recede from the self-evident, the path may become more difficult, and the progress slower. However, it is unjustifiable to follow the agnostic road and assign closed boundaries to our cognitive powers, for it is possible to pass gradually from one object to another without discontinuity, and there is a relation between science and metaphysics. The same instruments, principles, and methods that are recognised in the various sciences will carry us higher and higher, even to the Absolute, the First Cause, the Source of all reality. Induction will lead us from the effect to the cause, from the imperfect to the perfect, from the contingent to the necessary, from the dependent to the self-existent, from the finite to the infinite.[11] This same process by which we know God's existence cannot fail to manifest something, even if little, of His nature and perfections. That we know Him imperfectly, by way chiefly of negation and analogy, does not deprive this knowledge of all value. We can know God only so far as He manifests Himself through His works which dimly mirror His perfections, and so far as our finite mind will allow. This knowledge will necessarily remain infinitely far from being comprehension, but it is misleading to identify the unknowable with the incomprehensible. Seeing 'through a glass' and 'in a dark manner' is far from the vision 'face to face' of which our limited mind is incapable without a special light from God Himself. Nevertheless, it is knowledge of Him who is the source both of the world's intelligibility and truth, and of the mind's intelligence.

The Realist Perspective

Realism[12] is the metaphysical bridge which guarantees the true relation between the mind and reality and is thus the right approach to link reason with Christian belief in God. To highlight what is meant by realism, it is helpful to contrast it with nominalism, positivism, pragmatism, idealism and nihilism. Realism affirms the existence of universals against nominalism. Against positivism, realism proposes that reality extends beyond that which the natural sciences can measure. It affirms the validity of objective truth in its own right against a merely pragmatist or utilitarian view. Realism affirms against idealism that the external world is not simply the projection of the mind. Against nihilism, realism affirms that the world makes sense and has meaning.

The difference from *nominalism* is seen in a controversy which centred around the status of universals. Plato's solution of the question of universals resulted in absolute realism, in which there were two levels of reality: the first, that of absolutely real being that corresponds to the judgement of identity and the second, in which reality shares in the being of forms corresponding to the judgement of participation. In Plato's absolute realism, the universal concept in all its universality is being and the rôle of the mind is solely to discern this being.

In the early Middle Ages, there featured an exaggerated realism or ultra-realism. In this approach, 'our generic and specific concepts correspond to a reality existing extramentally in objects, a subsistent reality in which individuals share.'[13] In his debate with the ultra-realist William of Champeaux, Peter Abelard distinguished between the logical and real orders without any denial of the objective foundation of the universal concept. Abelard was part of the movement which led to Thomistic moderate realism, where the objectivity of real species and natures was held. Scotus went further along the realist road, since for him 'the universals were real entities apart from their existence in individuals,' while for St Thomas 'the universals are virtually present in individuals, from which they are abstracted by our intellect.'[14]

However, in the fourteenth century a different solution to the problem of universals was given by William of Ockham (1280–1349), and this solution was not in the direction of realism. For Ockham and the nominalists, there are no universal realities outside the mind. Man only encounters individually existing entities without being able to arrive at a unity of meaning for a group of individually existing entities which have something in common.

The universal was reduced to a word (whether mental, spoken or written) which is itself an individual entity.

Auguste Comte (1798–1857), the founder of *positivism*, formulated the 'positive philosophy,' which in conjunction with the positive sciences would give the complete answer to all the questions concerning man and the cosmos. For Comte, knowledge is obtained solely from sense experience through the scientific method. Now the objects of science are empirical facts and a system of relationships between these facts. Since, for Comte, the laws express only extrinsic relationships, they do not provide explanations for phenomena in terms of intrinsic principles. John Stuart Mill (1806–1873) carried further the positivism of Comte. His theory of knowledge was phenomenalism, in which only sense data was admissible and reality was not something independent of the mind, but a complex of actual and possible sensations. As well as the phenomenalist variant of positivism, there is also the physicalist approach (espoused by Reichenbach, by Neurath and the early Carnap), in which conceptual statements had to be translated into statements about external or experimental events. For Bridgman, all concepts must be related to performable experimental operations; thus the meaning of a concept is seen in terms of the corresponding set of operations. This approach is operationalism (or operationism), somewhat analogous to instrumentalism.

The philosophical heir to positivism and neo-positivism is scientism which 'refuses to admit the validity of forms of knowledge other than those of the positive sciences.' Scientism

> relegates religious, theological, ethical and aesthetic knowledge to the realm of mere fantasy .... Science would thus be poised to dominate all aspects of human life through technological progress. The undeniable triumphs of scientific research and contemporary technology have helped to propagate a scientistic outlook, which now seems boundless, given its inroads into different cultures

and the radical changes it has brought. And since it leaves no space for the critique offered by ethical judgement, the scientistic mentality has succeeded in leading many to think that if something is technically possible it is therefore morally admissible.[15]

Realism is also to be contrasted with *instrumentalism*, a pragmatist view of knowing. This is related to linguistic analysis, which in turn was a development of logical positivism. In logical positivism, the only meaningful statements were considered to be either empirical propositions which could be verified by sense experience or formal definitions, tautologies and linguistic conventions. In linguistic analysis, on the other hand, it was the use rather than the meaning of language which was the central focus. While logical positivists regard sentences as having only one rôle, that of reporting empirical facts, the linguistic analysts acknowledge the variety of functions served by language. When linguistic analysis is applied to the language of science it usually encourages an instrumentalist view of science, very often to be found among philosophers of science today. For the instrumentalist, scientific laws are aids to the investigator, scientific theories are judged according to their usefulness rather than according to their truth, and scientific concepts are related in a functional way to observations, but the concepts themselves do not need to be reducible to observations. Instrumentalists ascribe more to the rôle of the knower than do positivists. The former create conceptual schemes and models, albeit for pragmatic reasons; the latter merely record and organise data. 'In contrast to positivists, instrumentalists do not require that concepts should correspond to observables, and they make no effort to eliminate theoretical terms; in contrast to realists, however, they do *not* insist that there are *real entities* corresponding to concepts. Laws are invented, not discovered.'[16] Yet instrumentalists do not hold, with the idealists, that concepts originate from the mind imposing its own structure on experience.

Next, epistemological realism is to be contrasted with *idealism*. The realist sees the ultimate factor in being as existing beyond or outside the mind, whereas the idealist maintains that the ultimate principle and the philosophical point of departure is the mind. The idealist sees the structures of theory as entirely imposed by the mind on the chaos of sense data. Therefore idealism puts even more stress than does instrumentalism on the rôle of the knower. All the various forms of idealism are opposed to realism inasmuch as they assert that reality proceeds from intelligence or from spirit and is ultimately just another dimension of mind.

We have seen a gradation in the foregoing positions in the contribution to knowledge of the subject and the object, of the knower and the reality known. The realist asserts against the nominalist that a universal concept can be arrived at; against the positivist he asserts that the real cannot be reduced to the observable. The realist opposes the instrumentalist by affirming that valid concepts are true as well as useful. Against the idealist, the realist maintains a correpondence between concepts and the structure of events in the cosmos. For the realist, the object, not the subject, makes the main contribution to knowledge, or put in another way, being is prior to knowing.

Realism, however, comes in many shapes and forms, which can be conveniently grouped into scholastic and non-scholastic varieties. As to the non-scholastic forms of realism, most reflect the influence of Kant, such as the philosophies of H. Bergson, W. James and G. Santayana. Certain tendencies in the phenomenology of F. Brentano, E. Husserl and M. Scheler can be said to be realist, but it is a realism of essence that prescinds from a realism of existence. According to the scholastic viewpoint, the realist philosophies of G. E. Moore, B. Russell, A. N. Whitehead, S. Alexander and N. Hartmann also make too great a separation between essence and existence. Among scholastic versions of realism, the line of St Thomas expounded in the last century by J. Maritain and E. Gilson differs from

the various schools of transcendental Thomism, as exemplified in the writings of J. Maréchal, B. Lonergan and K.
Rahner.[17] The aim of transcendental Thomism has been to
attempt to graft together the philosophy of St Thomas
with the thought of Kant and other idealists as well as
with existentialist thought like that of M. Heidegger. Here
'transcendental' means 'knowledge that does not derive
from experience but is given a priori by the human
subject.'[18]

Realism must also be seen in contrast to *nihilism*. Certain
extreme forms deny any sense or meaning to the cosmos,
such as found in the views of F. Nietzsche. Existentialism
as exemplified by the writings of J. P. Sartre, M Heidegger
and R. Bultmann tends to deny the essences of things, and
undermines the continuity in space, time and reality and
so paves the way for a rejection of the sense of purpose in
life. Darwinists and neo-Darwinists who base their vision
of the evolution of life on chance often display a nihilist
tendency. Nihilism is a

> philosophy of nothingness .... Its adherents claim that the
> search is an end in itself, without any hope or possibility of
> ever attaining the goal of truth. In the nihilist interpreta-
> tion, life is no more than an occasion for sensations and
> experiences in which the ephemeral has pride of place.
> Nihilism is at the root of the widespread mentality which
> claims that a definitive commitment should no longer be
> made, because everything is fleeting and provisional ....
> Indeed, still more dramatically, in this maelstrom of data
> and facts in which we live and which seem to comprise the
> very fabric of life, many people wonder whether it still
> makes sense to ask about meaning. The array of theories
> which vie to give an answer, and the different ways of
> viewing and of interpreting the world and human life,
> serve only to aggravate this radical doubt, which can easily
> lead to scepticism, indifference or to various forms of
> nihilism .... According to some of them, the time of
> certainties is irrevocably past, and the human being must
> now learn to live in a horizon of total absence of meaning,

where everything is provisional and ephemeral. In their destructive critique of every certitude, several authors have failed to make crucial distinctions and have called into question the certitudes of faith.[19]

For some thinkers, nihilism has been justified by 'the terrible experience of evil which has marked our age. Such a dramatic experience has ensured the collapse of rationalist optimism, which viewed history as the triumphant progress of reason, the source of all happiness and freedom; and now ... one of our greatest threats is the temptation to despair.'[20] Nihilism often involves a denial of the principles of causality and of finality as well as the analogy of being.

Realist logic also implies the acceptance of certain basic principles, for all reality and thought is based on them and cannot contradict them. First, the Principle of Identity states that A is A. It simply affirms that a thing is what it is, is one with itself. A dog is a dog. A man is a man. Every act of every man accords with this principle. It is self-evident. Second, the Principle of Non-Contradiction states that A is not non-A. This principle denies that a thing is its own opposite. A dog is not a non-dog. This means that while a dog is a dog it cannot be anything else. By having the nature of dog it excludes everything else, namely what is non-dog. To assert that a thing is both what it is and not what it is clearly absurd. Non-contradiction is the essential precondition for a thing to exist or to be conceivable. Third, the Principle of the Excluded Middle proposes that between A and non-A there is no middle term. This principle states that there is no middle ground between something and its contradictory opposite. It has many applications. For example, a thing is either a tree or it is not. If it is not a tree then it is something else. But there is no middle term between be and be-not, between yes and no. If we cancel out tree and non-tree, which, in contradictory opposition, is everything other than tree, there is nothing left. Similarly, in biology we see that a thing is either living or non-living. There is nothing in between. A living thing is either a knower or a non-knower. This is the dividing line between plants which have no knowledge and things higher than plants. If a thing appears at first to be a plant but exhibits definite signs of sense knowledge it is an animal. There is no third thing between plant and animal because there is no middle ground between knower and non-knower, between being and non-being. This principle can be applied also to the distinction between rational animal (man) and irrational animal, and between Creator and creature.

Analogy

Realist philosophy opens the door to analogy and also guarantees it. Analogy indicates first, a property of beings and second, a process of reasoning. As a property, analogy denotes a certain similarity mixed with difference. This similarity may be founded entirely or chiefly upon a conception of the mind; in this sense we say that there is analogy between the light of the sun and the light of the mind, between a lion and a courageous man, between an organism and society. This kind of analogy is the source of metaphor. The similarity may be founded on the real existence of similar properties in objects of different species, genera, or classes; those organs, for instance, are analogous, which, belonging to beings of different species or genera, and differing in structure, fulfil the same physiological functions or have the same connections. As a process of reasoning, analogy consists in concluding from some similarity under certain aspects to another similarity under other aspects. Analogical reasoning is a combination of inductive and deductive reasoning. Based on a mere conception of the mind, it may suggest, but it does not prove; it cannot give conclusions, but only comparisons. Based on real properties, it is more or less conclusive according to the number and significance of the similar properties and according to the paucity and insignificance of the dissimilar properties. From a strictly logical point of view, analogical reasoning can furnish only probable conclusions and hypotheses. Such is the case for most of the theories in physical and natural sciences, which remain hypothetical so long as they are merely the result of analogy and have not been verified directly or indirectly.

Analogy in Scholastic philosophy was considered in depth by Pseudo-Dionysius, St Albert the Great, and St Thomas Aquinas. As a metaphysical property, analogy is not a mere likeness between diverse objects, but a proportion or relation of object to object. It is, therefore, neither a merely equivocal or verbal coincidence, nor a fully univocal participation in a common concept; but it partakes of the one and the other.[21] Two kinds of analogy may be distinguished. First, two objects can be said to be analogous on account of a relation which they have not to each other, but to a third object. For example, there is analogy between a climate and the appearance of a person, in virtue of which these two objects are said to be healthy. This is based upon the relation which each of them has to the person's health, the former as a cause, the latter as a sign. This may be called indirect analogy. Second, two objects again are analogous on account of a relation which they have not to a third object, but to each other. Climate, nourishment, and external appearance are termed healthy on account of the direct relation they bear to the health of the person. Here health is the basis of the analogy. This second sort of analogy is twofold. Two things are related by a direct proportion of degree, distance, or measure: e.g., 6 is in direct proportion to 3, of which it is the double; or the healthiness of a remedy is directly related to, and directly measured by, the health which it produces. This analogy is called *analogy of proportion*. Or, the two objects are related one to the other not by a direct proportion, but by means of another and intermediary relation. The analogy between corporal and intellectual vision is of this sort, because intelligence is to the mind what the eye is to the body. This kind of analogy is based on the proportion of proportion; it is called *analogy of proportionality*.[22]

As human knowledge proceeds from the data of the senses directed and interpreted by reason, it is evident that man cannot arrive at a perfect knowledge of the nature of God which is essentially spiritual and infinite. Yet the various elements of perfection, dependence, and limitation, which exist in all finite beings, while they enable us to prove the existence of God, furnish us also with a certain knowledge of His nature. Dependent beings must ultimately rest on something non-dependent, relative beings on that which is non-relative, and, even if this non-dependent and non-relative Being cannot be conceived directly in itself, it is necessarily conceived to some extent through the beings which depend on it and are related to it. Our knowledge of God in this world comes in three ways, affirmation, negation and eminence. First, the way of affirmation or causality takes as its starting point that God is the efficient cause of all things, and that the efficient cause contains in itself every perfection which lies in the effect. God must therefore possess every true perfection of His creatures. Finite beings are produced according to a certain plan and in view of a certain end. Thus they have a cause which possesses in itself a power of efficiency, exemplarity, and finality, with all the elements which such a power requires like intelligence, will and personality. In this approach the perfection of the finite is affirmed of God as its cause. This process of reasoning is known as the positive way.[23] On the other hand, the process of reasoning from the effects to the First Cause involve eliminating all the defects, imperfections, and limitations which are in the effects just because they are effects, such as change, limitation, time, and space. This way denies to God every imperfection which is found in creatures and is called the negative way.[24] While the positive way underscores the immanence of God within His creation, the negative way indicates His complete transcendence over His creation.[25] These two processes lead to the idea that the perfections thus affirmed of God, as First and Perfect Cause, cannot be attributed to Him in the same sense that they have in finite beings, but only in an absolutely excellent or supereminent way.[26] We can thus conceive and name God in an 'analogical way'. The perfections manifested by creatures are in God, not merely nominally (*equivoce*) but really and positively, since He is their source. Yet, they are not in Him as they are in the creature, with a mere difference of degree, nor even with a mere specific or generic difference (*univoce*), for there is no common concept including the finite and the Infinite. They are really in Him in a supereminent manner (*eminenter*) which is wholly incommensurable with their mode of being in creatures.[27] We can conceive and express these perfections only by an analogy; not by an analogy of proportion, for this analogy rests on a participation in a common concept, and, as already said, there is no element common to the finite and the Infinite; but by an analogy of proportionality. These perfections are really in God, and they are in Him in the same relation to His infinite essence that they are in creatures in relation to their finite nature. We must affirm, therefore, that all perfections are really in God, infinitely. This *infinitely* cannot be defined or expressed; we can say only that it is the absolutely perfect way, which does not admit any of the limitations which are found in creatures. Hence our conception of God, though very positive in its objective content, is, as represented in our mind and expressed in our words, more negative than positive. When speaking about God, our language uses human modes of expression; nevertheless it really does attain to God Himself, though unable to express him in his infinite simplicity.[28] Thus 'between Creator and creature no similitude can be expressed without implying an even greater dissimilitude'[29] and that 'concerning God, we cannot grasp what He is, but only what He is not, and how other beings stand in relation to Him.'[30]

Causality

Cause, as the correlative of effect, is understood as being that which in any way gives existence to, or contributes towards the existence of, any thing; that which produces a result; or that to which the origin of any thing is to be ascribed. The description just given is that of cause taken in the philosophical sense, as well as in its ordinary signification in popular language, for, strictly speaking, cause, being a transcendental, cannot receive a logical definition. It is the description also commonly advanced as a preliminary to the investigation of the nature of causality, in the schools. Although the ideas of cause and of causality are quite obviously among the most familiar that we possess, since they are involved in every exercise of human reasoning, and are presupposed in every form of argument and by every practical action, a very great vagueness attaches to the popular concept of them and a correspondingly great ambiguity is to be found in the use of the terms expressing them. All mankind by nature attributes to certain phenomena a causative action upon others. This natural attribution of the relationship of cause and effect to phenomena is anterior to all philosophical statement and analysis. Objects of sense are grouped roughly into two classes: those that act and those that are acted upon. No necessarily conscious reflection seems to enter into the judgement that partitions natural things into causes and effects. However, when we proceed to ask ourselves precisely what we mean when we say, for example, that A is cause and B effect, that A causes B, or that B is the result of A, we raise the question of causality.

Aristotle grouped causes into four classes, namely matter, form, moving or efficient cause, and final cause. His teaching was then incorporated by the medieval schools. With certain important modifications concerning the eternity of the material cause, the substantiality of certain formal causes of material entities, and the determination of the final cause, the fourfold division was handed on to the Christian teachers of patristic and scholastic times. The phenomena of which Aristotle was bent on discovering the causes, were not merely the accidental changes of things, but their more deeply rooted substantial changes. It was to substantial change that he especially directed his attention; and modem science has shown how right he was, by discovering that chemical or substantial changes are at the root of many phenomena the accidental nature of which were taken for granted at his time, such as combustion for example.

When a thing is changed substantially, something must remain throughout the change in order to justify the reality of the change. If, for example, when a piece of coal is changed into ashes, nothing whatsoever remained in the ashes that was in the piece of coal, there would be no connection between the two; ashes could not then be said to have been formed out of coal; the coal would have simply disappeared and ashes appeared from nowhere. The *material* cause is precisely that which remains, and is called the primary matter of things. It is considered as something undetermined and potential which can exist in different ways according to the different determining elements which make it exist in one way rather than in another. The *formal* cause is that which makes the material cause exist in one particular manner, that which makes one thing a piece of coal and another ashes. It is a determining and actual element. The *efficient* cause is the active power which makes it possible for the formal cause to be united to the material one. The *final* cause is the purpose for which the change is effected. According to St Thomas Aquinas, 'goodness, since it has the aspect of desirable, implies the idea of a final cause, the causality of which is first among causes.'[31]

The study of the final cause is called teleology which holds that there is purpose and design in every event and in every action. This purpose drives the agent to act and is for this reason called a cause. The drive to reach a goal is due to an interior and immanent impulse in all living beings. This impulse is more or less immanent according to the degree of perfection of their life. Other beings are driven towards their goal by exterior agents, for example an arrow, which is driven towards the target by the bow. Only intelligent beings are conscious of the purpose of their actions and can act for a deliberate motive. The purpose and design of all other agents is chosen and determined by the First Cause and Author of their nature. Teleology is opposed to those systems which hold that events are due to a blind and casual force.

This concept of causality is happily wedded to a common sense view of reality, and is based upon the observation, by the senses, of individual cases of causal action in the phenomenal world.[32] It squares well with the natural sciences and is agreement with the common experience of mankind. Beyond this, it provides a suitable account of the manner in which an observation of individual cases can become an intellectual concept. Also, it proceeds farther along the lines traced by common sense, in its analyses and syntheses, until it has presented natural knowledge as a complete and organised whole. It is particularly in the Scriptures that this holistic approach to knowledge may be encountered as will be seen in the next chapter.

Notes

[1] See Vatican I, *Dei Filius*, Chapter III, Canon 5 which condemns the error according to which 'Catholics could have a just reason for suspending their judgement and calling into question the faith they have received under the teaching authority of the Church, until they have completed a scientific demonstration of the credibility and truth of their faith.' English translation from ND130.

[2] The origin of this expression is the Stoic phrase, *zoon logicòn*, which Seneca uses: '... rationale animal est homo' (*Epistulae morales ad Lucilium* 46:63). In Christian usage, the word is deepened in meaning through belief in the immortality of the soul. Cf. S. L. Jaki, *The Road of Science and the Ways to God* (Edinburgh: Scottish Academic Press, 1978), p. 253, and also footnote 30, pp. 427–428.

[3] The Latin word *res* can be seen to be related to *h-ra-is*, itself a

derivative from *hir*, equivalent to the Greek *cheír* (hand); hence *res* is 'that which is handled', and means an object of thought, in accordance with that practical tendency of the Roman mind to treat all realities as tangible.

4　Besides using reason (*Vernunft*) as distinguished from the faculties of understanding (*Verstand*) and judgement (*Urteilskraft*), Kant employed the word in a transcendental sense, as the function of subsuming under the unity of the ideas the concepts and rules of the understanding.

5　J. H. Newman, Sermon XI 'The Nature of Faith in Relation to Reason' §6 in *Fifteen Sermons Preached Before the University of Oxford* (London: Rivingstons, 1872), p. 206.

6　See p. 64 below.

7　This is a faculty analogous to the Aristotelian *phrónesis*, or prudence or practical wisdom. See Aristotle, *The Nicomachean Ethics*, Book 6, v. For the illative sense see J. H. Newman, *The Grammar of Assent* (London: Burns, Oates and Company, 1870) pp. 336–378, and especially pp. 351–352 where Newman lists its characteristics: 'First, viewed in its exercise, it is one and the same in all concrete matters, though employed in them in different measures. We do not reason in one way in chemistry or law, in another in morals or religion; but in reasoning on any subject whatever, which is concrete, we proceed, as far indeed as we can, by the logic of language, but we are obliged to supplement it by the more subtle and elastic logic of thought; for forms by themselves prove nothing.

Secondly, it is in fact attached to definite subject-matters, so that a given individual may possess it in one department of thought, for instance, history, and not in another, for instance, philosophy.

Thirdly, in coming to its conclusion, it proceeds always in the same way, by a method of reasoning, which, as I have observed above, is the elementary principle of that mathematical calculus of modern times, which has so wonderfully extended the limits of abstract science.

Fourthly, in no class of concrete reasonings, whether in experimental science, historical research, or theology, is there any ultimate test of truth and error in our inferences besides the trustworthiness of the Illative Sense that gives them its sanction; just as there is no sufficient test of poetical excellence, heroic action, or gentleman-like conduct, other than the particular mental sense, be it genius, taste, sense of propriety, or the moral sense, to which those subject-matters are severally committed. Our duty in each of these is to strengthen and perfect the special faculty which is its living rule, and in every case as it comes to do our best. And such also is our duty and our necessity, as regards the Illative Sense.'

8　See chapter 9 below for further detail on this point. See also A. J.

Rahilly, 'Reason' in *The Catholic Encyclopaedia* 12 (New York; Robert Appleton Co., 1911) pp. 673–675.

9   St Thomas Aquinas, *Summa Theologiae*, I, q. 12, a. 4.

10 St Augustine, *De Trinitate*, Book 9, c. 12, n. 18 in *PL* 42, 970. The Latin phrase is 'unde liquido tenendum est quod omnis res quamcumque cognoscimus, congenerat in nobis notitiam sui. Ab utroque enim notitia paritur, a cognoscente et cognito.'

11 Some of these processes will be employed in the proofs of the existence of God, as will be seen in chapter 7 below. See also C. A. Dubray, 'Knowledge' in *The Catholic Encyclopaedia* 8 (New York: Robert Appleton Co., 1910) pp. 673–675.

12 See my *Mystery of Creation* (Leominster: Gracewing, 1995) pp. 2–5.

13 See F. Copleston, *A History of Philosophy*, vol. II, 'Augustine to Scotus,' (New York: Image Books, 1985), p. 140.

14 E. Gilson, *The Unity of Philosophical Experience* (Westminster, Maryland: Christian Classics, 1982), p. 66.

15 Pope John Paul II, Encyclical Letter *Fides et Ratio* 88

16 I. G. Barbour, *Issues in Science and Religion* (New York: Harper and Row, 1971), p. 164.

17 See S. L. Jaki, Introduction to E. Gilson *Methodical Realism* (Front Royal, Virginia: Christendom Press, 1990), pp. 11–14; Idem, *The Keys of the Kingdom* (Chicago: The Franciscan Herald Press, 1986), pp. 155–160.

18 A.A. Maurer, *About Beauty. A Thomistic Interpretation* (Houston, Texas: Center for Thomistic Studies, 1983), p. 15.

19 Pope John Paul II, Encyclical Letter *Fides et Ratio* 46.3, 81.1.

20 Ibid., 91.2–91.3.

21 Cf. St Thomas Aquinas, *Summa Theologiae*, I, q. 13, aa. 5, 10; also *De potentia*, q. 7, a. 7.

22 Cf. St Thomas Aquinas, *De veritate*, q. 2, a. 11; *De veritate*, q. 23, a. 7, ad 9.

23 The Latin expression is *via positiva*. See L. de Raeymaeker, *The Philosophy of Being* (St Louis, Missouri: Herder, 1966), p. 306. See also Pseudo-Dionysius, *De Divinis Nominibus* c. 1, sect. 6, in *PG* 3, 595; see also, St Thomas Aquinas, Summa Theologiae, I, q. 3, a. 3; q. 13, a. 12. This approach is also sometimes described as 'the way of causality' (*via causalitatis*).

24 The Latin expression is *via negationis*. Cf. Pseudo-Dionysius, *De Divinis Nominibus* c. 1, sect. 6, in *PG* 3, 595; see also St Thomas Aquinas, *Summa Theologiae*, I, q. 3, a. 1; q. 13, a. 1. Idem, *Summa Contra Gentiles*, Book 1, c. 14.

25 See M. Artigas, *The Mind of the Universe. Understanding Science and Religion* (Philadelphia and London: Templeton Foundation Press, 2000), p. 329: 'To say that God is transcendent has two related but different meanings. On the one hand, it means that God is different

from the created world. On the other, it means that we cannot completely conceptualise God.'

26 The Latin expression is *via eminentiae*. Cf. Pseudo-Dionysius, *De Divinis Nominibus* c. 1 sect. 41, in *PG* 3, 516, 590; c. 2, sect. 3, 8, in *PG* 3, 646, 689. See also St Thomas Aquinas, *Summa Theologiae* I, q. 13, a. 8; II–II, q. 27, a. 4. Idem, *In I Sententiarum* Distinctio 3, Prologus; Distinctio 3, q. 1, a. 2.

27 Cf. St Thomas Aquinas, *Summa Theologiae*, I, q. 13, a. 5, 6; Idem, *Summa Contra Gentiles*, Book 1, cc. 22–25; Idem, *In I Sententiarum*, Distinctio 13, q. 1, a. 1.

28 See *CCC* 43

29 Lateran IV, caput II. *De errore abbatis Ioachim, De Trinitate* as found in DS 806.

30 St Thomas Aquinas, *Summa Contra Gentiles*, Book 1, c. 30. See also Idem, *Summa Theologiae*, I, q. 3, the whole question; q. 13, aa. 2, 3, 5, 12. See also R. A. Knox, *The Hidden Stream* (London: Burns Oates, 1952), p. 38: 'Our intellects stammer and boggle when they try to reach the truth about Divine things, not because the other world is a reflection of ours, but because ours is a reflection, and how pale a reflection, of the other.'

31 St Thomas Aquinas, *Summa Theologiae*, I, q. 5, a. 2.

32 The principle axioms of causality can be summed up as follows:

1. Whatever exists in nature is either a cause or an effect. (See St Thomas Aquinas, *Summa Contra Gentiles*, Book 3, chapter 107, n. 3.)

2. No entity can be its own cause. (See St Thomas Aquinas, *Summa Contra Gentiles*, Book 2, chapter 21.)

3. There is no effect without a cause.

4. Given the cause, the effect follows and when the cause is removed, the effect ceases. This axiom is to be understood of causes efficient in act, and of effects related to them not only in becoming but also in being. (See St Thomas Aquinas, *Summa Contra Gentiles*, Book 2, c. 25.)

5. An effect requires a proportionate cause. This axiom is to be understood in the sense that actual effects respond to actual causes, particular effects to particular causes, and so forth. (See St Thomas Aquinas, *Summa Contra Gentiles*, Book 2, chapter 21.)

6. The cause is by nature prior to its effect. Priority is not necessarily understood here as relating to time. (See St Thomas

Aquinas, *Summa Contra Gentiles*, Book 2, chapter 21; Idem, *Summa Theologiae* III, q. 62, a. 6; Idem, *De potentia*, q. 3, a. 13; Idem, *De veritate*, q. 28, a. 7.)

7. The perfection of the effect pre-exists in its cause. (See St Thomas Aquinas, *Summa Theologiae*, I, q. 6, a. 2.)

8. Whatever is the cause of a cause (precisely as cause) is the cause also of its effect. This axiom enunciates a truth with regard to series of connected causes formally acting by their nature. (See St Thomas Aquinas, *Summa Theologiae*, I, q. 45, a. 5.)

9. The first cause (in any order of causes dependent one on the other) contributes more to the production of the effect than the secondary cause.

CHAPTER 2

SCRIPTURAL SOURCES

*The preaching of Christ crucified and risen is the reef upon which
the link between faith and philosophy can break up, but it is also
the reef beyond which the two can set forth upon the boundless
ocean of truth. Here we see not only the border between reason
and faith, but also the space where the two may meet.*

Pope John Paul II, *Fides et Ratio* 23

*Nothing is therefore more natural for a Catholic than to find
natural theology in the Bible.*

Stanley Jaki, *Bible and Science*

Human beings have always looked for God in various
ways, often as a result of asking questions dealing with
ultimate realities, like the origin of the world, the origin of
mankind, the meaning of life, of suffering, of love and of
death. In many and varied approaches, throughout
history down to the present day, people have expressed
their quest for God in their religious beliefs and behaviour: in their prayers, sacrifices, rituals, meditations, as
well as in philosophical reasoning about God. These forms
of religious expression, despite the ambiguities they often
brought with them, are so universal that one may well call
man a 'religious being'[1] as well as a thinking being.

According to the Scriptures and Christian tradition,
'God, the source and end of all things, can be known
with certainty from the things that were created.'[2]

Nevertheless, in practice, outside the Judaeo-Christian tradition, the rational side of religion has not been very keenly felt. This could be due to the irrationality of belief in most religions outside Christianity and Judaism.[3] To some extent Islam respects human reason. For example, in the Koran expressions of a rational and ordered cosmos are found:

> O men, adore your Lord who has created you and those who were before you, and fear God, who has made the earth a carpet for you and of the sky a castle, and has made water come down from the sky with which to extract from the earth those fruits that are your daily food.[4]

Islam however contains many elements which militate against a rational approach to faith. One is that three of the ninety-nine names of Allah imply that there is no resemblance at all between Him and His creatures which effectively means that the way of analogy is closed off.[5] Moreover, some passages of the Koran smack of voluntarism, or the tendency to stress strongly the divine Will at the expense of divine Rationality. This is expressed by the very frequent use in the Koran of the phrase 'Allah does what He pleases.' For example 'He chastises whom He pleases; and forgives whom He pleases.'[6] Furthermore, the following verse of the Koran also carries a voluntarist touch: 'Allah makes whom He pleases err and He guides whom He pleases.'[7]

It is important to defend the capacity of human reason to know God, since from this capacity flows the possibility of speaking about Him to all peoples and cultures, and therefore of discourse with people of other religions, of discussions involving philosophers and scientists, as well as with agnostics and unbelievers.[8] Now and again outside the Judaeo-Christian tradition, valid attempts have been made to read the book of nature in order to arrive at an affirmation of the Creator of the universe. Of all the ancient philosophers, Aristotle drew closest to the proclamation of God through human reason:

For the most divine science is also most honourable; and this science alone must be, in two ways, most divine. For the science which it would be most meet for God to have is a divine science, and so is any science that deals with divine objects; and this science alone has both these qualities; for (1) God is thought to be among the causes of all things and to be a first principle, and (2) such a science either God alone can have, or God above all others.[9]

Aristotle arrived at the point where his idea of God compelled wonder:

If, then, God is always in that good state in which we sometimes are, this compels our wonder; and if in a better this compels it yet more. And God is in a better state. And life also belongs to God; for the actuality of thought is life, and God is that actuality; and God's self-dependent actuality is life most good and eternal. We say therefore that God is a living being, eternal, most good, so that life and duration continuous and eternal belong to God; for this is God.[10]

Nevertheless, it is in the Old and New Testaments that we have the most penetrating insights into the relationship between faith and reason in the search for God.

Old Testament

The book of Genesis recounts how God made man and woman in His own image and likeness, and made them for communion with Himself, a communion of grace and faith. 'God created man in the image of Himself, in the image of God He created him, male and female He created them' (Gn 1:27). This threefold expression of the creation of the human person signifies that God is responsible for the creation of man's body, of man's soul and also for the differentiation between man and woman. It further signifies that God's image is found in man's body, man's soul and equally in man and in woman. Moreover, this creation

in the image of God reflects the supreme rationality of
God and so also implies the human powers of reason. In
order to be masters of creation (Gn 1:28–30), man and
woman were endowed with sufficient reason to know
what they were doing. Nevertheless, God also imposed a
limit on the knowledge that Adam and Eve were allowed
to access: 'But of the tree of the knowledge of good and
evil you are not to eat; for, the day you eat of that, you are
doomed to die' (Gn 2:17). This limit indicates that man and
woman were unable of themselves to discern and decide
for themselves what was good and what was evil, but
required guidance from a higher source. Instead of
obeying God's command, they gave way to the tempta-
tions of the devil and were deceived into considering
themselves sovereign and autonomous, and into imagin-
ing that they could ignore the knowledge which comes
from God. The devil tempted our first parents to commit a
sin similar to his own. In the theology of some of the
Eastern Churches, the first sin, rather than being simply of
pride and disobedience, consists rather in the lowering of
man from the divine and the eternal to the human and the
temporal spheres. The divine plan was that man should
know the earthly realities only after having known the
heavenly and divine mysteries. However man gave way to
the devil's temptation and preferred first to know the
things of earth represented by eating of the tree of the
knowledge of good and evil. All men and women were
caught up in this primal disobedience, which wounded
reason so that thereafter its path to full truth would be
strewn with obstacles.[11] St Thomas indicated that, as a
result of the Fall, the will suffered a greater wound than
the intellect.[12] This clouding of the intellect and weakening
of the will represent only a *relative* and not an *absolute*
deterioration of human nature, and one which is *extrinsic*
to the human faculties.[13] The human person can still know
natural truths (including religious ones) through reason,
and can perform morally good actions.

However it is effectively in the Wisdom literature that

the intimate relationship between the knowledge of God imparted by faith and the knowledge of Him conferred by reason becomes apparent.[14] The author of the book of Ecclesiasticus, Jesus Ben Sirach, expresses a theme common to all the Wisdom literature, namely the figure of the wise man who loves the truth and seeks it:

> Happy the man who meditates on wisdom, and reasons with good sense, who studies her ways in his heart, and ponders her secrets. He pursues her like a hunter, and lies in wait by her path; he peeps in at her windows, and listens at her doors; he lodges close to her house, and fixes his peg in her walls; he pitches his tent at her side, and lodges in an excellent lodging; he sets his children in her shade, and camps beneath her branches; he is sheltered by her from the heat, and in her glory he makes his home (Si 14:20–27).

The Israelite mind did not traditionally proceed to knowledge by way of abstraction, but approached life in its concrete reality. The Semitic concept of knowledge is one which is global and concrete, in complementarity with the Greek idea which is more abstract. As time went on, contact with the Egyptian and Greek cultures stimulated the Hebrew mind to approach reality also from the abstract viewpoint. However, any interchange with other cultures was purified of those elements which would have corrupted the faith of the Chosen People. Moreover, the Hebrew world of the Old Testament brings its own distinctive offering to ways of knowing. What is specific to the biblical text is the conviction that there is a profound and indissoluble unity between the knowledge of reason and the knowledge of faith. The world and all that happens within it, including history and the fate of peoples, are realities to be observed, analysed and assessed with all the resources of reason, but always in the context of faith in God the Creator and Guarantor of the Covenant. God has created the cosmos in wisdom and has impressed upon this cosmos rationality and coherence: 'In wisdom, the Lord laid the earth's foundations, in understanding He spread out the heavens. Through His knowledge the depths were cleft open, and the clouds distil the dew' (Pr 3:19–20). Thus the world and the events of history cannot be understood in depth without professing faith in the God who is at work in them. Faith sharpens the inner eye, opening the mind to discover the treasure of the workings of Providence within the flotsam and jetsam of daily events. With the light of reason, human beings can know which path to take, but they can follow that path to its end, quickly and unhindered, only if with a rightly tuned spirit they search for it within the horizon of faith. This message is echoed in the Book of Proverbs: 'The human heart may plan a course, but it is the Lord who makes the steps secure' (Pr 16:9). Therefore, reason and faith cannot be separated without diminishing the capacity of men and women to know themselves, the world and God in an appropriate way.[15]

In the Old Testament, there is no opposition between faith and reason. Nevertheless, there is an awareness of the difference and relatedness of these two realms of human experience. The Book of Proverbs underlines this difference: 'To conceal a matter, this is the glory of God, to sift it thoroughly, the glory of kings' (Pr 25:2). Through the Revelation received from God, the people of Israel understood that, if reason were to be fully true to itself, and not be damaged or deformed then it must respect certain basic rules:

> The first of these is that reason must realise that human knowledge is a journey which allows no rest; the second stems from the awareness that such a path is not for the proud who think that everything is the fruit of personal conquest; a third rule is grounded in the 'fear of God' whose transcendent sovereignty and provident love in the governance of the world reason must recognise.[16]

When these rules are abandoned, the human person perverts reason and becomes 'the fool'. For the Bible, in this foolishness there lies a threat to life. The fool thinks that he knows many things, but really he is incapable of fixing his gaze on the things that truly matter. Therefore he can neither order his mind (Pr 1:7) nor assume a correct attitude to himself or to the world around him. Thus when he claims that 'God does not exist' (cf. Ps 14:1), he shows with conclusive clarity just how deficient his knowledge is and just how far he is from the full truth of things, their origin and their destiny.

The relation of reason with Revelation gives to reason a clearer picture of its own value. The results of the process of human reasoning acquire a deeper meaning when they are set within the larger horizon of faith, as is seen in the book of Proverbs: 'The Lord guides the steps of the powerful: but who can comprehend human ways?' (Pr 20:24). What God bestows by His grace is itself a stimulus for knowledge: 'The fear of Yahweh is the beginning of knowledge' (Pr 1:7; cf. Si 1:14). The wisdom which comes from God transcends man, so that he will always return to the fountain of knowledge to drink further (cf. Si 24:21-22).

God has created the human person as a searcher on the pilgrimage towards knowledge and wisdom:

> The first principle of wisdom is: acquire wisdom; at the cost of all you have, acquire understanding! Hold her close, and she will make you great; embrace her, and she will be your pride' (Pr 4:7-8).

This is demanding and tiring, indicating that man must search patiently among the folds of reality for the truth. 'Wisely I have applied myself to investigation and exploration of everything that happens under heaven. What a wearisome task God has given humanity to keep us busy!' (Qo 1:13). The process of acquiring knowledge and wisdom is almost endless, likened to the great quantity of the drops of rain or sand in the sea:

All wisdom comes from the Lord, she is with Him for ever. The sands of the sea, the drops of rain, the days of eternity – who can count them? The height of the sky, the breadth of the earth, the depth of the abyss – who can explore them? Wisdom was created before everything, prudent understanding subsists from remotest ages. For whom has the root of wisdom ever been uncovered? Her resourceful ways, who knows them? (Si 1:1–6).

Qoheleth introduced some interesting nuances regarding faith and reason. He pointed out the difficulty and, it seems, even the futility of human knowledge:

I have applied myself to understanding philosophy and science, stupidity and folly, and I now realise that all this too is chasing after the wind. Much wisdom, much grief; the more knowledge, the more sorrow (Qo 1:17–18).

At the same time, he avoided agnosticism, or a denial that we can have valid knowledge about God and creation, by his praise of wisdom:

Wisdom is as good as a legacy, profitable to those who enjoy the light of the sun. For as money protects, so does wisdom, and the advantage of knowledge is this: that wisdom bestows life on those who possess her (Qo 7:11–12).

The limits of human knowledge even in the natural order are always stressed: 'You do not understand how the wind blows, or how the embryo grows in a woman's womb: no more can you understand the work of God, the Creator of all' (Qo 11:5).

In the Psalms, an indication is to be found of how the mystery of reason penetrates the mystery of creation, the cosmos and above all the creation of the human person. Nevertheless, the Psalmist shows that God's work cannot be comprehended by reason alone:

> You created my inmost self,
> knit me together in my mother's womb.
> For so many marvels I thank You;
> a wonder am I, and all Your works are wonders.
>
> You knew me through and through,
> my being held no secrets from You,
> when I was being formed in secret,
> textured in the depths of the earth.
>
> Your eyes could see my embryo.
> In your book all my days were inscribed,
> every one that was fixed is there.
>
> How hard for me to grasp Your thoughts,
> how many, God, there are!
> If I count them, they are more than the grains of sand;
> if I come to an end, I am still with You (Ps 139: 13–18).

The book of Job also portrays an interesting perspective on human capacity for knowing God. It makes clear that we do have valid knowledge of God, for example through a consideration of His work of creation. Nevertheless this knowledge is limited and incomplete:

> Yes, the greatness of God exceeds our knowledge, the number of His years is past counting.
> It is He who makes the raindrops small and pulverises the rain into mist.
> And the clouds then pour this out, sending it streaming down on the human race.
> And who can fathom how He spreads the clouds, or why such crashes thunder from His tent?
> He spreads a mist before Him and covers the tops of the mountains.
> By these means, He sustains the peoples, giving them plenty to eat.
> He gathers up the lightning in His hands, assigning it the mark where to strike (Job 36: 26–32).

Moreover, in the face of suffering and its origin and purpose, knowledge of God is challenged, so that Job, through his process of purification arrives at a realisation of the inadequacy of his former knowledge and passes from a notional to a real assent of God. 'Before, I knew you only by hearsay but now, having seen you with my own eyes, I retract what I have said, and repent in dust and ashes' (Jb 42:5–6).

A search for God bestows benefits also on human understanding, 'for those who seek the Lord understand everything' (Pr 28:5), and 'those who trust in Him will understand the truth' (Ws 3:9). In a sense, God offers a share in His own infinite knowledge and understanding when He confers the gift of wisdom:

> But the One who knows all discovers her, He has grasped her with His own intellect, He has set the earth firm for evermore and filled it with four-footed beasts, He sends the light – and it goes, He recalls it – and trembling it obeys; the stars shine joyfully at their posts; when He calls them, they answer, 'Here we are'; they shine to delight their Creator. It is He who is our God, no other can compare with Him (Ba 3:32–36).

In the book of Wisdom, knowledge as the fruit of reason involved a painstaking investigation of the world, the human being and history, in a way which is open to what is received from Revelation. Indeed, even in seeking the fruits of rational endeavour, people sought the help of God, avoiding any exaggerated autonomy between two spheres of activity:

> May God grant me to speak as He would wish and conceive thoughts worthy of the gifts I have received, since He is both guide to Wisdom and director of sages; for we are in His hand, yes, ourselves and our sayings, and all intellectual and all practical knowledge. He it was who gave me sure knowledge of what exists, to understand the structure of the world and the action of the

elements, the beginning, end and middle of the times, the alternation of the solstices and the succession of the seasons, the cycles of the year and the position of the stars, the natures of animals and the instincts of wild beasts, the powers of spirits and human mental processes, the varieties of plants and the medical properties of roots. And now I understand everything, hidden or visible, for Wisdom, the designer of all things, has instructed me (Ws 7:15–21).

In the book of Wisdom is to be found a vision which affirms a rationally ordered universe, a world picture in stark contrast to that of the pagan neighbours of Israel like Egypt and Babylon where a magical and superstitious view of the cosmos dominated the understanding: 'You, however, ordered all things by measure, number and weight' (Ws 11:20). The truly realist world picture of ancient Israel, as described in the book of Wisdom paved the way of reason so that it was to become a sure road towards the affirmation of God:

Yes, naturally stupid are all who are unaware of God, and who, from good things seen, have not been able to discover Him-who-is, or, by studying the works, have not recognised the Artificer. Fire, however, or wind, or the swift air, the sphere of the stars, impetuous water, heaven's lamps, are what they have held to be the gods who govern the world. If, charmed by their beauty, they have taken these for gods, let them know how much the Master of these excels them, since He was the very source of beauty that created them. And if they have been impressed by their power and energy, let them deduce from these how much mightier is He that has formed them, since through the grandeur and beauty of the creatures we may, by analogy, contemplate their Author. Small blame, however, attaches to them, for perhaps they go astray only in their search for God and their eagerness to find Him; familiar with His works, they investigate them and fall victim to appearances, seeing so much beauty. But even so, they have no excuse: if they are capable of acquiring enough knowledge to be able to investigate the world, how have they been so slow to find its Master? (Ws 13:1–9).

The idea of 'analogy' is thus present in the book of Wisdom at this point, as a fundamental basis for human knowing of God. This is the only point in the Old Testament where the expression is to be found.[17]

The 'book of nature' thus represents a first stage of divine Revelation. If the cosmos is read with the proper tools of human reason within a realist perspective it can be a stepping stone to knowledge of the Creator. If human beings with their intelligence fail to recognise God as Creator of all, it is not because they lack the means to do so, but because a disordered will and clouded intellect place an impediment in the way.[18] In some of the prophetic literature also, there is an indication of the stupidity of ignoring the Creator's hand at work in His creation. For example, the prophet Isaiah points out: 'What perversity this is! Is the potter no better than the clay? Can something that was made say of its maker, "He did not make me"? Or a pot say of the potter, "He does not know his job"? (Is 29:16).'

In the Old Testament context, faith liberated reason in such a way that reason is enabled to attain rightly what it seeks to know and to place it within the ultimate order of things, in which everything acquires true meaning. In brief, human beings attain truth by way of reason because, enlightened by faith, they discover the deeper meaning of all things and most especially of their own existence.[19]

New Testament

Pontius Pilate's question when faced with Jesus Christ was 'What is truth?' (Jn 18:38). This question has been repeated down the centuries by searchers and sceptics alike. However, Christ Himself is the final and definitive answer to the question for He is 'the Way, the Truth and the Life'(Jn 14:6). In the New Testament, Christ employs various images for Himself which are based on analogy. For example in the parable of the Vine and the branches: 'I am the vine, you are the branches. Whoever remains in me, with me in him, bears fruit in plenty; for cut off from me you can do nothing' (Jn 15:5). This image is a very powerful indication of communion within the Church, and at the same time a eucharistic allusion.

The episode of the miraculous catch of fish recounted by St Luke can be taken as a powerful image for the relationship between faith as personal commitment and reason. 'Jesus said to Simon Peter, "Put out into deep water and pay out your nets for a catch." Simon replied, "Master, we worked hard all night long and caught nothing, but if You say so, I will pay out the nets." And when they had done this they netted such a huge number of fish that their nets began to tear, so they signalled to their companions in the other boat to come and help them; when these came, they filled both boats to sinking point. When Simon Peter saw this he fell at the knees of Jesus saying, "Leave me, Lord; I am a sinful man"' (Lk 5:4–8). In this image of the intellectual search for God, the net of the mind must go into deep waters, since God is not to be found in superficialities. St Peter trusts the words of Christ, even though, humanly speaking, they seem to be unreasonable, because he had worked all night and caught nothing. The key is this: 'If You say so, I will pay out the nets.' Afterwards St Peter felt ashamed that he had not trusted Christ fully, and expressed the sentiment that he was a sinful man. By analogy, casting out into the depths of God with the intellect brings about, by the grace of Christ, a process of conversion of the intellect. A further example of an episode of coming to faith through a process of interaction with empirical reason, was Christ's appearance to doubting Thomas. This apostle missed the earlier appearance of Christ, and did not believe the others but required empirical evidence that the Lord was indeed risen: 'Unless I can see the holes that the nails made in his hands and can put my finger into the holes they made, and unless I can put my hand into his side, I refuse to believe' (Jn 20:25). When Thomas did see the Lord and was invited, to his embarrassment, to put his hand into the Risen Christ's wounded side, he arrived at faith and Jesus said to him: 'You believe because you can see me. Blessed are those who have not seen and yet believe' (Jn 20:29).

In St Paul's letters the very specific nature of Christian wisdom is outlined. In this context there emerges in a poignant manner the contrast between 'the wisdom of this world' and the wisdom of God revealed in Jesus Christ. The depth of revealed wisdom disrupts the cycle of our habitual patterns of thought, which are in no way able to express that wisdom in its fullness. The crucified Son of God is the historic event upon which every attempt of the mind to construct an adequate explanation of the meaning of existence upon merely human argumentation comes to grief. The true key-point, which challenges every philosophy, is Jesus Christ's death on the Cross. It is here that every attempt to reduce the Father's saving plan to purely human logic is doomed to failure. St Paul emphasised that Christ sent him to preach the Gospel 'not by means of wisdom of language, wise words which would make the cross of Christ pointless' (1 Co 1:17). The Apostle paraphrases a passage in the book of the prophet Isaiah, and exclaims: 'As scripture says: I am going to destroy the wisdom of the wise and bring to nothing the understanding of any who understand'(1 Co 1:19; See Is 29:14). When St Paul stated that 'God has shown up human wisdom as folly' (1 Co 1:20), this does not mean that it is without value, but rather that God wished to save believers through the 'folly of the Gospel' (1 Co 1:21). The content of this Gospel is the crucified Christ, 'to the Jews an obstacle they cannot get over, to the Gentiles foolishness, but to those who have been called, whether they are Jews or Greeks, a Christ who is both the power of God and the wisdom of God' (1 Co 1:23–24). This shows that 'God's folly is wiser than human wisdom' (1 Co 1:25). The approach of the negative way is portrayed here, namely that God's Wisdom so transcends human wisdom, that the one seems almost totally dissimilar from the other. At the same time, St Paul's adoption of the human categories of wisdom and folly to describe the disparity between human wisdom and Divine Wisdom implies some kind of analogy, so that there is a positive way as well, a resemblance between the two orders of knowledge.[20] At the same time, 'it is not the wisdom of words, but the Word of Wisdom which Saint Paul offers as the criterion of both truth and salvation.'[21] The wisdom of the Cross, therefore is a challenge to reason which does not destroy human thinking but rather purifies, elevates and transforms it, heals it and redeems it, so that it can rise higher. This is a very specific aspect of Christian understanding of faith and reason, in contrast to other approaches where reason is regarded as irrelevant, unhelpful or an obstacle in the search for divine realities.

When St Paul visited Athens on one of his missionary journeys, he used one of the religious monuments as a convenient starting-point to establish a common base for his preaching of the Truth. He exclaimed:

> Men of Athens, I have seen for myself how extremely scrupulous you are in all religious matters, because, as I strolled round looking at your sacred monuments, I noticed among other things an altar inscribed: To An Unknown God. In fact, the unknown God you revere is the one I proclaim to you. Since the God who made the world and everything in it is Himself Lord of heaven and earth, He does not make his home in shrines made by human hands. Nor is He in need of anything, that He should be served by human hands; on the contrary, it is He who gives everything – including life and breath – to everyone. From one single principle He not only created the whole human race so that they could occupy the entire earth, but He decreed the times and limits of their habitation. And He did this so that they might seek the deity and, by feeling their way towards Him, succeed in finding Him; and

indeed He is not far from any of us, since it is in Him that
we live, and move, and exist, as indeed some of your own
writers have said: 'We are all His children' (Ac 17:23–28).

The truth that God is 'not far from any of us' is an expression of His immanence within His creation, the theological
basis for searching for God through His creation, and at
the same time the foundation for using human categories
to express divine truths. A well-known and classic
passage from St Paul's letter to the Romans deals with this
fundamental capacity of human reason to search for God.
The passage recalls the flavour of a similar passage from
the book of Wisdom (Ws 13:1–9) cited above:

> The retribution of God from heaven is being revealed
> against the ungodliness and injustice of human beings who
> in their injustice hold back the truth. For what can be
> known about God is perfectly plain to them, since God has
> made it plain to them: ever since the creation of the world,
> the invisible existence of God and His everlasting power
> have been clearly seen by the mind's understanding of
> created things. And so these people have no excuse: they
> knew God and yet they did not honour Him as God or give
> thanks to him, but their arguments became futile and their
> uncomprehending minds were darkened. While they
> claimed to be wise, in fact they were growing so stupid
> that they exchanged the glory of the immortal God for
> an imitation, for the image of a mortal human being, or
> of birds, or animals, or crawling things. That is why
> God abandoned them in their inmost cravings to filthy
> practices of dishonouring their own bodies – because they
> exchanged God's truth for a lie and have worshipped and
> served the creature instead of the Creator, who is blessed
> for ever. Amen (Rm 1:18–25).

Through the mediation of His creation, God arouses in
reason an intuition of His power and His divinity.
Elsewhere in the New Testament, an idea of the Creator
responsible for His creation is presupposed as in the Letter
to the Hebrews: 'Every house is built by someone, of

course; but God built everything that exists' (Heb 3:4). The process of reasoning starts from the human experience that every house has been built by someone, therefore the cosmos must have been created by God. This seems to endow human reason with a capacity which overcomes its natural limitations. The concept is not limited to sensory knowledge, but goes on from the data provided by the senses to reach the cause lying at the origin of all perceptible reality. St Paul effectively affirms that this passage from creation to Creator would have been very straightforward had the Fall not occurred. However, because of the disobedience by which man and woman chose to bypass their relation to the One who had created them, this easy access to God through their reasoning power diminished. As a result of the desire to exercise reason without reference to God, the eyes of the mind were no longer able to see clearly: reason became more and more enslaved to its own confusion.[22] Along with the incapacity to know God with ease, the fallen state of man brought a difficulty in arriving at moral truths, which reason should be able to see as connected with man's nature. Thus anarchy gave way to tyranny. The coming of Christ was to redeem and heal reason from this weakness, setting it free from the bondage in which it had been held captive. As Jesus said: 'If you make my word your home you will indeed be my disciples; you will come to know the truth, and the truth will set you free' (Jn 8:31–32).

Faith, although primarily connected with eternal life, has a real effect on the here and now, and on the human capacity of reason in the present context. This vision has its basis in the passage where Christ says to His followers that setting their hearts first on God's Kingdom will have beneficial effects not only in heaven, but also here upon earth: 'Set your hearts on His Kingdom first, and on His righteousness and all these other things will be yours as well' (Mt 6:33). The followers of Christ are promised something of a reward in this life (despite persecutions) as well as a reward in the life to come: 'And everyone who has left houses, brothers, sisters, father, mother, children or land for the sake of my name will be repaid a hundred times over and also inherit eternal life' (Mt 19:29).[23] This healing of the powers of reason is one of the blessings which the Gospel is bringing as it spreads throughout the world (cf. Col 1:6). In this way, 'God works with those who love Him, those who have been called in accordance with His purpose, and turns everything to their good' (Rom 8:28).

St Paul elucidated how the validity of the Mystery of Christ does not depend upon 'brilliance of oratory or wise argument' (1 Co 2:1), and he did not wish to convince his hearers using philosophical argument (1 Co 2:4). Rather it is the power of the Holy Spirit which supplies conviction to the Christian message. In his way, Christian faith does not depend 'on human wisdom but on the power of God' (1 Co 2:5). Nevertheless a knowledge and a wisdom are involved in St Paul's proclamation, a knowledge of Christ crucified and of 'the mysterious wisdom of God that we talk, the wisdom that was hidden, which God predestined to be for our glory before the ages began' (1 Co 2:7). This knowledge and wisdom are not accessible to the mind which is locked in its own natural categories, to the mind which has not recognised the power of the crucified Christ. St Paul made clear that there is an order of knowledge which transcends reason, namely the gift of revelation, 'God has given revelation through the Spirit, for the Spirit explores the depths of everything, even the depths of God' (1 Co 2:10). St Paul employs a human analogy to indicate that only the Spirit of God knows the depths of God. Just as a human individual knows himself through his own spirit, within him; 'in the same way, nobody knows the qualities of God except the Spirit of God' (1 Co 2:11). Human reason is surpassed when it comes to framing categories for what God has revealed. Christ blessed His Father for 'for hiding these things from the learned and the clever and revealing them to little children' (Lk 10:21; see also Mt 11:25).

Revelation cannot therefore be simply expressed 'in the terms learnt from human philosophy, but in terms learnt from the Spirit, fitting spiritual language to spiritual things' (1 Co 2:13). Human language is not incapable of expressing divine revelation, but rather revelation itself must reshape this human language into a new wineskin in order to enable it to contain the new wine of divine truths (Mt 9:17). Here is implied that revelation brings about a conversion of the intellect, a real change which does not destroy the power of reason, but enables the Christian to put on 'the mind of Christ' (1 Co 2:16). The mind must be renewed by a spiritual revolution, so that the Christian 'could put on the New Man that has been created on God's principles, in the uprightness and holiness of the truth' (Ep 4:23). This spiritual revolution enables one to live by the truth and in love (Ep 4:15). The gift of the Holy Spirit enables the believer to understand and appreciate the gifts of God, and to 'assess the value of everything' (1 Co 2:15). This revelation is a wisdom, but one which is not recognised by the intellectual authorities of this present passing world. It is a wisdom which also looks forward to a completion in the glory of heaven where God has prepared for those who love Him, 'what no eye has seen and no ear has heard, what the mind of man cannot visualise' (1 Co 2:9). This type of expression had already been used by the prophet Isaiah in the Old Testament to express the coming of Christ: 'Never has anyone heard, no ear has heard, no eye has seen any god but You act like this for the sake of those who trust Him' (Is 64:3).

The Apostle also taught that reason is perfected by love, and that reason without love remains sterile:

> Though I command languages both human and angelic – if I speak without love, I am no more than a gong booming or a cymbal clashing. And though I have the power of prophecy, to penetrate all mysteries and knowledge, and though I have all the faith necessary to move mountains – if I am without love, I am nothing (1 Co 13:1–2).

Love, however, is based on truth in which it rejoices. St Paul seems to imply that while imperfect knowledge will be done away with, 'love never comes to an end' (1 Co 13:8). He adopts the two famous analogies of the growth of a child and the reflection in a mirror to express the pilgrimage towards heavenly perfection:

> When I was a child, I used to talk like a child, and think like a child, and argue like a child, but now that I am an adult, all childish ways are put behind me. Now we are seeing a dim reflection in a mirror; but then we shall be seeing face to face. The knowledge that I have now is imperfect; but then I shall know just as fully as I am myself known (1 Co 13:11–12).

This latter analogy of the mirror implies that there will be a heavenly form of knowledge, one which is perfect. St John also illustrates the way of love which starts from the brother whom we can see, proceeding from the visible creation towards God, a process which tellingly also lies at the basis of rational proofs for the existence of God: 'Anyone who says "I love God" and hates his brother, is a liar, since whoever does not love the brother whom he can see cannot love God whom he has not seen' (1 Jn 4:20).

St Paul illustrates how the problem of non-belief can come about when the Gospel appears veiled or hidden in its meaning to the unbelievers whose minds have been blinded by the god of this world, so that they cannot see shining the light of the gospel of the glory of Christ, who is the image of God (2 Co 4:4). Once again, this text implies that a conversion of intellect is required in order that reason may approach the threshold of faith. This process of conversion is not without a struggle in which the Apostle employs powerful military imagery:

> The weapons with which we do battle are not those of human nature, but they have the power, in God's cause, to demolish fortresses. It is ideas that we demolish, every presumptuous notion that is set up against the knowledge of God, and we bring every thought into captivity and obedience to Christ (2 Co 10:4–5).

The Apostle exhorts the presiding elders, the forerunners of the bishops,[24] to have a firm grasp of the unchanging message of the tradition, so that they can be counted on both for giving encouragement in sound doctrine and for refuting those who argue against it (Tt 1:9). This capacity for encouraging sound doctrine and refuting error necessarily involved the use of reason and elementary philosophy, in order to enable his hearers to grasp his points in ways they could understand. The reason for this struggle (see Col 2:1) lies in the fact that the word of God transcends merely human thought; it is not the word of any human being, but God's word, a power that is working among believers (see 1 Th 2:13). Nevertheless there is a real and valid knowledge involved in understanding the mystery of God, and here are hid 'all the jewels of wisdom and knowledge' (Col 2:3). When the Christian is filled with knowledge of the mystery of Christ, his mind is 'filled with everything that is true, everything that is honourable, everything that is upright and pure, everything that we love and admire – with whatever is good and praiseworthy' (Ph 4:8). Here the light of Christ scatters the shadows of doubt from the mind of the believer. Moreover he or she is protected against deceptive and specious arguments (Col 2:4), and cannot be imprisoned by the 'empty lure of a "philosophy" of the kind that human beings hand on, based on the principles of this world and not on Christ' (Col 2:8).

St Paul also speaks of a 'reasonable service'[25] which the Christian is expected to offer to God: 'I urge you, then, brothers, remembering the mercies of God, to offer your bodies as a living sacrifice, dedicated and acceptable to God; that is the kind of worship for you, as sensible people' (Rm 12:1). This implies a worship of God which involves both the mind and the heart, therefore the power of reason cannot be left out of the relationship with God. For the knowledge of the truth leads to true religion (Tit 1:1), and this knowledge of Christ spreads like a pleasant fragrance (2 Co 2:14). This knowledge is based on love which enables the Christian in union with all God's holy people to acquire the strength to grasp the breadth and the length, the height and the depth; so that, knowing the love of Christ, which is beyond knowledge, he or she may be filled with the utter fullness of God (Eph 3:18–19). Knowledge and love of Christ are therefore correlative and the one needs the other; knowledge without love is sterile and love without knowledge can be misguided.[26] This knowledge of the Mystery of Christ also has an eschatological dimension, which leads to the final revelation of the Lord when He comes in glory at the end of the ages. This knowledge and complete understanding foster a growth towards true discernment, so that the Christian will be innocent and free of any trace of guilt when the Day of Christ comes (Ph 1:9–10).

In apostolic times there existed a sect of spirituals (*pneumatikoi*), who regarded as inferior those who were not completely liberated from matter; they rejected marriage because of its connection with matter (see 1 Tm 4:3). The spirituals preceded the Gnostics of the second century. Gnosticism, derived from the Greek word *gnosis* (knowledge) claimed a superior, secret understanding of things. It was a system based on an elitist human striving for philosophical knowledge rather than on faith; in Gnosticism, the distinction between the eternal uncreated Supreme Being and all other beings was blurred or erased. The production of matter was conceived of in terms of a downward emanation from God. St Paul warned Timothy of the dangers of this type of system:

My dear Timothy, take great care of all that has been entrusted to you. Turn away from godless philosophical discussions and the contradictions of the 'knowledge' which is not knowledge at all; by adopting this, some have missed the goal of faith' (1 Tm 6:20–21).

Perhaps in the same context, St Paul also warns about avoiding 'godless philosophical discussions' which 'only lead further and further away from true religion' (2 Tm 2:16).

St Peter encouraged a reasoned hope as well as a reasoned faith, so indicating that Christian hope, like faith, is not irrational but can be proclaimed in rational categories, though the mystery of hope is beyond reason: 'Simply reverence the Lord Christ in your hearts, and always have your answer ready for people who ask you the reason for the hope that you all have' (1 Pt 3:15). St Peter employs the Greek word λόγος for 'reason', and this expression has various shades of meaning in the New Testament, including a word of speech spoken by a living voice embodying a conception or idea, a matter under discussion, the power of reason, and the mental faculty of thinking. The meaning becomes especially powerful in St John's writings, where it refers to the Word of God, the Second Person of the Blessed Trinity, who to win human salvation assumed human nature as Jesus the Christ. St James indicates that true wisdom comes from God, and this gift is given when it is asked for 'with faith, and no trace of doubt, because a person who has doubts is like the waves thrown up in the sea by the buffeting of the wind' (Jm 1:6). Both gifts of faith and reason come down from above, from the Father of all light; with Him there is no such thing as alteration, no shadow caused by change (Jm 1:17). The next chapter will examine how ideas concerning the interaction of faith and reason developed in the first centuries of Christianity.

Notes

1. *CCC* 28
2. Vatican I, *Dei Filius* Chapter II in ND 113. See also Canon 1 in ND 115. See also chapter 7 below where we deal with proofs of the existence of God.
3. More will be said about the irrational element in religion in chapter 8.
4. *The Koran*, Sura 2, verses 21–23.
5. The names in question are Name 10 'Al-Mutakabbir – The One who

is distinct from the attributes of the creatures and from resembling them.' Name 36 'Al-'Ali – The One who is distinct from the attributes of the creatures.' Name 78 'Al-Muta'ali – The One who is distinct from the attributes of the creation.'

6   *The Koran*, Sura 5, verse 40.

7   Ibid., Sura 14, verse 4; see Sura 35, verse 8.

8   See *CCC* 39.

9   Aristotle, *Metaphysics*, Book 1, 2.

10   Ibid., Book 12, 7.

11   See Pope John Paul II, *Fides et Ratio* 22. See also P. Haffner, *Mystery of Creation* (Leominster: Gracewing, 1995), p. 119.

12   See St Thomas Aquinas, *Summa Theologiae* I-II°, q. 83, aa. 3–4.

13   See Pope John Paul II, *Discourse at General Audience* 8 October 1986 §7 in *IG* 9/2 (1986) p. 972. There is discussion as to whether the wound to human nature consists simply of the loss of preternatural gifts or of an intrinsic but accidental weakening. The Thomist approach considers that a person born in original sin compares to the human being in the state of pure nature as a person stripped of his clothes is to a naked person. Those who admit some intrinsic weakening use the analogy between the healthy man (before the Fall) and the sick person (in original sin).

14   Pope John Paul II, *Fides et Ratio* 16.

15   Ibid.

16   Ibid., 18.

17   In the Greek text, the word is ἀναλόγως which literally means 'proportionally.' See chapter 1, pp. 19–22 above for a presentation of analogy.

18   See Pope John Paul II, *Fides et Ratio* 19.

19   Cf. Ibid., 20

20   See chapter 1, pp. 21–22 above for a description of the positive and negative ways.

21   Pope John Paul II, *Fides et Ratio* 23

22   See ibid., 22.

23   Cf. Mk 10:29–30; Lk 18:29–30; 1 Tim 4:8. See also Second Vatican Council, *Gaudium et Spes* 38.2: 'Constituted Lord by his resurrection and given all authority in heaven and on earth, Christ is now at work in the hearts of all men by the power of his Spirit; not only does he arouse in them a desire for the world to come but he quickens, purifies and strengthens the generous aspirations of mankind to make life more humane and conquer the earth for this purpose.'

24   For a description of the development of sacred orders in the primitive Church, see my work, *The Sacramental Mystery* (Leominster: Gracewing, 1999) pp. 170–173.

[25] The Greek expression is λογικὴν λατρείαν which literally means 'reasonable worship'. Cardinal Ratzinger indicates the importance of this expression as that which distinguishes Christian worship, with Christ the Logos at the centre, from ancient pagan cults. See J. Ratzinger, *Introduzione allo spirito della liturgia* (Cinisello Balsamo: Edizioni San Paolo, 2001), pp. 42–47.

[26] See chapter 9 below for further discussion of this theme.

CHAPTER 3

PATRISTIC PATHS

For as the pomegranate, with the rind containing it, has within it many cells and compartments which are separated by tissues, and has also many seeds dwelling in it, so the whole creation is contained by the spirit of God, and the containing spirit is along with the creation contained by the hand of God. As, therefore, the seed of the pomegranate, dwelling inside, cannot see what is outside the rind, itself being within; so neither can man, who along with the whole creation is enclosed by the hand of God, behold God.

Theophilus of Antioch, *To Autolycus*

And since no one can scale a precipice unless there be jutting ledges to aid his progress to the summit, I have here set down in order the primary outlines of our ascent leading our difficult course of argument up the easiest path; not cutting steps in the face of the rock, but levelling it to a gentle slope, that so the traveller, almost without a sense of effort may reach the heights.

St Hilary of Poitiers, *On the Trinity*

Very early on in Christian tradition, the place of reason and philosophy in relation to God began to be developed. A certain dividing line between a positive and a negative approach to philosophy is to be found in many Christian thinkers, since in several authors two tendencies live together as it were: the Christian, full of reservations about a philosophy permeated with paganism, and the Greek, which instead is imbued with it. Christian reflection made use of ancient Greek philosophy, in which Aristotelian thought was perhaps the most compatible with Christian doctrine, but which had nevertheless to be purified in order to be adopted in some aspects by Christian thinkers. As regards Platonic notions, these underwent profound changes, especially with regard to concepts such as the immortality of the soul, the divinization of man and the origin of evil.[1]

In the anonymous *Epistle to Diognetus*, sometimes attributed to Mathetes, and composed around the year AD 130, one finds a clear idea of the relationship between Christians and the surrounding world, which also indicates, on the one hand, that their way of life has not been humanly devised and, on the other, manifests an openness to philosophy:

> For the Christians are distinguished from other men neither by country, nor language, nor the customs which they observe. For they neither inhabit cities of their own, nor employ a peculiar form of speech, nor lead a life which is marked out by any singularity. The course of conduct which they follow has not been devised by any speculation or deliberation of inquisitive men; nor do they, like some, proclaim themselves the advocates of any merely human doctrines. But, inhabiting Greek as well as barbarian cities, according as the lot of each of them has determined, and following the customs of the natives in respect to clothing, food, and the rest of their ordinary conduct, they display to us their wonderful and confessedly striking method of life.[2]

This document clearly indicates that faith must be reasonable and represents an important testimony since the author was in direct contact with the Apostles: 'I do not speak of things strange to me, nor do I aim at anything inconsistent with right reason; but having been a disciple of the Apostles, I am become a teacher of the Gentiles.'[3] A profound insight is offered regarding the two trees in the garden of Eden, the one being of knowledge and the other of life. The fact that God from the beginning planted both trees in the midst of paradise indicates that knowledge is the way to life, but because our first parents did not use this knowledge properly, they were, through the fraud of the Serpent, stripped naked. For neither can life exist without knowledge, nor is knowledge secure without life. Hence both trees were planted close together. The Christian by his rebirth has become a paradise of delight, being in himself a tree bearing all kinds of produce and flourishing well, being adorned with various fruits; thus knowledge and life must be linked.[4]

The Christian West

St Irenaeus of Lyons (130–202) refuted the Gnostic heresy, which was perhaps the first one concerning reason and faith in the history of the Church. Gnosticism, derived from the Greek word *gnosis* (knowledge), claimed a superior secret understanding of things. It was a system based on philosophical knowledge rather than on faith, where the distinction between the eternal, uncreated, Supreme Being and all other beings was blurred or erased. The production of matter was conceived of in terms of a downward emanation from God or as the work of a demiurge. The fact that the Gnostics belittled matter meant that they could not accept the Incarnation. Thus their knowledge of God was based on what they could acquire through their secret and elitist understanding of things rather than through revelation received from Christ. In contrast to the Gnostics, the Church dismantled barriers of race, social status and gender, and proclaimed from the first the equality of all men and women before God. One important implication of this touched the realm of truth. The elitism which had hallmarked the ancients' search for truth was clearly abandoned. Since access to the truth enables access to God, it must be denied to none.[5]

St Irenaeus declared that God should not be sought after

by means of numbers, syllables, and letters, as did the
Gnostics. For a system does not spring out of numbers, but
numbers from a system; nor does God derive His being
from things made, but things made derive their being
from God. For all things originate from one and the same
God.[6] St Irenaeus reminded his readers that man is infinitely inferior to God and cannot have experience or form
a conception of all things like God. Thus a due humility is
required in the search for knowledge concerning God.[7]
Therefore, truth and the testimony concerning God should
be the criteria in the search for knowledge about God; this
attitude towards investigation of the mystery of the living
God should lead to an increase in the love of Him who has
done, and still does, such great marvels. St Irenaeus
pointed out that even with respect to creation, the knowledge of some things belongs only to God, while others
come within the range of human knowledge; similarly, in
regard to the mysteries in the Scriptures, some can be
explained by the grace of God, while others must be left in
the hands of God. In this way, not only in the present
world, but also in that which is to come, God should for
ever teach, and man should for ever learn the things
taught him by God. Thus, perfect knowledge cannot be
attained in the present life: many questions must be
submissively left in the hands of God.[8] St Irenaeus
declared, in a well-known passage, that the Word of God
was made Man, born of the Virgin Mary, recapitulating in
Himself His own handiwork, and bringing salvation to it.[9]
This recapitulation of the human being by Christ must also
include a redemption of the human mind, enabling it to
receive knowledge of God.

An apparently total rejection of Greek philosophy was
most vividly exemplified in Tertullian's exclamations:

> What does Athens have in common with Jerusalem? What
> concord is there between the Academy and the Church?
> What between heretics and Christians? Our instruction
> comes from 'the porch of Solomon,' who had himself

taught that 'the Lord should be sought in simplicity of heart.' Away with all attempts to produce a mottled Christianity of Stoic, Platonic, and dialectic composition![10]

Tertullian's apparent distrust of reason could be a factor in the formation of the rigorist stance which he took in later life, and his joining of the Montanist sect. On the other hand, in Tertullian's *Apology*, addressed to the supreme authorities of the Empire about the year 200, his attitude to the question of the use of reason is more nuanced, and he indicates ways of arriving at the existence of God through reason:

> The object of our worship is the One God, He who by His commanding word, His arranging wisdom, His mighty power, brought forth from nothing this entire mass of our world, with all its array of elements, bodies, spirits, for the glory of His majesty; whence also the Greeks have bestowed on it the name of cosmos. The eye cannot see Him, though He is spiritually visible. He is incomprehensible, though in grace He is manifested. He is beyond our utmost thought, though our human faculties conceive of Him. He is therefore equally real and great .... This it is which gives some notion of God, while yet beyond all our conceptions; our very incapacity of fully grasping Him affords us the idea of what He really is. He is presented to our minds in His transcendent greatness, as at once known and unknown. And this is the crowning guilt of men, that they will not recognise One, of whom they cannot possibly be ignorant. Would you have the proof from the works of His hands, so numerous and so great, which both contain you and sustain you, which minister at once to your enjoyment, and strike you with awe; or would you rather have it from the testimony of the soul itself? Though under the oppressive bondage of the body, though led astray by depraving customs, though enervated by lusts and passions, though in slavery to false gods; yet, whenever the soul comes to itself, as out of a surfeit, or a sleep, or a sickness, and attains something of its natural soundness, it speaks of God .... O noble testimony of the soul by nature Christian![11]

The interesting element in Tertullian's standpoint is that he considers both an interior way of discussion to arrive at the existence of God and also an exterior way. These two ways are complementary and will be a keynote in all subsequent thought both in the Christian West and in the Christian East. In general, as regards demonstrations of God's existence, the Greek Fathers preferred the cosmological proofs of God which proceed from external experience: the Latin Fathers preferred the psychological proofs which flow from inner experience.

Around AD 305, Lactantius wrote the tract *On the Workmanship of God*, addressed to his pupil Demetrianus. According to Lactantius, God the Creator has endowed man with perception and reason, so that it might be evident that the human person derives from Him, because He Himself is intelligence, He Himself is perception and reason. God did not bestow that power of reason upon the other animals. However, God created the human being without those defences imparted to other animals, because wisdom was able to supply those things which the condition of nature had denied to him. He made him naked and defenceless, because he could be armed by his talent, and clothed by his reason. It is wonderful how the absence of those things which are given to the brutes contributes to the beauty of man. For if He had given to man the teeth of wild beasts, or horns, or claws, or hoofs, or a tail, or hairs of various colours, the human being would have been a misshapen animal. Man was formed to be an eternal and immortal being; God did not arm him, as the others, without, but within; nor did He place his protection in the body, but in the soul: since it would have been superfluous, when He had given him that which was of the greatest value, to cover him with bodily defences, especially when they hindered the beauty of the human body.[12]

St Hilary of Poitiers (315–367), a great Western Church Father also dealt with the relationship between faith and reason. His argument for a natural affirmation of the existence of God lies in the recognition of beauty in the cosmos. The Creator of great things is supreme in greatness, the Maker of beautiful things is supreme in beauty. Since the work transcends our thoughts, all thought must be transcended by the Maker. Thus heaven and air and earth and seas are beautiful: the whole universe is beautiful, hence the Greek expression *cosmos* which signifies order. However, if human thought can appraise this beauty of the universe by a natural instinct, must not the Lord of this universal beauty be recognised as Himself most beautiful amid all the beauty that surrounds Him? For although the splendour of His eternal glory overtaxes our mind's best powers, it cannot fail to see that He is beautiful. We must in truth confess that God is most beautiful, with a beauty which, though it transcend our comprehension, evokes our perception.[13] At the same time, Hilary is very definite about the obedience of steadfast faith which 'rejects the vain subtleties of philosophic enquiry' and embraces a truth lying beyond the grasp of reason which 'refuses to be vanquished by treacherous devices of human folly, and enslaved by falsehood.'[14] Faith will not confine God within the limits imposed by our common reason. The deeds of God, carried out in a manner beyond our comprehension, cannot be understood by our natural faculties, for the work of the Infinite and Eternal can only be grasped by an infinite intelligence. Hence, just as the truths that God became man, that the Immortal died, that the Eternal was buried, do not belong to the rational order but are a unique work of power, so on the other hand it is an effect not of intellect but of omnipotence that He Who is man is also God, that He Who died is immortal, that He Who was buried is eternal.[15]

St Hilary accepts the use of analogical expressions when speaking about God, but stresses that these are neither perfect nor complete. There can be no comparison between God and earthly things, yet the weakness of our understanding forces us to seek for illustrations from a lower sphere to explain our meaning about loftier themes.

The course of daily life indicates how our experience in ordinary matters enables us to form conclusions on unfamiliar subjects. St Hilary thus regards any comparison as helpful to man rather than as descriptive of God, since it suggests, rather than exhausts, the sense that we seek.[16] Considering Christ's expression concerning His Father: 'the Father is in me and I am in the Father' (Jn 10:38), Hilary affirms that here God's power brings within the range of faith's understanding an expression which is in itself beyond our comprehension. 'Thus truth beyond the dull wit of man is the prize of faith equipped with reason and knowledge; for neither may we doubt God's Word concerning Himself, nor can we suppose that the devout reason is incapable of apprehending His might.'[17] When St Hilary tried to defend the true faith concerning the Holy Trinity, he admitted:

> my brain whirls, my intellect is stunned, my very words must be a confession, not that I am weak of utterance, but that I am dumb. Yet a wish to undertake the task forces itself upon me; it means withstanding the proud, guiding the wanderer, warning the ignorant. But the subject is inexhaustible; I can see no limit to my venture of speaking concerning God in terms more precise than He Himself has used. He has assigned the Names Father, Son and Holy Spirit, which are our information of the Divine nature .... All is ineffable, unattainable, incomprehensible. Language is exhausted by the magnitude of the theme, the splendour of its brightness blinds the gazing eye, the intellect cannot compass its boundless extent. Still, under the necessity that is laid upon us, with a prayer for pardon to Him Whose attributes these are, we will venture, enquire and speak.[18]

The most famous Doctor of the patristic period in the Western Church was St Augustine (354–430), who in his own life had experienced various philosophies first hand, before he finally came to Christian faith. His encounter with different currents of thought left him unsatisfied and his reason found its true home only in the Catholic Church:

> From this time on, I gave my preference to the Catholic faith. I thought it more modest and not in the least misleading to be told by the Church to believe what could not be demonstrated – whether that was because a demonstration existed but could not be understood by all or whether the matter was not one open to rational proof – rather than to have a rash promise (from the Manichaeans) of knowledge with mockery of mere belief, and then afterwards to be ordered to believe many fabulous and absurd myths impossible to prove true.[19]

St Augustine was the first to formulate concisely the mutual relations between reason and faith: 'I believe in order to understand; and I understand, the better to believe.'[20] At the same time, he elucidated the place which authority held in faith: 'What we believe we owe to authority, what we know we owe to reason.'[21]

St Augustine developed the interior way of seeking God, which did however depend on a reflection on exterior created reality:

> I asked the heavens, the sun, moon, and stars; and they answered, 'Neither are we the God whom you seek.' And I replied to all these things which stand around the door of my flesh: 'You have told me about my God, that you are not He. Tell me something about Him.' And with a loud voice they all cried out, 'He made us.' My question had come from my observation of them, and their reply came from their beauty of order. And I turned my thoughts into myself and said, 'Who are you?' And I answered, 'A man.' For see, there is in me both a body and a soul; the one without, the other within. In which of these should I have sought my God, whom I had already sought with my body from earth to heaven .... But the inner part is the better part; for to it, as both ruler and judge, all these messengers of the senses report the answers of heaven and earth and all the things therein, who said, 'We are not God, but He

made us.' My inner man knew these things through the ministry of the outer man, and I, the inner man, knew all this – I, the soul, through the senses of my body.[22]

St Augustine also suggested how the Holy Trinity leaves an image impressed upon the human person, who if he reflects upon himself realises that he is, he knows, and he wills.[23] To be, to know and to will are dim analogies, but valid ones which can be used to illustrate the mystery of the Father, the Son and the Holy Spirit. The very fact that St Augustine hazards such an analogy, indicates his desire to propose a rational approach to faith. He pointed out that faith is reasonable, by using an analogy between human faith and divine faith. In human relationships people accept on trust, by human faith, certain things which are unseen. Why is it therefore not possible also to accept by divine faith what God reveals? St Augustine refutes the attitude of those unbelievers who seem through prudence to be unwilling to believe what they cannot see, since in their human activities they believe even those things which are not seen.[24] He shows how absurd is the attitude of those who only believe what they see; they seem almost to be precursors of modern empiricists or positivists. Citing the example of friendship, St Augustine argues that one cannot see the will and affections of a friend, but one still believes in him or her. One's own will and the will of the friend are instead perceived by the mind, by the power of reason. He retorts to the precursors of the positivists:

> You discern your friend's face with the faculties of your own body, you discern your own faith through the powers of your own mind; but you do not love your friend's faith, unless there exists in you that faith, through which you believe that which is in him but which you do not see.[25]

He remarks that if faith be taken away from human affairs, great disorder and fearful confusion must follow. If people cease to believe what they do not see, who will love anyone with mutual affection, since love itself is invisible?[26] St Augustine concludes that we certainly ought to believe certain temporal things, which we do not see, in order that we may merit to see eternal things also, which we believe. He adopts the analogy of human faith within friendship and thus applies it to supernatural faith. The wills of friends, which are not seen, are believed through symbols which are seen. In a similar way, the Church, which is now seen, is a guarantee of those past things unseen, and a herald of those future things which have not yet been revealed. St Augustine proposed that if we believe lesser authorities in our everyday life, should be not accept the higher authority of God?[27]

According to this great Doctor of the Church, it is the authority of God revealing Himself in Christ which provides a healing and a purification of the intellect. This authority raises the mind from dwelling merely on the earth, and helps it to turn from the love of this world to love of the True God. There exists a happy conspiracy between the outward form of all things which assuredly flows from some fountain of truest beauty, and the inward conscience, which both exhort the mind to seek God, and to serve God. The same God Himself offered some authority, whereby, as on a safe staircase, we may be lifted up unto God. One external proof of this authority is through the visible miracles which Christ performed: the sick were healed, the lepers were cleansed; walking was restored to the lame, sight to the blind, hearing to the deaf. The men of that time saw water turned into wine, five thousand filled with five loaves, seas crossed on foot, the dead rising again. Some of these wonders provided more for the good of the body, others more for the good of the soul but all were carried out for the good of men by their witness to God's authority.[28] St Augustine also mentioned that faith also in a certain sense 'prepares for reason'[29] namely it grants wisdom and health to the intellect and brings the reasoning power to a greater perfection.

Boethius (480–524) was a Latin Christian philosopher

who was distinctly optimistic concerning the capabilities of human reason in its quest for God. His basis was that the universe is rational because it has been created by God who is supremely rational, as exemplified in the following verse:

> O You who govern the universe by everlasting reason,
> sower of earth and heaven,
> You who from eternity order time to pass
> and remaining stable give movement to all things.
> Neither external causes nor envy impelled You to create
> a true work of changing matter, for within Yourself You
>   are the perfect Good.
> You lead all things to follow a heavenly model.
> In perfect beauty, Your mind rules a world of beauty,
> shaping all in a like image, and bidding the perfect whole
>   to complete its perfect parts.
> All the first principles of nature You bind together in
>   perfect numerical harmony,
> so that each may be balanced with its opposite:
> cold with heat, and dryness with moisture together;
> thus fire may not fly upward too swiftly because too
>   purely,
> nor may the weight of the solid earth drag it down and
>   overwhelm it.[30]

Boethius also anticipated the thought of St Anselm in his ontological argument for the existence of God when he declared: 'The common conception of the human spirit proves that God, the principle of all things, is good; for since nothing better than God can be thought of, who may doubt that He, than Whom there is nothing better, must be good?'[31] Boethius opposed chance explanations of the universe, which were in vogue during his time, much as they are today. 'If chance is defined as an outcome of random influence, produced by no sequence of causes, I am sure that there is no such thing as chance, and I consider that it is but an empty word .... For what place can be left for anything happening at random, so long as

God controls everything in order? It is a true saying that nothing can come out of nothing.'[32] Boethius was also most famous for his affirmation, in a classical passage, that the eternity of God also lies within reach of human reason:

> Then that God is eternal
> is the judgement by the common reason of all peoples.
> Then let us consider what eternity may be;
> for this will make clear to us at once
> divine nature and knowledge.
> Then eternity is at once
> the total and perfect possession of interminable life.
> This is more clearly evident
> from comparison of the temporal.
>
> For whatever lives in time
> proceeds from the past through the present into the future
> and there is nothing established in time
> which can grasp at once the entire space of its life,
> but in fact it does not yet apprehend tomorrow
> while it has already lost yesterday;
> And in this time of today
> your life is no more than a changing, passing moment.
>
> So what comprehends and so possesses at once
> the entire fullness of interminable life,
> to whom nothing of the future may be absent
> nor has anything of the past vanished,
> is rightly asserted to be eternal
> and it must be both present in control of itself
> to always stand by itself
> and have present the infinity of passing time.[33]

St Isidore of Seville (560–636) marked the end of the age of the Fathers of the Church, and in many ways represented a bridge between the patristic epoch and the Middle Ages. He warned against laziness of the intellect in relation to faith and encouraged study, reading and prayer to arrive at a deeper understanding of what God has revealed:

Some people are naturally endowed with intelligence but they neglect the pursuit of reading and they despise by their neglect the things which they might have been able to know by reading. On the other hand, some people have a love of knowledge, but are hindered through a slowness of understanding; but they do manage through constant reading to acquire the wisdom which the cleverer people in their idleness do not. Just as the one who is slow at understanding, nevertheless gains the prize for good study because of his application, so the one who neglects the natural ability to understand, which he has been given by God, stands as a culprit to be condemned, since he despises the gift he has received, and sins through idleness.[34]

An episode is recounted whereby Isidore once noticed water dripping on a rock near where he sat. The drops of water that fell repeatedly carried no force and seemed to have no effect on the solid stone. And yet he saw that over time, the water drops had worn holes in the rock. Isidore realised that if he kept working at his studies, his seemingly small efforts would eventually pay off in great learning. His encyclopaedia of knowledge, the *Etymologies*, contained all the learning that was available at the time and was a popular textbook for nine centuries. Isidore was therefore called 'The Schoolmaster of the Middle Ages.' He also wrote books on grammar, astronomy, geography, history, and biography as well as theology. When the Arabs brought the study of Aristotle back to Europe, this was nothing new to Spain because Isidore's open mind had previously reintroduced the philosopher to students there. He stated that 'The more conscientious one is in becoming familiar with the sacred writings, the richer an understanding one will draw from them: just as when the earth is cultivated to a greater extent, the more abundant is its harvest.'[35] St Isidore is now the patron saint of information technology.

The Christian East

An openly constructive dialogue with Greek philosophy was undertaken by St Justin (100–165). He based his discourse upon the creation of the universe out of nothing by God:

> For as in the beginning He created us when we were not, so do we consider that, in like manner, those who choose what is pleasing to Him are, on account of their choice, deemed worthy of incorruption and of fellowship with Him. For the coming into being at first was not in our own power; and in order that we may follow those things which please Him, choosing them by means of the rational faculties He has Himself endowed us with, He both persuades us and leads us to faith.[36]

Reason in Justin's vision therefore plays an important part in the process of coming to faith. Justin also proposed a theory of the seeds of the Word. In this perspective, the eternal Word of God who manifested Himself prophetically and in figure to the Jews, also showed Himself partially to the Greeks in the form of seeds of truth.

> We worship and love the Word who is from the unbegotten and ineffable God, since also He became man for our sakes, that, becoming a partaker of our sufferings, He might also bring us healing. For all the writers were able to see realities darkly through the sowing of the implanted word that was in them. For the seed and imitation imparted according to capacity is one thing, and quite another is the thing itself, of which there is the participation and imitation according to the grace which is from Him.

Justin concludes that, since Christianity is the historical and personal manifestation of the Word in His totality, it follows that 'everything beautiful that was said by anyone belongs to us Christians.'[37] St Justin continued to hold Greek philosophy in high esteem after his conversion, but insisted that he had found in Christianity 'the only sure and profitable philosophy.'[38] The worship offered to Christ must be reasonable, since the Christian has learned that He is the Son of the true God Himself.[39]

St Justin's approach was developed by the school of Alexandria, and in the first instance by Clement (160–215). Here not only is Greek philosophy not rejected, but it is actually seen as a help in defending the faith: 'Greek philosophy, with its contribution, does not strengthen truth; but, in rendering the attack of sophistry impotent and in disarming those who betray truth and wage war upon it, Greek philosophy is rightly called the hedge and the protective wall around the vineyard.'[40] Clement in a magnificent manner distinguishes and explains the various characteristics of faith, knowledge and wisdom. Knowledge is a perfecting of man as man, and is further elevated 'by acquaintance with divine things' conformable to itself and to the divine Word. Faith is perfected by knowledge, and this faith, without searching for God, confesses His existence, and glorifies Him. It is from this faith, and in accordance with the faith, that this knowledge regarding God is through His grace to be acquired as far as possible. Knowledge (*gnosis*) differs from the wisdom (*sophia*), which is the result of teaching. It is undoubtedly belief in God which is the basis of knowledge. 'Faith is then, so to speak, a comprehensive knowledge of the essentials; and knowledge is the strong and sure demonstration of what is received by faith, built upon faith by the Lord's teaching, carrying the soul on to certainty, knowledge, and comprehension. And, in my view, the first saving change is that from heathenism to faith ... and the second, that from faith to knowledge. And the latter terminating in love, thereafter gives the loving to the loved, that which knows to that which is known.'[41]

Origen (185–253) carried forward the thought of the Alexandrian school in regard to the rôle of reason. He stressed the importance of reason to access the Scriptures, in which the accounts related in the Gospels concerning

Jesus invite thinking people to more than a 'simple and unreasoning faith.' What is required is insight into the meaning of the writers, so that the purpose with which each event has been recorded may be discovered.[42] Origen observed that it is much more consonant with the spirit of Christianity to give assent to doctrines upon grounds of reason and wisdom than on that of faith alone, and that it was only in certain circumstances that the approach of naked faith was desired by Christianity, in order not to leave men altogether without help, as is shown by St Paul when he wrote: 'Since in the wisdom of God the world was unable to recognise God through wisdom, it was God's own pleasure to save believers through the folly of the gospel (1 Co 1:21).'[43] In one of his most beautiful passages from the *Commentary on the Song of Songs*, Origen links reason and love describing how God wounds the soul which loves Him with His arrow of love, His own Word. Here are linked a reflection upon the beauty of creation, leading to the Word, through Whom all things were made, as well as a love which perfects reason:

> And the soul is moved by heavenly love and longing when, having clearly beheld the beauty and the fairness of the Word of God, it falls deeply in love with His loveliness and receives from the Word Himself a certain arrow and wound of love ... If, then, a man can so extend his thinking as to ponder and consider the beauty and the grace of all the things that have been created in the Word, the very charm of them will so smite him, the grandeur of their brightness will so pierce him as with *a chosen arrow* – as says the prophet – that he will suffer from the arrow Himself a saving wound, and will be kindled with the blessed fire of His love.[44]

Origen then proposes an analogy between Solomon and Christ, and the Queen of Sheba and the Church. The Queen, like the Church, is chosen from the nations. The Queen came to hear the wisdom of Solomon; the Church also comes to hear the wisdom of the true Solomon, and of the true Peace-Lover, Our Lord Jesus Christ. 'She too at first comes *trying Him with riddles and with questions,* which had seemed to her insoluble before; and He resolves all her perplexity concerning the knowledge of the true God, and concerning the created things of the world, the immortality of the soul, and the future judgement, all of which ever remained doubtful and uncertain for her and for her teachers, at least for the Gentile philosophers.'[45] Origen elucidated how the Wisdom of Christ transcends all the thought of pagan philosophers. For when the Queen, as type of the Church, spoke to Solomon (as a type of Christ) she was amazed and exclaimed: 'The report is true which I heard in my own country concerning Your word and concerning Your prudence. For because of Your word, which I recognised as the true word, I came to You. For all the words that were said to me, and which I heard while I was in my own country, from worldly teachers and philosophers were not true words. That only is the true word, which is in You.'[46]

One of the most outstanding exponents of the Antiochene school of theology regarding reason and faith was Theophilus of Antioch, active during the second half of the second century. In his reply to Autolycus, an idolater who scorned Christians, he formulated many rational demonstrations of God's existence. In reply to the retort of his opponent, 'Show me your God,' Theophilus replied: 'Show me yourself as a man, and I will show you my God.' The eyes of the soul are capable of seeing, and the ears of the heart are able to hear; for as those who look with the eyes of the body perceive earthly objects and what concerns this life, and discriminate at the same time between things that differ, whether light or dark, white or black, deformed or beautiful, well-proportioned and symmetrical or disproportioned and awkward, or monstrous or mutilated; and as in like manner also, by the sense of hearing, we discriminate either sharp, or deep, or sweet sounds; so the same holds good regarding the eyes of the soul and the ears of the heart, that it is by them we are able to behold God. For God is seen by those who are enabled to see Him when they have the eyes of their soul opened: for all have eyes; but in some they are covered, and do not see the light of the sun. Yet it does not follow, because the blind do not see, that the light of the sun does not shine; but let the blind blame themselves and their own eyes. Theophilus linked with sin the incapacity for seeing God with the eyes of the soul. When there is rust on the mirror, it is not possible that a man's face be seen in the mirror; so also when there is sin in a man, such a man cannot behold God. As when a film of impurity on the eyes prevents one from beholding the light of the sun: so also do iniquities envelop man in darkness, so that he cannot see God.[47] For Theophilus, 'the appearance of God is ineffable and indescribable, and cannot be seen by eyes of flesh. For in glory He is incomprehensible, in greatness unfathomable, in height inconceivable, in power incomparable, in wisdom unrivalled, in goodness inimitable, in kindness unutterable.'[48] At the same time, he outlined how God may be known through His creation.

Theophilus elaborated the analogy between the human soul and God. For just as the soul in man is invisible to men, but is perceived through the motion of the body, so God cannot indeed be seen by human eyes, but is beheld and perceived through His providence and works. Just as any person, when he sees a ship on the sea rigged and in sail, and making for the harbour, will clearly deduce that there is a captain in her who is steering her; so also we must perceive that God is the governor of the whole universe, though He be not visible to the eyes of the flesh, since He is incomprehensible. For if a man cannot look upon the sun, though it be a very small heavenly body, on account of its exceeding heat and power, how shall not a mortal man be much more unable to face the glory of God, which is unutterable?[49] However, in order to make the deduction from the creation to its Creator, the human person needs a healing of the intellect because of the blindness of the soul, and the hardness of the heart. If there is a desire at least for healing, the Physician will soothe the eyes of the soul and of the heart. God is the Physician who heals through His word and wisdom.[50] Finally, Theophilus provides some examples to indicate that the Christian doctrine of the resurrection of the body is reasonable. Through His creation God provides many analogies of resurrection, so that we may see that the resurrection is indeed reasonable. One example is seen in the 'dying' of seasons, and days, and nights, and how these also 'rise again'. A further picture is found in the seed of wheat which, when it is cast into the earth, first dies and rots away, then is raised, and becomes a stalk of corn. The work of resurrection is going on in man, even though he be unaware of it. For when someone has fallen sick, and lost flesh, and strength, and beauty; but then received again from God mercy and healing, and recovered also physical strength, that person has in a sense experienced a prefiguration of the resurrection. In all these things, the wisdom of God shows that He is able to effect the general resurrection of all men.[51]

St Athanasius of Alexandria (296–373) was another Eastern Father who was a staunch defender of reasoned faith. He demonstrated the illogical nature of idol worship, indicating that no part of the creation can be a god because of the mutual dependence of those parts. For if a man take the parts of creation separately, and consider each by itself, for example the sun by itself alone, and the moon apart, and again earth and air, and heat and cold, separating them from their mutual conjunction, he will certainly find that not one is sufficient for itself, but all are in need of one another's assistance, and subsist by their mutual help. For the sun is carried round along with, and is contained in, the whole heaven, and can never go beyond its own orbit, while the moon and other stars testify to the assistance given them by the sun: while the earth again evidently does not yield its crops without rains, which in their turn would not descend to earth without the assistance of the clouds; but not even would the clouds ever appear of themselves and subsist, without the air.[52] Neither can the cosmic totality be God, for that would make God consist of dissimilar parts, and subject Him to possible dissolution. For if the combination of the parts makes up the whole, and the whole is combined out of the parts, then the whole consists of the parts, and each of them is a portion of the whole. However this is very far removed from the conception of God. For God is a whole and not a number of parts, and does not consist of various elements, but is Himself the Maker of the system of the universe.[53]

Athanasius asserted that 'the soul of man, being intellectual, can know God of itself, if it be true to its own nature.'[54] By affirming the existence of the rational human soul, Athanasius proposed a stepping stone to the contemplation of the Creator. The existence of the human soul is proved by the essential difference between man and the animals. The human person alone thinks of things external to himself, and reasons about things not actually present, and exercises reflection, and chooses by judgement the better of alternative reasonings. For the irrational animals see only what is present, and are impelled solely by what meets their eye, even if the consequences to them are injurious, while man is not impelled toward what he sees merely, but judges by thought what he sees with his eyes. In order to illustrate his point, Athanasius adopts the example of a lyre in the hands of a skilled musician. For each string of this musical instrument delivers its proper note, high, low, or intermediate, sharp or otherwise, yet their scale is indistinguishable and their time not to be recognised, without the artist. For only then is the scale evident and the time right, when the player holding the lyre plucks the strings and touches each in tune. In like manner, the senses are deployed in the body like the strings in a lyre; when the skilled intelligence presides over them, then too the soul distinguishes and knows what it is doing and how it is acting. This characteristic is specific to mankind, and this is what is rational in the soul of man and of woman, and shows that it is truly distinct from what is to be seen in the body.[55]

For Athanasius, only when the soul gets rid of the stains of sin is it able to know God directly, and then its own rational nature is once more the image of the Word of God, in whose likeness it was created. However, he pointed out that even if the soul cannot pierce the cloud which sin draws over its vision, it nevertheless can attain to the knowledge of God from the things which are seen, since creation, as though in written characters, declares in a loud voice, by its order and harmony, its own Lord and Creator.[56] St Athanasius proclaims that creation is a revelation of God, especially because of the order and harmony which pervades it. Anyone seeing the circle of heaven and the course of the sun and the moon, and the positions and movements of the other stars, as they take place in opposite and different directions, while yet in their difference all with one accord observe a consistent order, should be able to come to the conclusion that these are not ordered by themselves, but have a Maker distinct from themselves who orders them.[57] The great Eastern Doctor applies a similar musical analogy once again to illustrate that the harmony in nature is a reflection of the unity of God. If one were to hear from a distance a lyre, composed of many different strings, and marvel at the concord of its symphony, in that its sound is composed neither of low notes exclusively, nor high nor intermediate only, but all combine their sounds in equal balance; one would not fail to perceive from this that the lyre was not playing itself, nor even being struck by more persons than one, but that there was one musician, even if he did not see him, who by his skill combined the sound of each string into the tuneful symphony. In a similar manner, since the order of the whole universe is perfectly harmonious, without discord of the higher against the lower or the lower against the higher, and all things make up one order, it is consistent to think that the Ruler and King of all Creation is one and not many, Who by His own light illumines and gives movement to all.[58]

Finally, St Athanasius showed that the rationality and

order of the Universe indicate that it is the work of the Reason or Word of God. Three similes illustrate the power of the Word who guarantees rationality to the Universe. The first picture is that of a choir composed of different people, children, women, and old men, and those who are still young, and, when one, namely the conductor, gives the sign, each utters sound according to his nature and power, the man as a man, the child as a child, the old man as an old man, and the young man as a young man, while all make up a single harmony. The second image is that of the human soul which at the same time moves our several senses in a rational way according to the proper function of each, so that when some one object is present all alike are put in motion, and the eye sees, the ear hears, the hand touches, the smell takes in odour, and the palate tastes. The third example is that of a very great city, administered under the presence of the king who has built it; for when he is present and gives orders, and has his eye upon everything, all obey; some busy themselves with agriculture, others hasten for water to the aqueducts, another goes forth to procure provisions, one goes to the senate, another enters the assembly, the judge goes to the bench, and the magistrate to his court. The workman likewise settles to his craft, the sailor goes down to the sea, the carpenter to his workshop, the physician to his treatment, the architect to his building; and while one is going to the country, another is returning from the country, and while some walk about the town, others are going out of the town and returning to it again: but all this is going on and is organised by the presence of the one Ruler, and by his management. These similes show how we must conceive of the whole of creation: for by the power of the Word of God, all things simultaneously fall into order, and each discharge their proper functions, and a single order is made up by them all together.[59] The similes apply to the whole Universe, seen and unseen. By the power of the Divine Word of the Father that governs and presides over all, the heaven revolves, the stars move, the sun shines, the moon travels her circuit, the air receives the sun's light and the winds blow: the mountains are reared on high, the sea is rough with waves, the living things in it grow, the earth abides fixed, and bears fruit, and man is formed and lives and dies again, and all things whatever have their life and movement; fire burns, water cools, fountains spring forth, rivers flow, seasons and hours come round, rains descend, clouds are filled, hail is formed, snow and ice congeal, birds fly, creeping things move along, water-animals swim, the sea is navigated, the earth is sown and yields crops in due season, plants grow, and some are young, some ripening, others become old and decay, and while some things are vanishing, others are being generated and are coming to light.[60]

St John Damascene (676–770) wrote beautifully about the natural knowledge of God. The knowledge of God's existence has been implanted by Him in all human beings by nature. The creation also and its maintenance, and its government, proclaim the majesty of the Divine nature.[61] Despite this fact that the knowledge of the existence of God is implanted in the human being by nature, the wickedness of the Evil One has prevailed so mightily against man's nature as even to drive some into the pit of destruction whereby they deny the existence of God.[62] St John Damascene indicated that the Apostles convinced by means of miracles, but since he claimed not to have that gift, he proposed instead some rational demonstrations of God's existence. One example of his proofs was a precursor of one of St Thomas Aquinas' proofs.[63] It runs like this. All things that exist are either created or uncreated. If, then, things are created, it follows that they are also wholly mutable. For things whose existence originated in change, must also be subject to change, whether it be that they perish or that they become other than they are by an act of their wills. However, if things are uncreated they must, for consistency, be also wholly immutable. For things which are opposed in the nature of their existence must also be opposed in the mode of their existence, that is to say, must have opposite properties: who, then, will refuse to grant that all existing things, not only such as come within the province of the senses, but even the angels, are subject to change and transformation and movement of various kinds? For the things belonging to the rational world, namely angels and spirits and demons, are subject to changes of will, whether it is a progression or a retrogression in goodness, whether a struggle or a surrender; while the others suffer changes of generation and destruction, of increase and decrease, of quality and of movement in space. Things then that are mutable are also wholly created. However, things that are created must be the work of some Maker, and the Maker cannot have been created. For if He had been created, He also must surely have been created by someone, and so on till we arrive at something uncreated. The Creator, then, being uncreated, is also wholly immutable. And who could this be other than the Deity?[64]

The Fathers both of Eastern and of Western Christendom showed how reason, freed from the bondage of paganism, could find its way out of the blind alley of myth and superstition and be enlightened by the liberating force of the Gospel. Purified and rightly tuned, therefore, reason could rise to the higher planes of thought, providing a solid foundation for the perception of being, of the transcendent and of the absolute.[65] It was the task of the Scholastic Doctors to continue the task which the Fathers had begun.

Notes

[1]   See Pope John Paul II, *Fides et Ratio* 39.
[2]   *Epistle to Diognetus*, c. 5 in *PG* 2, 1173–1174.
[3]   Ibid., c. 11 in *PG* 2, 1183–1184.
[4]   Cf. ibid., c. 12 in *PG* 2, 1185–1186.
[5]   See Pope John Paul II, *Fides et Ratio* 19.
[6]   See St Irenaeus, *Adversus haereses* Book II, chapter 25, 1 in *PG* 7, 798.
[7]   See ibid., chapter 25, 3 and 4 in *PG* 7, 799.
[8]   See ibid., chapter 28, 1–3 in *PG* 7, 804–806.

[9]   See ibid., Book III, chapter 22, 1–2 in *PG* 7, 955–958.

[10]   Tertullian, *De Praescriptione Haereticorum*, chapter 7 in *PL* 2, 20.

[11]   Idem, *Apology*, 17 in *PL* 1, 375–377.

[12]   See Lactantius, *On the Workmanship of God*, chapter 2 in *PL* 7, 14–16.

[13]   See St Hilary of Poitiers, *On the Trinity*, Book I, n. 7 in *PL* 10, 30.

[14]   Ibid., n. 13 in *PL* 10, 34.

[15]   See ibid. in *PL* 10, 35.

[16]   See ibid. n. 19. in *PL* 10, 38–39.

[17]   Ibid., n. 22 in *PL* 10, 39.

[18]   Ibid., Book II, n. 5 in *PL* 10, 54.

[19]   Saint Augustine, *Confessions*, Book 6, chapter 5, 7 in *PL* 32, 722.

[20]   Idem, *Sermon* 43, chapter 7, 9 in *PL* 38, 257–258. The Latin is 'Intellige, ut credas, verbum meum; crede, ut intelligas, verbum Dei.'

[21]   Idem, *De utilitate credendi* (On the profit of believing), 11, 25 in *PL* 42, 83. The Latin is 'Quod intelligimus igitur, debemus rationi: quod credimus, auctoritati.'

[22]   Idem, *Confessions*, Book 10, chapter 6, n. 9 in *PL* 32, 783.

[23]   Ibid., Book 13, chapter 11, n. 12 in *PL* 32, 849.

[24]   See St Augustine, *De fide rerum quae non videntur* (Concerning faith in things not seen), chapter 1 in *PL* 40, 171.

[25]   Ibid., chapter 3 in *PL* 40, 174.

[26]   Cf. Ibid., chapter 4 in *PL* 40, 176.

[27]   Cf. Ibid.

[28]   See St Augustine, *De utilitate credendi*, Book I, chapter 16, n. 34 in *PL* 42, 89–90.

[29]   Ibid., chapter 17, n. 35 in *PL* 42, 91. The Latin text runs: 'Nam si nulla certa ad sapientiam salutemque animis via est, nisi cum eos rationi praecolit fides; quid est aliud ingratum esse opi atque auxilio divino, quam tanto labore praedictae auctoritati velle resistere?'

[30]   Boethius, *Consolation of Philosophy*, Book 3, verse 9 in *PL* 63, 758–760.

[31]   Ibid., Book 3, prose 10 in *PL* 63, 765.

[32]   Ibid., Book 5, prose 1 in *PL* 63, 830–831.

[33]   Ibid., Book 5, prose 6 in *PL* 63, 858–859.

[34]   Saint Isidore, *Book 3 of the Sentences*, chapter 9, 5–8 in *PL* 83, 681–682.

[35]   Idem, *Book 3 of the Sentences*, chapter 9, 2 in *PL* 83, 681. The Latin is 'Quanto quisque magis in sacris eloquiis assiduus fuerit, tanto ex eis uberiorem intelligentiam capit; sicut terra, quae quanto amplius excolitur, tanto uberius fructificat.'

[36]   St Justin Martyr, *The First Apology*, 10 in *PG* 6, 341–342.

[37]   St Justin Martyr, *The Second Apology*, 13 in *PG* 6, 465–466.

[38]   Idem. *Dialogue with Trypho*, 8 in *PG* 6, 491–492.

[39]   Cf. Idem, *The First Apology*, 13 in *PG* 6, 345–348.

[40]   Clement of Alexandria, *Stromata*, Book I, c. 20 in *PG* 8, 817–818.

41   Ibid., Book VII, c. 10 in *PG* 9, 481–482.

42   See Origen, *Contra Celsum*, Book 1, n. 42 in *PG* 11, 737–738.

43   See Origen, *Contra Celsum*, Book 1, n. 13 in *PG* 11, 679–680.

44   See Origen, *Commentary on the Song of Songs*, Prologue 2 in *Ancient Christian Writers* vol. 26, Origen. *The Song of Songs Commentary and Homilies*, translated and annotated by R. P. Lawson (New York: Newman Press, 1956) pp. 29–30. See also the passage from the Song of Songs to which Origen refers, namely Ct 2:5, which in the Greek Septuagint reads: τετρωμένη ἀγάπης ἐγώ, or 'I am wounded by love.' The New Jerusalem Bible translation 'I am sick with love' is rather weaker. This passage has inspired many generations of Christian mystics besides Origen, including St Gregory of Nyssa, St Augustine, St Theresa of Avila and St John of the Cross to consider the wound of love. See also Is 49:2 'He made me into a sharpened arrow and concealed me in his quiver.'

45   Origen, *Commentary on the Song of Songs*, Book 2, 1 in *The Song of Songs Commentary and Homilies*, p. 98.

46   Ibid., p. 100. 1 K 10:6–8; 2 Ch 9:5–7.

47   See Theophilus of Antioch, *To Autolycus* Book I, n. 2 in *PG* 6, 1025–1028.

48   Ibid., n. 3 in *PG* 6, 1027–1028.

49   See Ibid., n. 5 in *PG* 6, 1031–1032.

50   See Ibid., n. 7 in *PG* 6, 1033–1036.

51   See Ibid., n. 13 in *PG* 6, 1041–1044.

52   See St Athanasius, *Against the Heathen* Part I, n. 27 in *PG* 25, 51–56.

53   See ibid., n. 28 in *PG* 25, 55–58.

54   Ibid., n. 30 in *PG* 25, 61–62.

55   See ibid., n. 31 in *PG* 25, 61–64.

56   See ibid., n. 34 in *PG* 25, 67–70.

57   See Ibid., n. 35 in *PG* 25, 69–72.

58   See Ibid., n. 38 in *PG* 25, 75–78.

59   See Ibid., n. 43 in *PG* 25, 85–88.

60   See Ibid., n. 44 in *PG* 25, 87–88.

61   See St John Damascene, *An Exposition of the Orthodox Faith* Book I, chapter 1, in *PG* 94, 789–790.

62   Ibid., Book I, chapter 3, in *PG* 94, 793–798.

63   See chapter 7, p. 185 and note 14 on pp. 211–212 below.

64   See St John Damascene, *An Exposition of the Orthodox Faith* Book I, chapter 3, in *PG* 94, 793–798.

65   See Pope John Paul II, *Fides et Ratio* 41.

CHAPTER 4

MEDIEVAL MEANING

Let us hasten from faith to knowledge. Let us endeavour so far as we can, to understand what we believe.
                              Richard of St Victor, *De Trinitate*

Now in those things which we hold about God there is truth in two ways. For certain things that are true about God wholly surpass the capability of human reason, for instance that God is Three and One: while there are certain things to which even natural reason can attain, for instance that God is, that God is One, and others like these, which even the philosophers proved demonstratively of God, being guided by the light of natural reason.

In the teaching of philosophy which considers creatures in themselves and leads us from them to the knowledge of God, the first consideration is about creatures, and the last of God: whereas in the teaching of faith which considers creatures only in their relation to God, the consideration about God takes the first place, and that about creatures the last. And thus faith is more perfect, as being more like God's knowledge; for He beholds other things by knowing Himself.
                              St Thomas Aquinas, *Summa Contra Gentiles*

The writings of Fathers of the Church like St Augustine, Pseudo-Dionysius the Areopagite and Boethius stimulated later thought on the rational component of belief in

God. Following their lead, the medieval Doctors developed earlier ideas, added to them and refined them and,
above all, elaborated them into a real organic synthesis of
reason and faith. The leading figure in this regard was St
Thomas Aquinas.

St Anselm

A consideration of the medieval contribution to the importance of reason for Christian faith begins with St Anselm,
Archbishop of Canterbury, Doctor of the Church
(1033–1109), who was a great exponent of relations
between reason and faith in the early Middle Ages. During
his period as Prior of Bec, he composed the *Monologium*
and the *Proslogium*. Anselm was situated in the first phase
of the controversy on universals, and countered the
extreme nominalism of Roscelin with a firm realism which
was also derived from his Platonist perspective. Anselm's
chief contribution in the relations between faith and
reason is the so-called ontological argument for the existence of God proposed in his *Proslogion* which will be
discussed later in greater detail.[1] For St Anselm, the
dynamism of faith is not in competition with the search
undertaken by reason. Reason is not asked to pass judgement on the contents of faith, something of which it would
be incapable, since this is not its purpose. Its function is
rather to find meaning, to discover explanations which
facilitate a certain understanding of the contents of faith.
St Anselm thus stressed the first part of the Augustinian
binomial: 'I believe in order to understand; and I understand, the better to believe.'[2] Anselm conveyed this with
his famous expressions 'faith seeking understanding,'[3]
and 'I believe in order that I may understand.'[4]

Saint Anselm maintained that the intellect must seek
that which it loves: the more it loves, the more it desires to
know. Whoever lives for the truth is reaching for a form of
knowledge which is fired more and more with love for

what it knows, at the same time admitting that it has not yet attained what it desires: 'To see You was I conceived; and I have yet to conceive that for which I was conceived'[5] The desire for truth, therefore, spurs reason always to go further; indeed, it is as if reason were overwhelmed to see that it can always go beyond what it has already achieved. It is at this point, though, that reason can learn where its path will lead in the end:

> I think that whoever investigates something incomprehensible should be satisfied if, by way of reasoning, he reaches a quite certain perception of its reality, even if his intellect cannot penetrate its mode of being .... But is there anything so incomprehensible and ineffable as that which is above all things? Therefore, if that which until now has been a matter of debate concerning the highest essence has been established on the basis of due reasoning, then the foundation of one's certainty is not shaken in the least if the intellect cannot penetrate it in a way that allows clear formulation. If prior thought has concluded rationally that one cannot comprehend how supernal wisdom knows its own accomplishments ..., who then will explain how this same wisdom, of which the human being can know nothing or next to nothing, is to be known and expressed?[6]

French Scholastics

Peter Abelard (1079–1142), notwithstanding some doubtful theological opinions, played a distinctive rôle in the development of medieval thought. Among his teachers was Roscelin the Nominalist. As regards the problem of Universals, Abelard took a position of uncompromising hostility to the crude nominalism of Roscelin on the one side, and to the exaggerated realism of William of Champeaux on the other. It seems that Abelard's doctrine, while bearing some similarities to nominalism, was very similar to the moderate realism which began to take root about half a century after his death. With regard to the relation between reason and revelation, between the sciences including philosophy, and theology, Abelard incurred in his own day the censure of mystic theologians like St Bernard, whose tendency was to disinherit reason in favour of contemplation and ecstatic vision. If the principles 'Reason aids Faith' and 'Faith aids Reason' are to be taken as the inspiration of scholastic theology, Abelard was typically inclined to emphasize the former, and not lay stress on the latter. His influence on the philosophers and theologians of the thirteenth century was, however, very great. It was exercised chiefly through Peter Lombard, his pupil, and other shapers of the *Books of the Sentences*.

An important figure in the condemnation of Abelard's theological errors was St Bernard of Clairvaux (1090–1153). In his mystical theology, he accords a more submissive rôle to reason, but nevertheless it has a place in his theological discourse. Bernard, one of the strongest personalities in history, who came down from the loftiest peaks of mysticism to share divine and human truth with the ecclesial and civil society of his time, as a true master of love and knowledge, described the five motives that lead human beings to study. There are people who only wish to know for the sake of knowing: this is base curiosity. Others desire to know in order that they themselves may be known: this is shameful vanity. Then there are those who acquire knowledge in order to re-sell it, and for example to make money or gain honours from it: their motive is distasteful. However some wish to know in order to edify: this is charity. Others desire knowledge in order to be edified: this is wisdom. Only those who belong to these last two categories do not misuse knowledge, since they only seek to understand in order to do good.[7]

According to this great Cistercian saint, we owe gratitude to God for three key gifts, which should be cherished without neglecting the Giver. These three gifts are dignity, wisdom and virtue. By dignity Bernard means free will, whereby the human person not only excels all other earthly creatures, but has dominion over them. Wisdom is the power whereby he recognises this dignity, and perceives also that it is no accomplishment of his own. Virtue impels man to seek eagerly for Him who is man's Source, and to lay fast hold on Him when He has been found. Bernard indicated how dignity without wisdom is worthless; and wisdom is harmful without virtue, and proposed this argument to illustrate his point:

> There is no glory in having a gift without knowing it. However to know only that you have it, without knowing that it is not of yourself that you have it, means boasting, rather than giving true glory to God. And so the Apostle Paul says to men in such cases, 'What have you got that was not given to you? And if it was given to you, why are you boasting as though it were your own?'(1 Co 4:7). He asks, Why do you boast? but goes on, as if you had not received it, showing that the guilt is not in glorying over a possession, but in glorying as though it had not been received. And rightly such glorying is called vain-glory, since it has not the solid foundation of truth. The Apostle shows how to discern the true glory from the false, when he says, 'If anyone wants to boast, let him boast of the Lord', that is, in the Truth, since our Lord is Truth (1 Co 1:31; Jn 14:6).[8]

St Bernard's approach to reason is one of humility, which he summarised succinctly: 'We must know, then, what we are, and that it is not of ourselves that we are what we are. Unless we know this thoroughly, either we shall not glory at all, or our glorying will be vain.'[9] The human being must know himself as the creature that is distinguished, by the possession of reason, from the irrational beasts. Otherwise if he starts to be confused with them and ignorant of his own true glory which is within, man can be held captive by his curiosity, in concerning himself with external, sensual things. St Bernard warns that we must be on our guard against this ignorance. He proposes that 'we must not rank ourselves too low; and with still greater care we must see that we do not think of ourselves more highly than we ought to think, as happens when we foolishly impute to ourselves whatever good may be in us.'[10] Even more important than avoiding these kinds of ignorance, it is essential to detest that presumption which would lead us to glory in goods which are not our own, knowing that they are not of ourselves but of God, and yet not fearing to rob God of the honour due to Him. In this case man sins not in ignorance but deliberately, usurping the glory which belongs to God. Pride only, the chief of all iniquities, can make us treat gifts as if they were rightful attributes of our nature, and, while receiving benefits, rob our Benefactor of His due glory. Thus, concludes St Bernard, to dignity and wisdom we must add virtue, the proper fruit of them both. Virtue seeks and finds Him who is the Author and Giver of all good, and who must be in all things glorified. When a person possesses virtue, then wisdom and dignity are not dangerous but blessed.

St Bernard also suggests that even those who do not know Christ are sufficiently taught by the natural law, and by their own endowments of soul and body, to love God for God's own sake. He asks:

What infidel does not know that he has received light, air, food, namely all things necessary for his own body's life, from Him alone who provides food for all living creatures (Ps 136:25), causes His sun to rise on the bad as well as the good, and sends down rain to fall on the upright and the wicked alike (Mt 5:45). Who is so impious as to attribute the singular pre-eminence of humanity to any other except to Him who says, in Genesis, 'Let us make man in our own image, in the likeness of ourselves' (Gn 1:26)? Who else could be the Bestower of wisdom, but He 'the teacher of all people?' (Ps 94:10). Who else could bestow virtue except the Lord of virtue? Therefore even the infidel who knows not Christ but does at least know himself, is bound to love God for God's own sake. He is unpardonable if he does not love the Lord his God with all his heart, and with all his soul, and with all his mind; for his own innate justice and common sense cry out from within that he is bound wholly to love God, from Whom he has received all things.[11]

St Bernard concedes however that it is hard, even impossible, for a man by his own strength or with the power of his free will to render all things to God from Whom they came, without rather turning them to his own advantage on his own account, even as it is written, 'they all want to work for themselves, not for Jesus Christ' (Phil 2:21).[12]

William of St Thierry (1085–1148), theologian and mystic, was a friend of St Bernard and was named after the monastery of St Thierry of which he was abbot. He also proposed some important ideas about the rôle of reason in searching for God. Interestingly, William posits a wisdom which lies between the wisdom of God, and the philosophy of this age or of the rulers of this age (1 Co 2:6), and this intermediate wisdom deals with that which is useful and honest, and is guided by prudence. Citing St Paul, 'knowledge puffs up, love is what builds up' (1 Co 8:1), William adds that reason without love tends to be vain and sterile.[13] He underscored that the human being was created with the capacity to know God through the natural light of reason and also to know some of His attributes in this way. Thus people have no justification for not making progress in the knowledge of God. William implies that faith and grace perfect wisdom, when he states that the wise soul, once it enjoys God alone, 'unveils man within man.'[14] The human person then becomes capable of seeing God's creation as He Himself sees it. Thus the wise soul carries a kind of reflection of the eternal light, and a mirror of the divine majesty; this soul manifests and expresses the goodness and justice of God before all of creation.[15]

St Albert the Great

St Albert the Great (1206–1280), a German scientist, philosopher, and theologian, was known as the *Doctor*

Universalis (Universal Doctor), since he was proficient in every branch of learning cultivated in his day. Albert was assiduous in developing the natural sciences; he was an authority on physics, geography, astronomy, mineralogy, chemistry, zoology and physiology. In some ways he stands at the beginning of the modern scientific movement.[16] He stressed the concrete and empirical approach to reality, and had no illusions about respecting the field belonging to science:

> In studying nature we have not to inquire how God the Creator may, as He freely wills, use His creatures to work miracles and thereby show forth His power: we have rather to inquire what nature with its immanent causes can naturally bring to pass.[17]

St Albert expressed contempt for everything that smacked of the superstitious or of the magical.[18] He demonstrated to the world that the Church is not opposed to the study of nature, that faith and science may go hand in hand. Above all, his impact on the study of philosophy and theology was highly significant. St Albert realised that Averroës, Abelard and others had absorbed false doctrines from the writings of Aristotle and so he attempted to purify the works of Aristotle from rationalism, Averroism, pantheism, and other errors, and thus utilise pre-Christian philosophy in the service of revealed truth. For Albert, all natural sciences should be the handmaids (*ancillae*) of theology, which is the superior and the mistress of all branches of knowledge.[19] Against the rationalism of Abelard and his followers, Albert pointed out the distinction between truths which are knowable through the natural light of reason and mysteries like the mystery of the Holy Trinity and the Incarnation which cannot be known without revelation.[20] St Albert the Great taught and directed a pupil, St Thomas Aquinas, who gave the world a concise, clear, and reasoned scientific exposition and defence of Christian Doctrine.

St Thomas Aquinas

St Thomas Aquinas (1225–1274), even as a child used to ask the question: 'What is God?' The Angelic Doctor enjoys pride of place in developing the relations between reason and faith which both come from God; hence he argued that there can be no contradiction between them.[21] The particular context of St Thomas was the early thirteenth century when the major works of Aristotle were made available in a Latin translation, accompanied by the commentaries of Averroës and other Islamic scholars. Aquinas opposed the two errors of Averroës: first, that philosophy and religion were in different spheres, so that what is true in religion might be false in philosophy; second, that all men share one soul. Under the leadership of Siger of Brabant, the Averroists asserted that philosophy was independent of revelation. Furthermore, there was the issue of rationalism which infected the University of Paris; this current was represented by Abelard and Raymond Lullus, and claimed that reason could know and prove all things, even the mysteries of the faith. With regard to pagan philosophy, St Thomas developed further the attitude of St Augustine, namely that where those philosophers suggested anything that was true and consistent with our faith, we must claim it from them as from unjust possessors. While some of the doctrines of the heathens are spurious imitations or superstitious inventions, which we must be careful to avoid, other concepts which they proposed can be used in the service of the truth.[22] St Thomas applied this principle, and whenever he encountered in pre-Christian philosophy something consistent with faith, he adopted it: and those things which he observed as contrary to faith he amended.[23]

Most profoundly, Thomas recognised that nature, the specific sphere of reason's investigation, could contribute to the understanding of God's Revelation. Faith therefore has no fear of reason, but seeks it out and has trust in it. Just as grace builds on nature and brings it to fulfilment, so faith builds upon and perfects reason.[24] The gifts of grace are added to nature in such a way that they do not destroy it, but rather perfect it. So too the light of faith, which is imparted to us as a gift, does not do away with the light of natural reason given to us by God. Even though the natural light of the human mind is inadequate to make known what is revealed by faith, nevertheless what is divinely taught to us by faith cannot be contrary to what we are endowed with by nature. If there was a real contradiction, one or the other areas of truth would have to be false, and since we have both of them from God, He would be the cause of our error, which is impossible. Rather, since what is imperfect bears a resemblance to what is perfect, what we know by natural reason has some likeness to what is taught to us by faith. While it is impossible that the contents of philosophy should be contrary to the contents of faith, the content of what can be grasped by reason falls short of what is revealed.[25]

Illumined by faith, reason is set free from the fragility and limitations deriving from the disobedience of sin and finds the strength required to rise to the knowledge of the Triune God. Although he emphasised the supernatural character of faith, the Angelic Doctor did not overlook the importance of its reasonableness; rather he plumbed the depths of this and explained its meaning. Faith is in a sense an 'exercise of thought'; and human reason is neither invalidated nor debased in assenting to the contents of faith, which are in any case attained by way of free and informed choice.[26] Aquinas developed the distinction between faith as a set of doctrines to be believed (*fides quae creditur*, the faith which is believed) and faith as personal commitment (*fides qua creditur*, the faith by which we believe).[27] The first aspect of faith is the objective content of Revelation, which comes from God the Father, through His Son in the power of the Holy Spirit, and is public and accessible to all. The second aspect is the subjective response of the believer to the objective content. Clearly, the second aspect presupposes the first. St Thomas also makes it clear that 'the act of the believer does not terminate in a proposition, but in a thing. For as in science we do not form propositions, except in order to have knowledge about things through their means, so is it in faith.'[28] The content aspect of faith is contained in articles of faith, professions of faith, and dogmatic definitions, and the whole content of Scripture, for example. The virtue of faith is the appropriate response to all those contents. However, in order to assent, we must be able to consider and understand what those articles mean. So faith presupposes reason. Only a rational being can be a believer. Only someone who understands the content of faith to some extent, can receive the gift of faith.

In the works of St Thomas, reason offers essentially three different types of service or ministry to faith. St Thomas' threefold illustration of the rôle of reason as a handmaid to faith, is a clear development of St Augustine's dictum that through knowledge 'the most wholesome faith is begotten ... is nourished, defended, and made strong.'[29] For Aquinas, first of all reason prepares the minds of people to receive the faith by proving the truths which belief presupposes, known as the preamble to the faith.[30] Second, reason should explain and develop the truths of faith and should propose them in scientific form. Third, reason should defend the truths revealed by Almighty God.[31]

The three approaches are exemplified in the two comprehensive syntheses of the Catholic faith written by Thomas. In the *Summa Contra Gentiles*, using arguments from authority, the Angelic Doctor established the truths contained in Christian Revelation which are inaccessible to natural reason alone.[32] The purpose was to demonstrate the truth of the Catholic faith using authority, when reason was no longer sufficient. However reason was still employed in order to refute errors and to furnish probable arguments. However, in the refutation of heresies, he adopted rational arguments taking authorities as premises, and often these authorities were accepted by the adversary. Arguments are marshalled to show the possibility or even the convenience of the revealed truths, drawing conclusions from them. On the other hand, the *Summa Theologiae* follows the second approach. This synthesis of Christian Doctrine is explicitly addressed to beginners in theology, and so to believers.[33] The purpose of the *Summa* is to offer them an understanding of what they believe, and not to establish what they believe. St Thomas' discourse and arguments are almost the same from one *Summa* to the other, but the difference is a difference of purpose: that of the two kinds of discussion. Even the revealed truths that are accessible to reason are rationally demonstrated in the *Summa Theologiae* as they were in the *Contra Gentiles*, the first one being the existence of God. Only now it is not a question of *establishing* the otherwise *believed* truth that God exists, it is more an exercise of *understanding* faith which tells us that God exists and that God's existence can be reached by natural reason. One could say that the *Summa Contra Gentiles* applies philosophy and Aristotelian metaphysics as a preamble to faith, and as part of theology, in order to establish the truth of the Catholic faith. On the other hand, the *Summa Theologiae* employs reason and Aristotelian metaphysics, in order to reach the understanding of the faith, or a *philosophy of faith*.

Aquinas argues not only that reason is presupposed by faith in order to understand the content of Revelation, but that one can also assent to part of this content on the basis of reason alone, and that once those articles are believed, one can draw rational conclusions from them. Thomas maintains that part of the content of faith (*fides quae*) can be accepted not by the virtue of faith, but by the exercise of natural reason. This portion of the deposit of Revelation can be *known* as well as *believed*. For Aquinas, this part is not small: it includes the existence of God, many of His attributes, the spirituality and immortality of the human soul, and much of what the Bible says of divine Providence and God's commandments, in particular the content of the Decalogue. Excluded from this potentially known portion of Revelation are the mysteries of the Christian faith, like the nature of the Holy Trinity, the Incarnation of the Son, and His work of Redemption, continued in the Sacraments. In particular, St Thomas indicates that the mystery of the Holy Trinity is reached only through faith. It is impossible to attain to the knowledge of the Trinity by natural reason. For man obtains the knowledge of God by natural reason from creatures. Now creatures lead us to the knowledge of God, as effects do to their cause. Accordingly, by natural reason we can know of God that only which of necessity belongs to Him as the principle of things. Now, the creative power of God is common to the whole Trinity; and hence it belongs to the unity of the essence, and not to the distinction of the persons. Therefore, by natural reason we can know what belongs to the unity of the essence of the Godhead, but not what belongs to the distinction of the Persons. 'Therefore, we must not attempt to prove what is of faith, except by authority alone, to those who receive the authority; while as regards others it suffices to prove that what faith teaches is not impossible.'[34]

Many articles of faith therefore could not be established on the basis of reason alone. Only one who accepts divine Revelation, and so only one who has been given the gift of faith, can assent to those articles.[35] As regards the content of those articles, reason is not confined simply to the capacity of grasping them. Instead, two functions of reason are at work here. The first one is the refutation of all arguments that would deny the content of faith. As truth is one, there can be no opposition between believing it by faith and holding it by reason.[36] Thus reason must be able to reveal as unsound and counter any argument which would contradict truths of faith. This does not mean that reason should be able to establish the denial of its conclusion (and so the truth of the article denied), but that it could discover the logical failure in the inference, or the falsity in the premises, and so the non-necessity of this conclusion. Thomas' position on the question of the eternity of the world is a case in point: reason cannot establish the truth believed by faith (namely that the world has a beginning), which is not a necessary but a contingent truth, but it can show that every argument to the contrary is inconclusive, and so that it has no necessity either. Generally, though not in this last case, reason can also give probable arguments in favour of what is believed.[37] The second task of reason relative to truths which can only be held by faith is the drawing of conclusions from these truths taken as premises.[38] In this way, reason can establish some consequences deriving from Revelation, or develop a synthetic unity within the faith. In the writings of St Thomas 'the demands of reason and the power of faith found the most elevated synthesis ever attained by human thought, for he could defend the radical newness introduced by Revelation without ever demeaning the venture proper to reason.'[39]

Aquinas often distinguishes two different modes of the knowledge of God. The first one proceeds from the created world to God, and the second one descends from God to human persons. This second mode can be direct, as in the case of the beatific vision, or indirect, as in the case of faith in divine Revelation received through the apostles. Thus Thomas arrives at three types of 'theology', the first 'natural theology', because it needs natural reason alone, the second one 'glorious theology', because it needs the light of glory, and the third one 'gracious theology', because it needs the gift of grace.[40] In our present situation in this world, only the first and third ways are available to us, which are 'theology working upwards' (natural theology) and 'theology working downwards' (gracious theology). Both theologies are also forms of rational arguments about the most fundamental aspects of reality.

St Thomas established that the act of faith resides in the intellect, but is motivated by the will. Since faith is a virtue, its act should be perfect. Now, for the perfection of this act proceeding from two active principles, each of these principles must be perfect. St Thomas adopts the image of a sawyer to illustrate this point: it is not possible for a thing to be sawn well, unless the sawyer possess the skill, and the saw be well fitted for sawing. 'To believe is an act of the intellect inasmuch as the will moves it to assent. And this act proceeds from the will and the intellect, both of which have a natural aptitude to be perfected in this way .... Now, to believe is immediately an act of the intellect, because the object of that act is 'the true,' which pertains properly to the intellect. Consequently faith, which is the proper principle of that act, resides in the intellect.'[41] The Angelic Doctor further specified the contribution of the intellect and the will to assent of faith:

> Now the object of faith can be considered in three ways. For, since 'to believe' is an act of the intellect, in so far as the will moves it to assent, the object of faith can be considered either on the part of the intellect, or on the part of the will that moves the intellect. If it be considered on the part of the intellect, then two things can be observed in the object of faith. One of these is the material object of faith, and in this way an act of faith is 'to believe in a God'; because, nothing is proposed to our belief, except in as much as it is referred to God. The other is the formal aspect of the object, for it is the medium on account of which we assent to such and such a point of faith; and thus an act of faith is 'to believe God,' since, the formal object of faith is the First Truth, to Which man gives his adhesion.... Third, if the object of faith be considered in so far as the intellect is moved by the will, an act of faith is 'to believe in God.' For the First Truth is referred to the will, through having the aspect of an end.[42]

St Thomas applies the respective rôles played by the intellect and will in the act of believing to the question of whether the assistance of reason diminishes the merit in believing. The act of faith can be meritorious, in so far as it is subject to the will, not only as to the use, but also as to the assent. Now human reason when it supports belief, may stand in a twofold relation to the will of the believer. First, as preceding the act of the will; as, for instance, when a man either has not the will, or not a prompt will, to believe, unless he be moved by human reasons: and in this situation human reason diminishes the merit of faith. Just as a man ought to perform acts of moral virtue, on account of the judgement of his reason, and not on account of a passion, so ought he to believe matters of faith, not on account of human reason, but on account of the Divine authority. Second, human reasons may be consequent to the will of the believer. For when a man's will is ready to believe, he loves the truth he believes, he thinks out and takes to heart whatever reasons he can marshal in support of it; and in this situation human reason does not exclude the merit of faith but is a sign of greater merit. In this case St Thomas sees an image of reason in the episode of the encounter between Christ and the Samaritan woman at the well (Jn 4:5–42). She encourages other Samaritans to believe in Christ, but these others affirm: 'Now we believe no longer because of what you told us; we have heard Him ourselves and we know that He is indeed the Saviour of the world.' (Jn 5:42). [43] St Thomas thus argues that the basis for belief is the authority of God who reveals. [44] Moreover, just as the faith cannot be proven solely by reason, because it lies beyond the power of the human intellect, in the same way, because of its truth, it cannot be contradicted by any necessary reason. [45]

St Thomas also discussed the distinction between demonstrative and persuasive reasoning in regard to the question of the merit of faith when reason is involved. He defined demonstrative reason as that which compels the mind's assent, and states that there can be no place in matters of faith for this kind of reasoning, but it can be adopted to disprove claims that faith is impossible. For although matters of faith cannot be demonstratively proved, neither can they be demonstratively disproved. If this sort of reasoning were brought forward to prove what is held on faith, the merit of faith would be destroyed, because the assent to it would not be voluntary but necessary. On the other hand, persuasive reasoning, drawn from analogies to the truths of faith, does not take away the nature of faith because it does not render them evident, for there is no reduction to first principles intuited by the mind. Neither does it deprive faith of its merit, because it does not compel the mind's assent but leaves the assent voluntary.[46]

The Angelic Doctor then indicated in a nuanced manner how faith is more certain than the knowledge which is acquired through the natural light of reason. Faith is more certain than the three virtues of wisdom, knowledge and understanding because it is founded on the Divine truth, whereas the three virtues are based on human reason. Secondly, certitude may be considered on the part of the subject, and thus the more a man's intellect lays hold of a thing, the more certain it is. From this viewpoint, faith is less certain, because matters of faith are above the human intellect, whereas the objects of the aforesaid three virtues are not. Other things being equal sight is more certain than hearing; but if the authority of the person from whom we hear greatly surpasses that of the seer's sight, hearing is more certain than sight: thus a man of little science is more certain about what he hears on the authority of an expert in science, than about what is apparent to him according to his own reason: and much more is a man certain about what he hears from God, Who cannot be deceived, than about what he sees with his own reason, which can be mistaken. The gifts of understanding and knowledge are more perfect than the knowledge of faith as regards their greater clearness, but not in regard to more certain adhesion: because the whole certitude of the gifts of understanding and knowledge, arises from the certitude of faith, even as the certitude of the knowledge of conclusions arises from the certitude of the assumptions. However, in so far as knowledge, wisdom and understanding are intellectual virtues, they are based upon the natural light of reason, which falls short of the certitude of God's word, on which faith is founded.[47] The Angelic Doctor also suggested how reason and faith both prepare for the light of glory:

Although the divinely infused light of faith is more powerful than the natural light of reason, nevertheless in our
present state we only imperfectly participate in it; and
hence it comes to pass that it does not beget in us real
vision of those things which it is meant to teach us; such
vision belongs to our eternal home, where we shall
perfectly participate in that light, where, finally, in God's
light we shall see light.[48]

St Bonaventure

While St Thomas followed an Aristotelian approach, the
Franciscan school of philosophy and theology tended to
follow Plato and St Augustine. One of the greatest exponents of this school was a contemporary of St Thomas, St
Bonaventure (1221–1274), Cardinal Bishop of Albano, who
was, for a time, Minister General of the Friars Minor. He
was known as the Seraphic Doctor and his *Breviloquium*
derives all things from God, while the *Itinerarium Mentis in
Deum* proceeds in the opposite direction, bringing all
things back to their Supreme End. St Bonaventure asserted
that God's existence could be proved from creatures as
Cause through effect, and affirmed that this mode of
knowledge is natural to man.[49] He enumerated six steps
carved out of the soul's powers through which we climb
from the depths towards the heights, from exterior things
towards interior ones, from temporal things towards
eternal ones. These steps are the sense, the imagination,
the reason, the intellect, the intelligence, and the apex of
the mind or the spark of synderesis. These steps are
planted in us by nature, deformed by fault, reformed by
grace; they are to be purified by justice, exercised by
knowledge, and perfected by wisdom.[50]

St Bonaventure proposed that God's existence is
certainly a truth which is naturally implanted in the
human mind.[51] However, in practice not everyone has a
clear knowledge of God from birth or from the use of

reason. Thus Bonaventure postulated an implicit knowledge of God in every human being which cannot be denied, and which becomes explicit mainly through interior reflection, as well as through consideration of the external world. Therefore, in St Bonaventure, the very arguments for God starting from His creation presuppose some awareness of Him. For instance, he illustrated how God has left in His creatures a sevenfold witness to His divine power, divine wisdom and divine goodness. First, the *origin* of things according to their creation, distinction and embellishment in so far as it considers the work of the six days of creation, proclaims the divine power, producing all things from nothing, the divine wisdom distinguishing all things clearly and the divine goodness adorning all things with generosity. Second, the *magnitude* of things according to the quantity of their length, breadth and depth; according to the excellence extending far, wide, and deeply, as is clear in the diffusion of light; according to the efficacy of their most interior, continual and diffuse activity, as is clear in the activity of fire, manifestly indicates the immensity of the power, wisdom and goodness of the Triune God who in all things by power, presence and essence exists as the One who is uncircumscribed. Third, their *multitude* according to their general, special and individual diversity in substance, in form or figure and efficacious beyond every human estimation, manifests the immensity of the aforesaid three conditions in God. Fourth, the *beauty* of things according to the variety of their lights, figures and colours in bodies simple, mixed and even connected, as in celestial and mineral bodies, as stones and metals, plants and animals, proclaims in an evident manner the aforesaid three characteristics. Fifth, the *fullness* of things, according to which matter is full of forms according to originative reasons; form is full of virtue according to active power; virtue is full of effects according to efficiency, and this declares the divine characteristics. Sixth, the manifold *activity* of things, according to that which is natural, according to that which is artificial, according to that which is moral, by its most manifold variety shows the immensity of His virtue, art, and goodness, which is for all things the cause of existing, the reason for understanding and the order of living. Seventh, their *order* according to the reckoning of duration and influence, that is by prior and posterior, superior and inferior, more noble and more ignoble, manifestly intimates in the Book of Creatures the primacy, sublimity and dignity of the First Principle, as much as it regards the infinity of His power; indeed the order of divine laws, precepts, and judgements in the Book of Scripture manifests the immensity of His wisdom; moreover the order of divine Sacraments, gifts and benefits in the Body of the Church indicates the immensity of His goodness, so that the order itself most evidently leads us by hand to the First and Most High, the Most Powerful, the Most Wise and the Best.[52]

Blessed John Duns Scotus

Blessed John Duns Scotus (1265–1308), known as the Subtle Doctor (*Doctor Subtilis*), was an important figure in medieval philosophical and theological development. He is the greatest champion of Franciscan Augustinianism. The reconstruction of Augustinianism by St Bonaventure, and the reformulation of Aristotelianism by St Thomas had already been established before Scotus began to teach. However, Scotus did not reproduce either of these currents of thought. Of Scotus it was written:

> He described the Divine Nature as if he had seen God; the celestial spirits as if he had been an angel; the happiness of the future state as if he had enjoyed them; and the ways of Providence as if he had penetrated into its secrets.

He was convinced that truth may shine more brightly as a result of profound investigation. In his teachings Scotus abandoned some theses that were dear to the Augustinian tradition, while he interpreted others in the light of the new contribution of Aristotelianism. From this treatment there flowed a new and original view of the major philosophical problems which has come to be known as Scotism. His principal work is the so-called *Opus Oxoniense*, an extensive commentary on the Sentences of Peter Lombard, written in Oxford. It is principally a theological work, but it contains many treatises, on logical, metaphysical, grammatical, and scientific topics, so that nearly his whole system of philosophy can be gleaned from this work. However, none of his writings plainly reveals a unified system; while several of them, owing no doubt to his early death, seem unfinished. His language is often obscure; a maze of terms, definitions, distinctions, and objections through which it is by no means easy to navigate. Nevertheless, there is in Scotus' teaching a crafted arrangement, and a logical development depicted in minute detail.

Regarding the concept of being, Scotus holds that it is univocal, as against St Thomas, who teaches that it is an analogous concept. Like St Thomas, Scotus held that intellectual cognition takes its origin from sensation through the process of abstraction. Scotus was a realist in philosophy, but he differed from Aquinas on certain basic issues. Some would say that Scotus went further along the realist road, since for him 'the universals were real entities apart from their existence in individuals,' while for St Thomas 'the universals are virtually present in individuals, from which they are abstracted by our intellect.'[53] A major point of difference concerned their views of perception. Scotus proposed that a direct, intuitive grasp of particular things is obtained both through the intellect and the senses. Aquinas maintained that the intellect did not directly know the singularity of material things but only the universal natures that are abstracted from sense perceptions. Scotus, in opposition to the Augustinian doctrine and in accord with Thomism, held that the existence of God is not intuitive, but is only demonstrable *a posteriori*.

Scotus maintained that reason is capable of arriving at the existence of God, many of his attributes and truths concerning Him, through a consideration of His actions.[54] He was optimistic about the rôle of reason in a discourse concerning God:

> Help me then, O Lord, as I investigate how much our natural reason can learn about that true being which You are if we begin with the being which You have predicated of Yourself.[55]

In particular, the Subtle Doctor proposed that through reason one could conclude that God is one, supreme, good, but not that God is a Holy Trinity.[56] Moreover, Scotus also differed from St Thomas on the demonstrability via natural reason of the omnipresence of God. For St Thomas, this divine attribute was within the capacity of reason to indicate, whereas for Blessed Scotus, it was not philosophically demonstrable.[57] Scotus was also concerned to use reason to support what faith already held:

> O Lord, our God, You have proclaimed Yourself to be the first and last. Teach your servant to show by reason what he holds with faith most certain, that You are the most eminent, the first efficient cause and the last end.[58]

Our natural knowledge of God depends on the capacity to form univocal concepts. Scotus affirmed that creatures which impress their own ideas on the intellect, can also impress the ideas of transcendent attributes which belong in common to them and to God.[59] However, it would not be possible to proceed from a knowledge of creation to the knowledge of God, were we not able to shape from creatures univocal concepts. When the intellect has formed these concepts, it can combine them to form a composite idea of God. Just as the imagination can combine the images of mountain and gold to form the image of a golden mountain, so can the intellect combine the ideas of goodness, supremacy and actuality to form the concept of a supremely good and actual being.[60] This image should not be taken to mean that Scotus regards the combining activity of the mind in natural theology as exactly parallel to the combining work of imagination; the former activity is governed by the objective truth, whereas the imaginative construction of a golden mountain is 'imaginary', that is, arbitrary.

A key point in the Scotist approach, in continuity with St Bonaventure and as distinguished from the Thomistic tradition, is the stress on human freedom and the primacy of human will and its acts of love over the power of the intellect; this primacy Scotus extends also to God. God has created the world through an act of His will. For Scotus there could not be free essences in secondary causes like man if these did not proceed from a free cause, namely from the divine Will. This Scotist voluntarism profoundly affects not only his cosmology but also his theory of knowledge and psychology. Everything becomes radically contingent. Thus God in creating has assigned to every being its own nature: to fire that of heating, to water that of being cold, to the air that of being lighter than earth, and so forth. However, since God is free, His will cannot be bound to any object. Hence it is not absurd that fire be cold, water hot, earth lighter than air; in other words, that the universe be ruled by laws opposite to those which presently govern it. A consequence of Scotus' voluntarist doctrine is that many metaphysical and theological truths which for St Thomas are demonstrable by reason are not so for Scotus once he advances the principle that the passage from effect to cause is not always legitimate. A case in point concerns the immortality of the soul, where the argument of St Thomas and of the entire Scholastic tradition is that the immaterial nature and hence the spirituality and immortality of the soul are deduced from the fact that the object of the intellect lies in the immaterial essences of things. Scotus accepted that reason could demonstrate the spirituality, individuality, substantiality, and unity of the soul, as well as its free will. In many of Scotus' writings he also affirmed that mere reason can come to know the immortality of the soul; in others he maintained the direct opposite. For Scotus, the rational deduction of the immortality of the human soul only enjoys the value of possibility, of non-repugnance. Since the will of God is not bound to any contingent thing, and is free to do anything that does not imply contradiction, Scotus concludes that the alternative is also possible; namely, that the soul could perish with the body. Hence Scotus affirms that we must rely upon faith for the truth of the immortality of the soul. It is faith which gives us the assurance that the immortality of the soul has real foundation.

Nevertheless, despite his voluntarism, Scotus demonstrated the dogmas of faith not only from authority but, as far as possible, from reason also. For him, theology presupposes philosophy as its basis. Facts which have God for their author and yet can be known by our natural powers, especially miracles and prophecies, are criteria of the truth of Revelation, religion, and the Church. Scotus strove to gain as thorough an insight as possible into the truths of faith, to disclose them to the human mind, to build truth upon truth, and from dogma to prove or to reject many a philosophical proposition. Scotus firmly emphasised the authority of Scripture, the Fathers, and the Church but he also attached much importance to natural knowledge and the intellectual capacity of the mind of angels and of men, both in this world and in the other. He was inclined to widen rather than narrow the range of attainable knowledge. He set great store upon mathematics, the natural sciences and especially upon metaphysics. The Subtle Doctor rejected every unnecessary recourse to Divine or angelic intervention or to miracles, and demanded that the supernatural and miraculous be limited as far as possible even in matters of faith.

Furthermore, Scotus, along with St Augustine and in opposition to Aristotle and St Thomas, affirms that virtue is an act of love which directs us to God. Finally he holds that the essence of eternal life does not consist, as St Thomas states, in the beatific vision of God, but in love of God. There is no contradiction here, for love and knowledge are not of the same order. Distinct acts of distinct faculties cannot be counterbalanced in such a way. In all created beings, the act of loving is really distinct from the act of knowledge. One and the same thing can be the object of knowledge and of love, but the viewpoint is different; for as regards knowledge, the thing is 'true', and as regards will, or love, it is 'good'. Considering the rational subject in the act of his intelligence, he knows God as Truth. Considering him in his act of love, he adheres to God as Goodness. There is no priority, but merely a difference in vantage point. The Beatific Vision is an act of possession of the unity of God by the soul, in the highest degree of its own unity. To put the same matter in other words, do we know in order to love, or do we love in order to know? These questions will be examined again later on.[61] As human persons, we possess both rational intellectual and rational appetitive faculties; these are coexisting and simultaneous. By our knowledge we are informed of the object of our love. By our love, we are attracted to the object of our knowledge. We can love only what we know. We can know only what we are in contact with affectively. Whenever we possess an object, we do so both through our intellect, by understanding the object, and through our will, by reacting affectively to it.

Consideration of the patristic and medieval reflection on the approach to God through reason and faith leads to the formulation of four basic positions. The first lays the stress on Revelation only, as exemplified by the positions of Tertullian, St Bernard, and some Franciscans. The idea is that Revelation has been given as a substitute for all other knowledge, including science, ethics, and metaphysics. Some exponents held that since God has spoken to us, it is no longer necessary for us to think. The only thing that matters is our salvation. This position maintained that no pagan philosopher said anything true of God, and that reason is dangerous, especially philosophy. Anything that distracts one from faith should be shunned. The second position accepted reason, but revelation must be given total priority. In this perspective are to be found St Augustine, St Anselm, and St Bonaventure among others. A certain degree of rationality was admitted as being natural and part of God's creation. Reason is necessary if only to understand the word of God. The Scriptures require some rational interpretation in order for them to be properly understood. Earlier pagan philosophies all had a kernel of truth. However, faith must be the starting point. The progression is from revelation to reason; unless one already believes one will never understand. The various thinkers are fairly unified in their initial assumptions but reason takes them to many different conclusions. A third position involved an almost total emphasis on reason, apart from revelation. In this camp fell Averroës, Siger of Brabant, Boethius, and Abelard for example. Faith was seen to be for the masses, and reason for the elite. While reason leads to knowledge and truth, revelation is the next best thing to reason. Some thinkers maintained that religion has a social rôle that even philosophy cannot fill. In the final school of thought a harmony of reason and Revelation was proposed by Alexander of Hales, St Albert the Great, St Thomas Aquinas, and Blessed John Duns Scotus. Everything in the cosmos has its proper place, and thus philosophical problems should be handled with philosophy, while theological problems ought to be dealt with by theology. Hence reason and revelation are two distinct species of knowledge, in which each should respect the appropriate function of the other. Faith involves assent to Revelation because it is revealed by God. Reason assents to what we perceive to be true through our mental powers. Revelation should not be taken for granted; for example, in the history of the Church, the spread of Christianity could not have happened by pure chance. Both reason and Revelation are seen to be in harmony, because not everyone can be a philosopher but everyone needs to be saved. This final fourth position is the one which is most fruitful in the relation between faith and reason. It is the approach which has consistently proved durable across the centuries. Nevertheless, after the golden epoch of medieval thought, certain perils were to appear on the horizon which were to undermine easy rational access to God, as will be seen in the next chapter.

Notes

1   See chapter 7, pp. 183–185 below.
2   St Augustine, *Sermon* 43, chapter 7, n. 9 in *PL* 38, 257–258.
3   St Anselm, *Proslogion*, Preface in *PL* 158, 225. The Latin expression is *fides quaerens intellectum.*
4   St Anselm, *Proslogion*, chapter 1 in *PL* 158, 227. The Latin expression is *credo, ut intellegam.*
5   St Anselm, *Proslogion*, chapter 1 in *PL* 158, 226. The Latin phrase is 'Ad te videndum factus sum; et nondum feci propter quod factus sum.'
6   Idem, *Monologion*, chapter 64 in *PL* 158, 210.
7   See St Bernard of Clairvaux, *Sermon XXXVI in Cantica Canticorum*, 3 in *PL* 183, 968.
8   St Bernard of Clairvaux, *On Loving God*, chapter 2, n. 3 in *PL* 182, 976.
9   Ibid., chapter 2, n. 4 in *PL* 182, 976.
10   Ibid., chapter 2, n. 4 in *PL* 182, 976–977.
11   Ibid., chapter 2, n. 6 in *PL* 182, 977–978.
12   See Ibid., chapter 2, n. 6 in *PL* 182, 978.
13   See William of St Thierry, *De natura et dignitate amoris*, 48 in Guglielmo di Saint-Thierry, *Opere* 3 (Rome: Città Nuova, 1998), p. 113.
14   Ibid., 50 in Guglielmo di Saint-Thierry, *Opere* 3, p. 114. The Latin expression is 'hominem in homine exuit.'
15   Ibid., in Guglielmo di Saint-Thierry, *Opere* 3, p. 115.
16   See E. A. Reitan, 'Nature, Place and Space: Albert the Great and the Origins of Modern Science' in *American Catholic Philosophical Quarterly* 70/1 (1996), pp. 83–101.
17   St Albert the Great, *De Coelo et Mundo*, I, tr. iv, 10.
18   See St Albert the Great, *De Mineralium* Book II, d. 3: where he states in relation to producing gold from lead, that art alone cannot produce a substantial form. 'Non est probatum hoc quod educitur

de plumbo esse aurum, eo quod sola ars non potest dare formam substantialem.'

19 See St Albert the Great, *Summa Theologiae*, Part 1, tr. 1, q. 6.

20 Ibid., Part 1, tr. 3, q. 13.

21 See St Thomas Aquinas, *Summa Contra Gentiles*, Book 1, chapter 7.

22 See St Augustine, *De doctrina Christiana*, chapter 40, n. 60 in *PL* 34, 63.

23 See St Thomas Aquinas, *Summa Theologiae*, I, q. 84, a. 5.

24 See St Thomas Aquinas, *Summa Theologiae*, I, q. 1, a. 8: 'cum enim gratia non tollat naturam sed perficiat.'

25 See St Thomas Aquinas, *Commentary on Boethius' De Trinitate*, Part 1, q. 2, a. 3.

26 See St Thomas Aquinas, *Summa Theologiae*, II–II, q. 2, a. 9. Cf. also Pope John Paul II, *Discourse to the Participants at the IX International Thomistic Congress* (29 September 1990) in *IP* 13/2 (1990), pp. 770–771.

27 See St Thomas Aquinas, *Summa Theologiae*, II–II, qq. 1–2.

28 St Thomas Aquinas, *Summa Theologiae*, II–II, q. 1, a. 2.

29 St Augustine, *De Trinitate*, Book 14, chapter 1, n. 3 in *PL* 42, 1037.

30 The notion of the preamble to the faith or *praeambula fidei* appears in the *Summa Theologiae*, II–II, q. 2, a. 10: 'On the other hand, though demonstrative reasons in support of the preambles of faith, but not of the articles of faith, diminish the measure of faith, since they make the thing believed to be seen, yet they do not diminish the measure of charity, which makes the will ready to believe them, even if they were unseen; and so the measure of merit is not diminished.'

In his *Commentary on Boethius' De Trinitate*, Part 1, q. 2, a. 3 St Thomas also wrote about the preamble of faith, as seen below in note 31.

31 St Thomas' threefold illustration of the influence of reason on faith is proposed in many places, especially in the following:

Summa Contra Gentiles, Book 1, chapters 1, 3–4, 7–8; *Summa Theologiae*, I, q. 1, aa. 1, 5, 8; q. 32, a. 1; q. 84, a. 5.

In the text of his *Commentary on Boethius' De Trinitate*, Part 1, q. 2, a. 3, Thomas distinguishes three uses of philosophy in theology: 'First, in order to demonstrate the preambles of faith, which we must necessarily know in the act of faith. Such are the truths about God that are proved by natural reason, for example, that God exists, that he is one, and other truths of this sort about God or creatures proved in philosophy and presupposed by faith.

Second, by throwing light on the contents of faith by analogies, as Augustine uses many analogies drawn from philosophical doctrines in order to elucidate the Trinity.

Third, in order to refute assertions contrary to the faith, either by showing them to be false or lacking in necessity.'

32 See St Thomas Aquinas, *Summa Contra Gentiles*, Book 4.

33 See St Thomas Aquinas, *Summa Theologiae*, Prologue.

34 St Thomas Aquinas, *Summa Theologiae*, I, q. 32, a. 1.

35 In *Summa Theologiae*, II–II, q. 1, a. 8, St Thomas says of the Creed's first article: 'By faith we hold many truths about God, which the philosophers were unable to discover by natural reason, for instance His providence and omnipotence, and that He alone is to be worshipped, all of which are contained in the one article of the unity of God.'

36 See St Thomas Aquinas, *Summa Contra Gentiles*, Book 1, chapter 7.

37 See St Thomas Aquinas, *Commentary on Book 1 of the Sentences*, Prologue, q. 1, a. 5; *Commentary on Book 3 of the Sentences*, d. 24, q. 1, a.3; *Commentary on Boethius' De Trinitate*, Part 1, q. 2, a. 1; *Summa Contra Gentiles* Book 1, chapter 8; *Summa Theologiae* I, q. 1, a. 8; II–II, q. 2, a. 10; III, q. 55, a. 5.

38 See St Thomas Aquinas, *Summa Theologiae*, I, q. 1, a. 2.

39 Pope John Paul II, *Fides et Ratio* 78.

40 See, for example, this threefold division in St Thomas' *Summa Contra Gentiles* Book 4, chapter 1.

41 St Thomas Aquinas, *Summa Theologiae*, II–II, q. 4, a. 2. See also *Ibid.*, q. 2, a. 1 where the Angelic Doctor points out that 'the intellect of the believer is determined to one object, not by the reason, but by the will, wherefore assent is taken here for an act of the intellect as determined to one object by the will.'

42 St Thomas Aquinas, *Summa Theologiae*, II–II, q. 2, a. 2.

43 See St Thomas Aquinas, *Summa Theologiae*, II–II, q. 2, a. 10.

44 See St Thomas Aquinas, *Summa Theologiae*, I, q. 1, a. 8.

45 See St Thomas Aquinas, *De rationibus fidei*, chapter 2: 'Quia tamen quod a summa veritate procedit falsum esse non potest, nec aliquid necessaria ratione impugnari valet quod falsum non est, sicut fides nostra necessariis rationibus probari non potest quia humanam mentem excedit, ita improbari necessaria ratione non potest propter sui veritatem.'

46 See St Thomas Aquinas, *Commentary on Boethius' De Trinitate*, Part 1, q. 2, a. 1, ad 5.

47 See St Thomas Aquinas, *Summa Theologiae*, II–II, q. 4, a. 8.

48 St Thomas Aquinas, *De Veritate*, q. 14, a. 9, ad 2. See also Ps 36:9.

49 See St Bonaventure, *Commentary on Book 1 the Sentences*, d. 3, q. 2: 'Utrum Deus sit cognoscibilis per creaturas.' In St Bonaventure, *Opera Omnia*, vol. 1 (Quaracchi: Collegio San Bonaventura, 1882), pp. 71–73.

50 See St Bonaventure, *The Journey of the Mind to God*, chapter 1, n 6, in St Bonaventure, *Opera Omnia*, vol. 5 (Quaracchi: Collegio San Bonaventura, 1891), p. 297. The Latin text runs: 'Iuxta igitur sex gradus ascensionis in Deum, sex sunt gradus potentiarum animae

per quos ascendimus ab imis ad summa, ab exterioribus ad intima, a temporalibus conscendimus ad aeterna, scilicet sensus, imaginatio, ratio, intellectus, intelligentia et apex mentis seu synderesis scintilla. Hos gradus in nobis habemus plantatos per naturam, deformatos per culpam, reformatos per gratiam; purgandos per iustitiam, exercendos per scientiam, perficiendos per sapientiam.'

By *synderesis* is meant a faculty or habit both of judging and of willing what is right. The faculty continues to exist despite the weakening of human nature brought about by the Fall. According to St Thomas Aquinas, it is practical reason: certain principles belonging to the practical side of reason which point out the right direction for action, just as the theoretical axioms of the understanding do for thinking. A different picture is given by St Bonaventure, who makes the distinction between conscience and synderesis rest upon the difference between judgement and will. God has implanted a double rule of right in human nature: one for judging rightly, and this is the moral strength of conscience; another for right willing, and this is the power of synderesis, whose function is to dissuade from evil and stimulate to good.

51 See St Bonaventure, *De Mysterio Trinitatis*, q. 1, a. 1, n. 10, in St Bonaventure, *Opera Omnia* vol. 5, p. 46. He used the expression 'quod Deum esse sit menti humanae indubitabile, tanquam sibi naturaliter insertum.'

52 See St Bonaventure, *The Journey of the Mind to God*, chapter 1, n. 14, in St Bonaventure, *Opera Omnia*, vol. 5, p. 299.

53 E. Gilson, *The Unity of Philosophical Experience* (Westminster, Maryland: Christian Classics, 1982), p. 66.

54 See Bd John Duns Scotus, *Reportata Parisiensia*, Prologue, 3, n. 6.

55 Bd John Duns Scotus, *A Treatise On God As First Principle*, 1.2.

56 See Bd John Duns Scotus, *Opus Oxoniense*, 1, 1, 2, n. 2.

57 See Bd John Duns Scotus, *Reportata Parisiensia*, I, 37, 2, nn. 6ff.

58 Bd John Duns Scotus, *A Treatise On God As First Principle*, 3.2.

59 See Bd John Duns Scotus, *Opus Oxoniense*, 1, 3, 2, n. 18.

60 See Bd John Duns Scotus, *Opus Oxoniense*, 1, 3, 2, n. 18.

61 See chapter 9 below.

CHAPTER 5

MODERN MEANDERING

I fled Him, down the nights and down the days;
I fled Him, down the arches of the years;
I fled Him, down the labyrinthine ways
Of my own mind; and in the mist of tears
I hid from Him, and under running laughter.
Up vistaed hopes I sped;
And shot, precipitated,
Adown Titanic glooms of chasmèd fears,
From those strong Feet that followed, followed after.
Francis Thompson, 'The Hound of Heaven'

St Paul, the learned Pharisee, was the first fruits of that gifted
company, in whom the pride of science is seen prostrated before
the foolishness of preaching. From his day to this the Cross has
enlisted under its banner all those great endowments of mind,
which in former times had been expended on vanities, or dissi-
pated in doubt and speculation.
John Henry Newman, *A University Sermon*
Preached on the Purification, 1843

The Breakdown of the Medieval Synthesis

William of Ockham (1280–1349), a Franciscan philosopher
and theologian is usually credited with bringing about the
breakdown of the medieval synthesis between faith and
reason; he was granted the title 'venerable beginner'

(*Venerabilis inceptor*), beginner of the modern epoch. In his philosophy, William urged a reform of Scholasticism both in method and in content, the purpose of which was simplification. This aim he formulated in the famous *Ockham's Razor*: 'Beings are not to be multiplied without necessity.'[1] Ockham combined with this tendency towards simplification a very marked inclination towards scepticism, or a distrust of the ability of the human mind to reach certitude in the most important areas of philosophy. In the process of simplification he rejected the distinction between essence and existence, and protested against the Thomistic doctrine of active and passive intellect. His scepticism appeared in a denial that human reason can prove either the immortality of the soul or the existence, unity, and infinity of God. These truths, Ockham proposed, are known to us by Revelation alone. In ethics he was a voluntarist, maintaining that any distinction between right and wrong depends on the will of God. William's best known contribution to Scholastic philosophy is his theory of universals, which is a modified form of nominalism, more closely allied to conceptualism than to nominalism of the extreme type. The universal, he says, has no existence in the world of reality. Real things are known to us by intuitive knowledge, and not by abstraction. The universal is the object of abstractive knowledge. Therefore, the universal concept has for its object, not a reality existing in the world outside us, but an internal representation which is a product of the understanding itself and which stands, in the mind, for the things to which the mind attributes it. Universals signify individual things and stand for them in propositions. For Ockham, only individual things exist, and by the very fact of a thing's existence it is individual. The nominalist spirit was 'inclined to analysis rather than to synthesis, and to criticism rather than to speculation.'[2] Thus Ockham attacked realism, especially that of Scotus, his teacher, who was not a nominalist and had deduced the objective existence of universals from the concepts originated under the operation of the objects.[3]

Ockham's idea of reality was incoherent in many ways, and this incoherence resulted from one of his basic principles, that God could produce in the human mind intuition of a non-existent object. Also 'every effect which God causes through the mediation of a secondary cause, He can produce immediately by Himself.'[4] These ideas lead to the concept that, for example, God separately created the stars and the effect of their light which we perceive. Ockham's tendency was thus to break up some supposed necessary conditions 'which might seem to limit in some way the divine omnipotence.'[5] This resulted in a cosmos which was split up into separate entities, each depending on God, but with no necessary connection between them. In a way, Ockham paved the way for absolutism, a philosophical and political concept in which the parts of a whole were cut off (*ab-solutus*) from each other. Politically, absolutism is rule not limited by any formal constraint, legal, constitutional or conventional; its power is unchecked, and its laws are the commands of the sovereign who is not subject to law. The theory of absolutism was embraced by the monarchs of early modern Europe who set aside Church constraints on their power. It is significant that Ockham himself sided with the Emperor Ludwig of Bavaria against Pope John XXII.

William of Ockham's approach featured consequences for the relations between God and His creatures. In particular, he did not think that the existence of God as the absolutely supreme, perfect and unique Being could be proved from philosophy. At he same time, he allowed a possibility that the first conserving cause of the universe could be proved, but nothing certain could be known about that cause from reason alone.[6] Furthermore, even from a theological point of view, according to Ockham, we cannot have certain knowledge of God's nature:

> We cannot know in themselves either the unity of God … or His infinite power or the divine goodness or perfection; but what we know immediately are concepts, which are

not really God but which we use in propositions to stand
for God.[7]

A consequence of this idea is that the non-believer can
attain all the knowledge, whether simple or complex,
which the believer can have; the difference lies in the
possession of faith. Thus Ockham's idea of theological
propositions seems very different from that of St Thomas
Aquinas, who maintained that faith does not stop at the
propositions but in the realities which they express.[8]
For Ockham, faith derives only from authority and
is not taught by reason, by experience, or by logic.
Ockham's radical stress on faith separated from reason in
some sense paved the way for the Reformers' motto of
faith alone.

  In Christianity before the Reformation, philosophy was
in all its variety almost always viewed as the handmaid of
theology. With the onset of the Reformation, this pleasant
cohabitation and fruitful collaboration was to change
dramatically. Martin Luther (1483–1546) inherited
Ockham's nominalist epistemology and also painted a
bleak picture of human nature, insisting strongly on the
total corruption of the human person as a result of original
sin. He regarded reason as so fallen that it was no longer
capable of metaphysical knowledge. As Chesterton was
later to remark, 'It was the very life of the Thomist teaching that Reason can be trusted: it was the very life of
Lutheran teaching that Reason is utterly untrustworthy.'[9]
For Luther, therefore, the existence of God was purely a
question of naked faith and blind obedience. This saving
faith is a pure gift of God for which there can be no
preparatory action in man either through mystical discipline and ecstasy or though demonstrative reason or good
works. The human person simply received this gift from
God and was incapable of making a response. Classical
Protestantism was thus, in principle, based upon *faith
alone*, the hearing of *scripture alone*, and the response lay in
the mystery of predestined election and vocation *by grace*

alone. Later on in Protestantism, some forms of rational reflection or voluntarist mysticism returned in the clothes of Pietism or Puritanism. A liberal wing also developed inside the Reformed tradition which allowed reason to roam where it willed, not taking into account the truths of the faith; this approach was typified by Adolf von Harnack.

The unified vision of faith and reason in the Patristic and Medieval period produced knowledge capable of reaching the highest forms of speculation in the search for God. This was compromised by systems which espoused the cause of rational knowledge radically fragmented from faith and intended to take the place of faith.[10] The progression of this drama of the separation of faith and reason passed through empiricism and rationalism. The empiricist movement gathered ground in the persons of Francis Bacon, Thomas Hobbes and Father Marin Mersenne; depth of understanding was limited with the empiricists, who restricted knowledge to sense perception. A further development of empiricism was presented by David Hume (1711–1776), who built his philosophy on sensationism. It was as if Hume were using sensory impressions as bricks to construct a philosophical house, yet using no mortar to cement these bricks together. For Hume, there were mental states but no mind, and, as a result, his theory of knowledge left no reliable means for dealing with objective reality. Hume has sometimes been regarded as a deist, but in fact he was what we would now call an agnostic. His posthumously published *Dialogues Concerning Natural Religion*[11] contain some of the most incisive criticism of the cosmological and the teleological arguments for the existence of God. In connection with the former he observed that a causal series is nothing over and above the members of the series, so that if we have explained the origin of each member, there is nothing left to explain. As for the teleological argument, we have no reason to suppose that order of the kind described in scientific laws existed always and everywhere in the universe.[12] The positivism of Auguste Comte and John Stuart Mill was a grandchild of empiricism, and here bare facts themselves imposed the only true conceptual system. No place was left for metaphysics, and so the road to God through a reflection on the world was closed off.

Descartes

In certain respects, the modern way of philosophy 'begins with Descartes, who split thought from existence and identified existence with thought itself.'[13] René Descartes (1596–1650) posited his basic philosophical first principle and starting point in the axiom 'I think, therefore I am.'[14] The Cartesian rationalist position made subjective consciousness absolute and rendered thought autonomous, in stark contrast to the Thomist approach in which mind and reality were linked in synthetic harmony.[15] Objectivity was lost in favour of human consciousness. Descartes thus put us 'on the threshold of modern immanentism and subjectivism.'[16] He surveyed the ancients and self-consciously proclaimed the need for a new method, indeed a new goal for philosophy and all learning. Rejecting the ancient philosophy, Descartes desired to found a new practical philosophy; by 'knowing the force and actions of the fire, water, air and stars, the heavens, and all other bodies that surround us, just as we understand the various skills of our craftsmen, we could make ourselves the masters and possessors of nature.'[17] The criterion for the new knowledge is therefore certitude which, at the same time, entails a scepticism towards traditional modes of opinion. For Descartes, provisional doubt was the essential means towards distinguishing the true from the false in the maze of contradictory opinions. He applied the analogy of builders who, in order to erect a high structure, begin by digging deep to discard the sand, so that the foundations may be laid on solid ground.[18] Descartes' philosophical road to God was not the one charted by Christian tradition, namely through reflection on the external cosmos. His approach was not one based on the evidence of the senses but was abstract and conceptual, founded on pure thought like mathematics. Evidence of God was found no longer in the cosmos, but inside the mind, where an innate idea of the Absolute Being was to be found: 'God, in creating me, placed this idea within me to be like the mark of the workman imprinted on his work.'[19] Descartes' radical dualism meant that 'the thinking soul also had to be distinct from the world of matter, including that living human body without which there was no experienced certainty about the reality of thinking.'[20] This lack of certainty surfaced in Cartesian methodical doubt, a disease which has plagued Western philosophy ever since. Spinoza and Malebranche were also early representatives of this rationalist tendency, which put an undue stress on the knowing mind. Spinoza, a Cartesian trapped in his own mind, could not cope with the fact that matter was a richly varied reality. Malebranche essentially parted company with the existence of the external world as he made it an object of faith. Furthermore, his occasionalism only undermined the vision of a coherently interconnected cosmos.[21]

Pascal

Jansenism, an erroneous system originating from Cornelius Jansen, Bishop of Ypres (died 1638), and continued by others, held that man was completely corrupted by the Fall, so that his freedom was severely compromised, some of God's commandments were impossible and good works by unbelievers were sinful. Jansenists held that Christ did not die for the whole human race, but only for a few privileged souls. They were pessimistic about the capacity of fallen human nature in general and the power of reason in particular. Blaise Pascal (1623–1662) was influenced by Jansenism as can be seen in some of his

writings. Pascal regards man as a Nothing in comparison
with the Infinite, an All in comparison with the Nothing, a
mean between nothing and everything. Since man is infinitely removed from comprehending the extremes, the
end of things and their beginning are hopelessly hidden
from him in an impenetrable secret; he is equally incapable of seeing the Nothing from which he was made, and
the Infinite in which he is swallowed up.[22] Pascal is rather
pessimistic concerning man's capacity for knowing:

> We sail within a vast sphere, ever drifting in uncertainty,
> driven from end to end. When we think to attach ourselves
> to any point and to fasten to it, it wavers and leaves us; and
> if we follow it, it eludes our grasp, slips past us, and
> vanishes for ever. Nothing stays for us. This is our natural
> condition and yet most contrary to our inclination; we
> burn with desire to find solid ground and an ultimate sure
> foundation whereon to build a tower reaching to the
> Infinite. But our whole groundwork cracks, and the earth
> opens to abysses.[23]

Pascal was distinctly reserved about proving the existence
of God from creation. Those who already have faith see at
once that all existence is none other than the work of the
God whom they adore. However, for those in whom this
light is extinguished, persons destitute of faith and grace,
who seeking with all their light whatever they see in
nature that can bring them to this knowledge, find only
obscurity and darkness. To tell them that they have only to
look at the smallest things which surround them, and they
will see God openly, to give them, as a complete proof of
this great and important matter, the course of the moon
and planets, and to claim to have concluded the proof with
such an argument, is to give them ground for believing
that the proofs of our religion are very weak. Pascal
claimed that Scripture speaks in a different way, saying
that God is a hidden God, and that, since the corruption of
nature, He has left men in a darkness from which they can
escape only through Jesus Christ, without whom all

communion with God is cut off.[24] However, Pascal nuanced his pessimistic view of reason: 'If we submit everything to reason, our religion will have no mysterious and supernatural element. If we offend the principles of reason, our religion will be absurd and ridiculous.'[25] Pascal further stressed the paradoxical element in the relationship between faith and reason by saying that the Christian religion teaches these two truths: that there is a God whom men can know, and that there is a corruption in their nature which renders them unworthy of Him. It is equally important for people to know both these points; and it is equally dangerous for man to know God without knowing his own wretchedness, and to know his own wretchedness without knowing the Redeemer who can free him from it. The knowledge of only one of these points gives rise either to the pride of philosophers, who have known God, and not their own wretchedness, or to the despair of atheists, who know their own wretchedness, but not the Redeemer.[26] Thus the Catholic religion is wise and foolish. Wise, because it is the most learned and the most founded on miracles and prophecies and the like. Foolish, because it is not all this which makes us belong to it. This makes us, indeed, condemn those who do not belong to it; but it does not cause belief in those who do belong to it. It is the cross that evokes belief.[27]

The Enlightenment

The Enlightenment[28] was a European intellectual, social and political movement of the seventeenth and eighteenth centuries in which ideas concerning God, reason, nature, and man were synthesised into a worldview that gained wide assent and that stimulated revolutionary developments in art, philosophy, and politics. The movement began in England in the seventeenth century (with Locke and the deists), and developed in France in the eighteenth century (under Bayle, Voltaire, Diderot, and other

Encyclopaedists) and also, especially under the impetus of the rationalist philosophy of Christian Wolff, in Germany (with Mendelssohn, Lessing). The period of history in which the movement predominated is known as the 'Age of Reason'. The concept of 'Enlightenment' sets up a false contrast with the hypothetical darkness of irrationality and superstition that supposedly characterised the Medieval era. This tendency to discredit the Middle Ages was a characteristic of Enlightenment and Masonic thought, in hostility to anything Christian. Kant, one of the last key Enlightenment figures, maintained that this period marked the emergence of man from his self-imposed infancy. Central to Enlightenment ideology was the exaltation of reason, often at the expense of faith. However, by exalting reason in an exaggerated fashion, reason itself was to be wounded. The synthetic vision of reason and faith emerging from the Middle Ages was eroded by the ravages of nominalism, of humanism, of neo-pagan Renaissance thought, and of the Protestant Reformation. Reason was applied in an increasingly autonomous way, whereby the reasoning process contained within itself its own guarantee of validity; this approach was later seen to be less than valid, when one considers Gödel's theorem.[29]

The Enlightenment was partly stimulated by the obvious success of reason in the natural sciences and mathematics, for example in Sir Isaac Newton's attempt to describe, in a few mathematical equations, the laws that govern the motion of the planets. The dominant concept of the cosmos as a mechanism governed by a few simple and discoverable laws led to a desire to establish a purely rational religion. The product of a search for a natural and purely rational religion was deism, which conflicted with Christianity for two centuries, especially in England and France. Deism is the false notion according to which, having created the world, God leaves it to its own devices, or at best allows it not to be destroyed. In this approach God is envisaged as a type of distant clock-maker Who, having 'wound up' the cosmos in the act of creation, there-after left the universe to its own devices. Deism leads to despair, for it encourages the idea that God has deserted the work of His own hands. Deism was related to the Masonic concept of the Supreme Being as the Architect of the cosmos. For the deist a very few religious truths sufficed, and they were truths perceived to be evident to all rational beings: the existence of one God, often conceived of as architect, the existence of a system of rewards and punishments administered by that God, and the obligation of men to virtue and piety. Beyond the natural religion of the deists lay the more radical products of Enlightenment exaggeration of reason in the religious sphere: scepticism, atheism, and materialism.

The Enlightenment fell victim to its own excesses. The more rarefied the religion of the deists became, the less it offered to those who sought solace or salvation. The cele-bration of abstract reason provoked a contrary reaction among thinkers who began exploring the world of sensa-tion and emotion in the cultural movement known as Romanticism. The French Revolution represented the beginning of anarchic nihilism: the negation of truth in the political order, the negation of justice in the social order and the negation of the adoration due to God in the divine order. The Reign of Terror that followed the French Revolution severely tested the belief that man could govern himself. By losing its reference point in faith, reason became progressively more irrational. The Enlightenment turned out to be one of the darkest ages mankind has known, also in terms of the intellectual chaos which followed in its wake. The heritage of the Enlightenment was a damaged faculty of reason in its search for God, precisely because of a proud exaltation of the intellect. Christ's words 'everyone who raises himself up will be humbled' (Lk 14:11, 18:14), came true histori-cally in this epoch.

From its beginnings, but especially from the late eigh-teenth century on, the Enlightenment was subjected to

serious criticism. Its suggestion that medieval philosophers accepted their beliefs on authority alone cannot be
justified by a reading of their works. Its wholesale rejection
of traditional beliefs and institutions is vulnerable to the
retort that the accumulated wisdom of past generations is
more likely to be correct than the ideas of an individual
philosopher. Its demand that an individual should subject
all his beliefs to criticism, and accept nothing on authority,
is countered by the disparity between any given individual's necessarily limited first-hand experience and the
range of knowledge now available to him. Its belittling of
the non-rational aspects of man and of the differences
between cultures, in favour of a narrowly defined rationality, met with criticism from later thinkers.

Although not as radical as Hume, Immanuel Kant
(1724–1804) enjoyed a much greater influence on subsequent developments. Kant originated from a Lutheran
Pietist background from which he inherited a certain
distrust of the power of reason. His *Critique of Pure Reason*
contains a devastating examination of the ontological,
cosmological, and teleological arguments. The work of
Hume and Kant helped to pave the way for agnosticism
and atheism. The Kantian experiment attempted to unite
rationalism and Hume's sensationist empiricism in a superior kind of phenomenalism. This was expressed in Kant's
distinction between the noumenological sphere of the
thing in itself (*Ding an sich*) which is inaccessible to reason,
and the phenomenal world which man perceives by virtue
of innate *a priori* knowledge. Reality loses its meaning if
Kant is right in claiming that the mind knows things by
imposing its own structure on reality. Kant was already a-
prioristic in his pre-Critique phase,[30] and in his
post-Critique phase, he held that the structure of the mind
determines the structure of reality so there can be no need
for observation and experiment: 'Whatever Kant's intentions, his "critical" work inevitably leads to the most
uncritical philosophical stance: subjective idealism, if not
plain solipsism.'[31] Mind and reality were being built as

two sides of an arch which never joined.[32] Kant denied in the name of 'pure reason' the passage from creation to God via the classical theistic proofs. On the other hand, in the name of 'practical reason' he reduced the postulation of God's existence to a mere consequence of the moral law. Kant's formulation encouraged the cause of anti-theistic philosophy. If, on the one hand, Kantian criticism marked the crossroads where the rationalism and empiricism which preceded it are fused together, it is also true that Kantian criticism contains within itself the seed of much subsequent philosophical thought, including contemporary philosophy. The two major philosophical movements of the last century, idealism and positivism, have their source in the teachings of Kant. Idealism, rejecting the noumenon entirely, reduces reality to the status of the phenomena of an impersonal 'ego' carrying out its activity dialectically. Positivism, on its part, reduces reality to the mere phenomena of matter. From idealism and positivism was to emerge later existentialism, a philosophy devoid of metaphysics and purporting to give knowledge of a world acting by means of immanent forces.

The Hegelians

Kant's German disciples Fichte, Schelling, and Hegel drifted into pantheism. Georg Wilhelm Friedrich Hegel (1770–1831) represented the apex of German idealism and immanentism in a dialectic system. Being was characterised in its development by three stages: being (thesis), non-being (antithesis), and becoming (synthesis). In other words, the preceding entity (being) is affirmed with its opposite (non-being) in a higher entity (becoming). Hegel founded a new concept of reality as the realisation and overcoming of opposites (being, non-being, synthesis). For Aristotle, the principle of identity could be formulated because the concept of being is always the same; A is equal to A, and A cannot be its negation (non-A) at the same time and in the same respect. According to Hegel, this logic is faulty because it misinterprets reality. For him reality is never identical with itself, but at every moment changes, passing from what it is to what it is not. Thus Hegel's philosophy is essentially contradictory. He proposed that the State is the living God, who concretises Himself in the spirit of the people (the 'national spirit'). The living God incarnates Himself now in this, now in that nation, according as the nation realises more perfectly than any other the ideal of civilisation. Hegel's views cannot be easily classified, chiefly because they are so obscure. He believed in something called the 'Absolute Idea', and some of his conservative followers, known as the 'Right Hegelians', had no difficulty identifying the Absolute Idea with a personal God. However, almost all his most famous students, known as 'Left Hegelians', were outspoken atheists. They included Marx, Engels, and Feuerbach. Hegel's concept of reality is immanentist, pantheist and tends towards non-theism. Faith was reduced to human confidence, subordinated or ancillary to science (reason's progeny); in the Hegelian idealism of the Right, to the State, or in the inverted Hegelian dialectical materialism of the Left, to service of the proletariat of the world.

The development of a good part of modern philosophy has thus seen it move further away from Christian Revelation, to the point of setting itself up quite explicitly in opposition. This process reached its apogee in the nineteenth century. Some representatives of idealism, like Hegel, sought in various ways to transform faith and its contents, even the mystery of the Death and Resurrection of Jesus, into dialectical structures which could be grasped by reason. Opposed to this kind of thinking were various forms of atheistic humanism like that of Marx, expressed in philosophical terms, which regarded faith as alienating and damaging to the development of a full rationality. They did not hesitate to present themselves as new religions serving as a basis for projects which, on the political and social plane, gave rise to totalitarian systems which have been disastrous for humanity.[33] Modern reason all too often forgot that the human mind should be regarded as 'neither an empiricist slave nor an idealist lawgiver with respect to nature, but a partner which teaches about nature by learning from it.'[34] This middle ground is the epistemology of classical scholastic philosophy in which the contingency of the universe means that one cannot have an *a priori* discourse about it, while its rationality makes it accessible to the mind but only in an *a posteriori* manner, with empirical investigation. Balance in this philosophical see-saw is provided by a realist metaphysics which lies at the basis of every rational affirmation of God the Creator.

Ontologism

Ontologism marked a further modern obstacle in the rational road to God as it rejected mediated knowledge of God. It originated in the thought of Malebranche (1638–1715) and was revived in the nineteenth century, by Gioberti (1801–1852) and in some ways by Antonio Rosmini (1797–1855). According to this theory, we know God immediately, or without the mediation of creation, not by abstraction, but by intuition. Knowledge of God is the first among human intuitions, and is the light in which we see all beings. Instead of rising from creatures to God, ontologism descends from God to creatures. For Gioberti the order of knowledge must correspond to the order of being. Now God is the first in the order of being (in the ontological order), thus He must also be first in the order of knowledge (the logical order). This system has been inspired to some extent by Kantian influences. Ontologism maintains that we have naturally some immediate consciousness, however dim at first, or some intuitive knowledge of God. It does not propose that we see Him in His essence face to face but that we know Him in His relation to creatures by the same act of cognition (according to

Rosmini, as we become conscious of being in general) and therefore that the truth of His existence is as much a datum of philosophy as is the abstract idea of being. The idea that in the order of created things there is immediately manifested to the intellect something divine in itself, such that it belongs to the divine nature, was condemned by Church authorities.[35] Ontologism flies in the face of Scripture, Tradition and experience which all describe a mediated knowledge of God. Philosophically, the system can easily degenerate into pantheism. Theologically, ontologism seems to jeopardize the distinction between the natural order founded on the mediated knowledge of God, and the supernatural order, founded on the vision of God. If this vision were connatural with the human soul, it is not easy to see how it could be a gratuitous gift of God.

Fideism and Traditionalism

Fideism embodied an approach to the knowledge of God which essentially appeared after the Enlightenment in reaction to rationalism.[36] However, it was made easier by the nominalist programme put in place by Ockham, and also has its roots in Lutheran and Jansenist thought. Fideism flourished in the nineteenth century and is still widely adopted at the present time. This view implies a mindset which, denying the power of unaided human reason to reach certitude, affirms that the fundamental act of human knowledge consists in an act of faith, and the supreme criterion of certitude is authority. Fideism comes in various strengths and different forms, according to the field of truth to which it is extended, and the various elements which constitute the given authority. For some fideists, human reason cannot of itself reach certitude in regard to any truth whatever; for others, it cannot reach certitude in regard to the fundamental truths of metaphysics, morality, and religion, while some maintain that we can give a firm supernatural assent to revelation on motives of credibility that are merely probable. Authority, which according to fideism is the rule of certitude, has its ultimate foundation in divine revelation, reserved and transmitted in all ages through society and manifested by tradition, common sense or some other agent of a social character.

Another related error concerning the knowledge of God also emerged in the nineteenth century. Known as *traditionalism*, it was a philosophical system which made tradition the supreme criterion and rule of certitude. According to this idea, human reason is radically unable on its own to know with certainty the fundamental truths of the philosophical, moral, and religious order. Hence the first act of knowledge must be an act of faith, based on the authority of revelation. This revelation is transmitted to us through society, and its truth is guaranteed by tradition or the general consent of mankind. Such is the philosophical system maintained chiefly, in its absolute form, by the Vicomte de Bonald and F. de Lamennais in their respective works, and, also in a milder form by Bautain, Bonetty and others. When viewed in its historical context, traditionalism appears as a reaction against the rationalism of the philosophers of the eighteenth century and the anarchic individualism of the French Revolution. Against these errors it pointed out and emphasised the weakness and insufficiency of human reason, the influence of society, education, and tradition on the development of human life and institutions. The reaction was extreme, and produced the opposite error.

According to Bonald, man is essentially a social being. His development comes about through society; and the continuity and progress of society are founded upon tradition. Now language is the instrument of social intercourse, and speech is as natural to man as is his social nature itself. Language could not have been discovered by man, for 'man needs signs or words in order to think as well as in order to speak'; that is 'man thinks his verbal expression before he verbally expresses his thought.'[37] Originally the fundamental elements of language, together with the thoughts which it expresses, were given to humanity by God the Creator.[38] These fundamental truths, absolutely necessary to the intellectual, moral, and religious life of man, must be first accepted by faith. They are communicated through society and education, and guaranteed by tradition or the universal reason of mankind. There is no other basis for certitude and there remains nothing, besides tradition, but human opinions, contradiction, and uncertainty.[39] The system proposed by Lamennais is very similar to that of Bonald. Our instruments of knowledge, namely sense, feeling, and reason, are fallible. For Lamennais, one of the characteristics of religion must be never to reason with people.[40] The rule of certitude therefore can only be external to man and it can consist only in the verification of the individual senses, feelings, and reasoning via the testimony of the senses, feelings, and reason of all other men; their universal agreement is the rule of certitude. Hence, to avoid scepticism, we must begin with an act of faith which comes before all reflection; this act of faith must be based upon the common consent or agreement of all, in the general reason. 'Such is', Lamennais concludes, 'the law of human nature', outside of which 'there is no certitude, no language, no society, no life.'[41] Bautain and Bonnetty are sometimes called moderate fideists, for, though they maintained that human reason is unable to know the fundamental truths of the moral and religious orders, they admitted that, after accepting the teaching of revelation concerning them, human intelligence can demonstrate the reasonableness of such a belief. Traditionalism is basically a kind of fideism, and as such is a denial of the reasonable nature of faith. More particularly, authority, whatever be the way or agency in which it is presented to us, cannot of itself be the supreme criterion or rule of certitude. For, in order to be a rule of certitude, it must first be known as valid, competent, and legitimate, and reason must have ascertained this before it is entitled to our assent.

John Henry Newman

Into the bleak scene of the place of reason in post-Enlightenment thought, some great luminaries stepped onto the stage. One of these was John Henry Newman (1801–1890). In the last of his University Sermons preached on the Feast of the Purification in 1843, Newman provided a penetrating analysis of the relations between faith and reason. His starting point was the scriptural passage: 'As for Mary, she treasured all these things and pondered them in her heart' (Lk 2:19). Newman proposed that Mary's faith 'did not end in a mere acquiescence in Divine providences and revelations: as the text informs us, she "pondered" them.'[42] He shows how Mary is a model for relating faith and reason:

> She does not think it enough to accept, she dwells upon it; not enough to possess, she uses it; not enough to assent, she develops it; not enough to submit the Reason, she reasons upon it; not indeed reasoning first, and believing afterwards, with Zacharias, yet first believing without reasoning, next from love and reverence, reasoning after believing.[43]

The genius of Newman's idea is that Mary comes to symbolise not only the faith of the unlearned, but of the doctors of the Church also, who need 'to investigate, and weigh, and define, as well as to profess the Gospel; to draw the line between truth and heresy; to anticipate or remedy the various aberrations of wrong reason; to combat pride and recklessness with their own arms; and thus to triumph over the sophist and the innovator.'[44] Newman illustrated how, gradually, 'the whole mind of the world ... was absorbed into the philosophy of the Cross, as the element in which it lived, and the form upon which it was moulded.'[45] Newman cited as evidence for the Church's triumph over the wisdom of the world, the great libraries where along the shelves, every name is, in one sense or other, a trophy set up in record of the victories of Faith and where at length 'a large fabric of divinity was reared, irregular in its structure, and diverse in its style, as beseemed the slow growth of centuries; nay, anomalous in its details, from the peculiarities of individuals, or the interference of strangers, but still, on the whole, the development of an idea, and like itself, and unlike anything else, its most widely-separated parts having relations with each other, and betokening a common origin.'[46] Newman carefully proposed that reason has not simply submitted to faith, but has ministered to it: 'It has illustrated its documents; it has raised illiterate peasants into philosophers and divines; it has elicited a meaning from their words which their immediate hearers little suspected. Stranger surely is it that St John should be a theologian, than that St Peter should be a prince.'[47]

Newman explained the difference between the fruitfulness of reason associated with faith and the sterility of reason when it serves heresy. The Gospel has a life in it which shows itself in progress; a truth, which has the token of consistency; a reality, which is fruitful in resources; a depth, which extends into mystery: for it represents what is actual, and has a definite location and necessary bearings and a meaning in the great system of things, and a harmony in what it is, and a compatibility in what it involves.[48] On the other hand the propositions of heresy are unfruitful; its formulae end in themselves, without development, because they are words; they are barren, because they are dead. If they had life, they would increase and multiply; or, if they do live and bear fruit, it is not life-giving. Heresy 'creates nothing, it tends to no system, its resultant dogma is but the denial of all dogmas, any theology, under the Gospel. No wonder it denies what it cannot attain.'[49]

Karl Adam

Another great luminary, Karl Adam (1876–1966) described how the Enlightenment uprooted man from his true soil.

After that age 'dethroned reason and dispossessed that power of thought which grasps the whole in one comprehensive view, to replace it by the power which pursues detail and difference, the interior economy of man, his spiritual unity, broke up into a mere juxtaposition of powers and functions.'[50] Adam depicted how Kant and his school made the transcendental subject the autonomous lawgiver of the objective world and even of the empirical consciousness itself, so that the whole consciousness of reality became paralysed with an unhealthy subjectivism. This approach, like a vampire, sucked all the blood out of resolution and action. 'The autonomous man, cut off from God, and the solitary man cut off from the society of his fellow-men, isolated from the community, is now severed also from his own empirical self. He becomes a merely provisional creature, and therefore sterile and unfruitful, corroded by the spirit of "criticism", estranged from reality, a man of mere negation.'[51] Adam affirmed how Catholicism involves the whole person, not simply pious feeling, but also the cool light of reason, and not reason only, but also the practical will, and not only the inner man of the intelligence, but also the outer man of the sensibility. Catholicism is positive and life-giving as it involves essentially affirmation without subtraction. On the other hand, 'all non-Catholic creeds are essentially anti-thesis, conflict, contradiction and negation. And since negation is of its very nature sterile, therefore they cannot be creative, productive and original, or at least not in the measure in which Catholicism has displayed these qualities throughout the centuries.'[52]

Atheism

The twentieth century witnessed what was perhaps the most lethal of all attacks on traditional belief in God, in terms of the 'semantic' challenge. It consisted of questioning the very intelligibility of statements about God. It

began in the 1930s with the verificationism of the Logical
Positivists, according to which statements about God are
meaningless since they are not even in principle verifi-
able.[53] Other modern objections to theism, the belief
supported by reason that God exists, are expressed in
various forms. One objection states that theism is
somehow incoherent, and does not square with the existence of evil, another that modern science has somehow
cast doubt upon it; a further opponent of theism would
object that it is in some way unreasonable or *irrational* to
believe in God, even if that belief should happen to be
true. In this context is to be found the *evidentialist* objection
to theism, namely that there is, at best, insufficient
evidence for the existence of God.

An expression of this evidentialist incapacity to reach
God through reason is found in thinkers like Bertrand
Russell, who would claim that a theist who has no
evidence has violated some kind of intellectual or cognitive duty. He has run contrary to an obligation laid upon
him, perhaps by society, or perhaps by his own nature as
a creature capable of grasping propositions and holding
beliefs. This obligation consists in proportioning beliefs to
the strength of the available evidence. An objection to this
evidentialist position is that often the standards for decid-
ing what type of evidence is to be admitted and what
strength of evidence is required for belief are in the hands
of atheists, who begin the discussion with their position
already decided. According to other opponents, the theist
without evidence is under a sort of illusion, a kind of
pervasive deception afflicting the great majority of
mankind over the greater period of time thus far allotted
to it. Thus Freud saw religious belief as 'illusions, fulfil-
ments of the oldest, strongest, and most insistent wishes of
mankind.'[54] He regarded theistic belief as a matter of
wish-fulfilment. Men are paralysed by and appalled at the
spectacle of the overwhelming, impersonal forces that
control our destiny, but mindlessly take no notice, no
account of us and our needs and desires; they therefore

invent a heavenly father of cosmic proportions, who exceeds our earthly fathers in goodness and love as much as in power. Religion for Freud is the 'universal obsessional neurosis of humanity', and it is destined to disappear when human beings learn to face reality as it is, resisting the tendency to edit it to suit our fancies. Freud proposed the disappearance of religion through psychoanalysis, which has taught us the intimate connection between the father complex and belief in God, and 'which has shown us that the personal God is logically nothing but an exalted father, and *daily* demonstrates to us how youthful persons lose their religious belief as soon as the authority of the father breaks down.'[55]

A similar sentiment is volunteered by Karl Marx:

The basis of irreligious criticism is: Man makes religion, religion does not make man .... Religion is the self-consciousness and self-esteem of man who has either not yet found himself, or has already lost himself again. But man is no abstract being encamped outside the world. Man is the world of man, the state, society. This state, this society, produce religion, an inverted world-consciousness, because they are an inverted world. Religion is the general theory of that world, its encyclopaedic compendium, its logic in a popular form, its spiritual *point d'honneur*, its enthusiasm, its moral sanction, its solemn complement, and its universal source of consolation and justification. It is the fantastic realisation of the human essence because the human essence has no true reality. The struggle against religion is, therefore, indirectly a fight against the world of which religion is the spiritual aroma. Religious distress is at one and the same time the expression of real distress and the protest against real distress. Religion is the sigh of the oppressed creature, the heart of a heartless world, just as it is the soul of soulless conditions. It is the opium of the people ....[56]

It is ironic that Marx refers to religion as the opium of the people, when in practice history has shown that Marxism itself has been and is that very opium of the people for its illusory means and ends. Both Freud and Marx dismiss God and religion with recourse to ideology rather than reason; in a sense they construct their own false religion to replace the true faith. It is ironic that Marx speaks here of a *perverted* world consciousness produced by a perverted world, because his system (and also that of Freud) is really the perversion of a correct, or right, or natural condition. It is the perspective of Marxist and Freudian materialism which brings about a sort of cognitive dysfunction, a certain lack of cognitive and emotional health. For it is healthy for human beings to affirm God's existence because we have a concept of the nature of the human person created by God in His image, and are endowed with a natural tendency to see God's handiwork in the cosmos.

Existentialism

Existentialism is a broad expression for the reaction, led by the Dane Søren Kierkegaard (1813–1855), against the abstract rationalism of Hegel's philosophy. Against Hegel's synthetic but artificial conception of 'absolute consciousness' within which all oppositions are supposedly reconciled, Kierkegaard insisted on the irreducibility of the subjective, personal dimension of human life. He formulated this concept in terms of the perspective of the 'existing individual', and it is from this particular use of the term 'existence' to describe a distinctively human mode of being that existentialism gets its name. Existentialism represents a series of interpretations of human existence in the world that stress its concreteness and its problematic character. According to Kierkegaard, the individual is aware of the fact that he exists, and this is a most terrible thing, for to exist is 'to stand out' or in a certain sense to be detached from God. Thus human existence denotes a detachment, an opposition to God. Kierkegaard was a Protestant, and followed the line of Luther, strongly accentuating the fallenness of man.

Human existence is in itself a mystery: on the one hand I cannot be nonexistent, and on the other, my existence is bathed in sin; I exist, and I am necessarily a sinner. The consciousness of this contradiction causes *Angst* (dread, anguish, anxiety) and this ends in despair; the individual accepts existence as a mystery which he cannot hope to fathom. Kierkegaard claimed that from the experience of contradicting opposites, from despair arises faith, and faith gives the individual the hope of redemption by means of grace. The person abandons himself or herself to God in the leap of faith, which is seen as detached from reason. Kierkegaard maintained that no one can create a life for themselves which will survive the vicissitudes of fortune without making this leap of faith, a personal commitment to the kind of life lived by Jesus Christ.

Martin Heidegger (1889–1976) followed Kierkegaard in applying the term *Existenz* to describe the mode of being that is distinctive of human life, and also held that the typical feature of human existence arises from the irreducibility of the practical concern we each face concerning our lives. There is no fixed human essence which gives a structure to human life that is independent of the engagements and goals which, by giving us a sense of our own practical identity, fill out our existence. What then motivates us to become authentic is the experience of *Angst*, which Heidegger interprets as an awareness of the precariousness of a life whose goals and values are not understood as arising from the structure of one's own existence. The existent reality should give us an understanding of the essence of reality, but being guided by no spiritual principle, Heidegger ends with destruction and death. Thus for Heidegger, existence in its attempt to transcend its limits ends in nothingness. Karl Jaspers (1883–1969) proposed that transcendence, as a unique and absolute Being, is always beyond and just outside the existent being. Every degree of human knowledge is a limitation of horizon beyond which there is something more. Knowledge is a subjective point of view belonging to the being in the world. It is also limited because of the existence of many subjective points of view. The transcendence of being is always something else, something more; and any attempt to attain it is destined to fail. An impassable barrier exists within my existence, a limit beyond which Transcendence (God) is found, inaccessible to my being in the world. However, the transcendent Being can be perceived in the form of 'ciphers' or symbolic characters expressed by the things of the world. Philosophy, in its search for being, reads these ciphers as possible traces of God (*'vestigia Dei'*), as signs and signals pointing toward the ultimate depth and plenitude of Being.

Gabriel Marcel (1889–1973), a dramatist and philosopher, a convert from Hegelianism to Roman Catholicism, is representative of the French Existentialists; he actually coined the term 'existentialism.' According to Marcel, philosophy is not research about being but an attempt to find being. Through my body I perceive surrounding objects. They represent a transcendent thing for me; but through the act of perception I am open to them and they are open to me. Thus the act of perception is an act of love. Through it I transcend myself; I enter into mysterious participation with objects. Through the act of perception objects become immanent in me. Now, the objects are no longer a third thing; they become the 'you' with whom I talk. From the 'you' of the finite things I ascend to God, the absolute You. Thus, I feel God as present to me and I invoke Him. The existence of God is an object of faith and not of reason; and faith is possible only when charity overcomes all impediments and all obstacles.

While for the philosopher Heidegger the existent is reduced to a being tending to death, for Jean-Paul Sartre (1905–1980), an outspoken atheist, the existent is identified with the series of phenomena which tell us of its existence. In other words, to be an existent means to be a series of separate appearances. Ordinarily, 'appearance' reveals the visible reality and what is hidden behind that appearance. This dualism was denied by Sartre and he maintained instead that appearance is the entire and only reality. As a result God, who cannot be phenomenal, does not exist. Sartre rejected theism because it is incompatible with free will in the somewhat peculiar sense in which he takes it to be a basic fact about human beings. If there were a God, he would create human beings with a 'nature' or 'essence', and this is incompatible with Sartre's view that in man existence precedes essence. This seems to mean that human beings do not have an essence until they have chosen their initial 'fundamental projects', Sartre's term for character traits. The problem with this idea is that, regardless of the extent and power of our volitions, ultimately we are also the result of our heredity and early environment. Like many other philosophers, Sartre failed to see this inescapable fact, which is reconcilable with free will, but is incompatible with Sartre's view that our character is self-chosen. As for free will as an argument against God's existence, it should be observed that even if Sartre's argument is otherwise valid, it would not show that there is no God, but only that God cannot have given human beings their 'essences'. Further, Sartre proposed that if God does not exist, all is permitted, hence freedom results in arbitrary acts in the carrying out of the project of existence. He argued that we choose our emotions as much as any other aspect of our life, and that the basic goals of our lives cohere around a fundamental project which is itself the product of an 'original choice', a choice which, since it provides us with all the motivations we have, must itself be unmotivated, or 'absurd'. This unattractive line of thought goes back to Kant. In Kant's case the implied threat of ethical nihilism is supposed to be averted by the requirements of the categorical imperative. Sartre's ethical theory is basically similar: although he celebrates the 'absurdity' of existentialist freedom, he actually only commends those exercises of this freedom which manifest respect for the freedom of others. The atheism and amoralism[57] of Sartre may be considered as the ultimate corruption of existentialism, and of philosophy in general.

Nihilism

The logical end of the road for modern philosophy came in the form of nihilism, a philosophy of nothingness which has been in vogue in our times, but also possesses ancient roots.[58] In addition to the fact that it conflicts with the demands and the content of the word of God, nihilism is a denial of objective truth and of the humanity and of the very identity of the human being. 'It should never be forgotten that the neglect of being inevitably leads to losing touch with objective truth and therefore with the very ground of human dignity. This in turn makes it possible to erase from the countenance of man and woman the marks of their likeness to God, and thus to lead them little by little either to a destructive will to power or to a solitude without hope. Once the truth is denied to human beings, it is pure illusion to try to set them free. Truth and freedom either go together hand in hand or together they perish in misery.'[59] In some ways, nominalism was already a first step on the road to nihilism, since the concern with being was progressively abandoned in the wake of nominalism. The exponents of the French Revolution killed the king, Freud attempted to eliminate the truth of fatherhood and Nietzsche and other modern nihilists wished to destroy any approach to God.[60] Friedrich Nietzsche (1844–1900) was the chief exponent of modern nihilism; he despised Judaism and Christianity and replaced God, the Creator of man, with the 'will to power' which, according to him, is the soul of the world and is scattered among individual men.[61] Each person is a centre of the 'will to power', and his existence can be represented as the will to dominate the whole universe. For Nietzsche, the whole is in me, and I am in the whole: what I do now is what I do forever. No moral, religious or scientific principle can oppose such a will to power; according to Nietzsche these principles were set up by the weak in order to defend themselves and to prevent the impetus of the will to power. Nietzsche despised reason as well as faith, and his works are full of deliberate contradictions. Instead he exalted chaos, disorder and irrationality, which was inserted into a world picture of hopeless eternal recurrence in the cosmos.[62] The tragic and evil impact of Nietzsche's thought was seen in Nazism, in which he was a favourite philosopher.

Gilson and Chesterton

In the twentieth century, the great figure who provided the antidote to nihilism by proposing a Christian philosophy was Etienne Gilson (1884–1978). On the one hand, philosophy, whether it is called Christian or not, can only be philosophy if its principles and arguments are not dependent upon the assent of Christian faith. Everyone agrees that every philosophical principle and every philosophical argument must be fully accessible to any man, whether he is a believer or not. On the other hand, everyone also agrees that philosophers bring certain experiences, opinions, views of the world, and so forth, to the study of philosophy. A philosopher's faith is surely a part of his general understanding of the world, and it is natural and good that such faith should help to direct and to inform the philosopher's thinking, about philosophy as about many other things. Gilson proposed this definition:

> I call 'Christian philosophy' any philosophy which, keeping well distinct the two formal orders [of revelation and of reason], considers Christian revelation as an indispensable aid to reason. Understood thus, this notion does not correspond to a simple essence that can be given an abstract definition; rather it corresponds to a concrete historical reality of which it indicates a description. It is but one kind within the genus of philosophy and denotes those systems of philosophy which would not have been what they were but for the fact that there existed a Christian religion and for the fact that they willingly submitted to its

influence. Insofar as they are concrete historical realities, these systems distinguish themselves one from another by their individual differences; insofar as they form one kind, they show common characteristics which justifies the grouping of them under one category.[63]

Three points are particularly interesting in this definition. First, the order of reason is to be distinguished from the order of revelation; formally, philosophy is always distinct from theology. Second, the expression *Christian philosophy* does not indicate a formal nature but is rather a term to specify concrete historical realities; it is a description rather than a definition. Third, the term indicates the sort of philosophy that results from the influence of Christianity; a philosophy that would not be what it is except for the influence of Christianity is a Christian philosophy. Gilson's understanding anticipates closely what is said by Pope John Paul II as regards *Christian philosophy*:

> In itself, the term is valid, but it should not be misunderstood: it in no way intends to suggest that there is an official philosophy of the Church, since the faith as such is not a philosophy [Gilson's first point]. The term seeks rather to indicate a Christian way of philosophising, a philosophical speculation conceived in dynamic union with faith [Gilson's second point]. It does not therefore refer simply to a philosophy developed by Christian philosophers who have striven in their research not to contradict the faith. The term Christian philosophy includes those important developments of philosophical thinking which would not have happened without the direct or indirect contributions of Christian faith [Gilson's third point].[64]

A further great luminary of the twentieth century was G.K. Chesterton (1874–1936). As a convert to Catholicism he championed a realist Christian philosophy in the line of St Thomas Aquinas. About him, Chesterton remarked that 'It will not be possible to conceal much longer from anybody the fact that St Thomas Aquinas was one of the great liberators of the human intellect .... It is true to say that Thomas was a very great man who reconciled religion with reason, who expanded it towards experimental science, who insisted that the senses were the windows of the soul and that the reason had a divine right to feed upon facts, and that it was the business of the Faith to digest the strong meat of the toughest and most practical of pagan philosophies.'[65] Chesterton illustrated how Thomas' argument for Revelation is not in the least an argument against reason. Rather, Thomas seems inclined to admit that truth could be reached by a rational process, if only it were rational enough; and also long enough. St Thomas is of an optimistic character, which led him rather to exaggerate the extent to which all men would ultimately listen to reason. In his controversies, he always assumed that they would listen to reason.[66] Chesterton pointed out that the Church was 'already beginning to appear as the only champion of reason in the twentieth century, as it was the only champion of tradition in the nineteenth.' The Church was taking this rôle precisely at the time that the higher mathematics was trying to deny that two and two make four and the higher mysticism to imagine something that is beyond good and evil. Amid all these anti-rational philosophies, ours will remain the only rational philosophy.[67]

For Chesterton, Christendom is in the literal sense a continent; it contains everything, even the things in revolt against itself. It is perhaps the most towering intellectual transformation of all and the one that it is hardest to undo even for the sake of argument.[68] He indicated that the history of sects and false religions 'is not one of straight lines striking outwards and onwards, though if it were they would all be striking in different directions. It is a pattern of curves continually returning into the continent and common life of their and our civilisation; and the summary of that civilisation and central sanity is the philosophy of the Catholic Church.'[69] With great perspicuity, Chesterton stresses the reasonableness of faith even when the reasons are not evident:

> I do not mean in the least that the Catholic Church is arbitrary in the sense of never giving reasons; but I do mean that the convert is profoundly affected by the fact that, even when he did not see the reason, he lived to see that it was reasonable. But there is something even more singular than this, which it will be well to note as a part of the convert's experience. In many cases, as a matter of fact, he did originally have a glimpse of the reasons, even if he did not reason about them; but they were forgotten in the interlude when reason was clouded by rationalism.[70]

In conclusion, this rapid survey of the history of philosophy reveals in modern times a growing separation between faith and reason. The rôle of philosophy has changed dramatically within modern culture. From universal wisdom and learning, it has been gradually consigned to a rather marginal position. Other forms of rationality have acquired an ever higher profile, and these are orientated not towards the contemplation of truth and the search for the ultimate goal and meaning of life; but instead they are directed towards the promotion of utilitarian ends, towards enjoyment or power. In the wake of these cultural shifts, some philosophers have abandoned the search for truth in itself and made their sole aim the attainment of a subjective certainty or a pragmatic sense of utility. This in turn has obscured the true dignity of reason, which is no longer equipped to know the truth and to seek the absolute.[71] In the modern secularized era, the idea of thought is no longer one of wisdom and contemplation, but of pragmatist power over nature, which then is considered as an object of conquest.[72] Knowledge is measured in terms of its usefulness, thus resulting in a type of consumerist materialism.

However, closer scrutiny shows that even in the philosophical thinking of those who helped drive faith and reason further apart, there were insights which corroborated realist philosophy, and could be used in a discourse concerning God the Creator. Such insights are found, for instance, in penetrating analyses of perception and experience, of the imaginary and the unconscious, of personhood and intersubjectivity, of freedom and values, of time and history. The theme of death also can become for all thinkers an incisive appeal to seek within themselves the true meaning of their own life. Deprived of what Revelation offers, reason has taken side-tracks which expose it to the danger of losing sight of its final goal. Deprived of reason, faith has stressed feeling and experience, and so runs the risk of no longer being a universal proposition. It is an illusion to think that faith, tied to weak reasoning, might be more penetrating; on the contrary, faith then runs the grave risk of withering into myth or superstition. By the same token, reason which is unrelated to an adult faith is not prompted to turn its gaze to the newness and radicality of being.[73] Therefore, the link between faith and reason needs to be solidly reinformed and reinforced so as to illustrate the glories of reason in the scientific sphere which will form the material of the next chapter.

Notes

[1]   Entia non sunt multiplicanda sine necessitate.
[2]   F. Copleston, *A History of Philosophy*, vol. III, *Ockham to Suarez* (New York: Image Books, 1985), p. 11.
[3]   See ibid., p. 51.
[4]   See William of Ockham, *Quodlibeta septem*, 6,6.
[5]   Copleston, *A History of Philosophy*, vol. III, *Ockham to Suarez*, p. 67.
[6]   See Copleston, *A History of Philosophy*, vol. III, *Ockham to Suarez*, p. 84.
[7]   William of Ockham, *Commentary on the First Book of the Sentences*, 3, 2, M.
[8]   See St Thomas Aquinas, *Summa Theologiae*, II–II, q. 1, a. 2. See also chapter 1, p. 92 above.
[9]   G. K. Chesterton, *St Thomas Aquinas* (New York: Doubleday, 1956), p. 33.
[10]   See Pope John Paul II, *Fides et Ratio* 45.

[11] See D. Hume, *Dialogues concerning natural religion* (New York: Social Sciences Publishers, 1948).

[12] For the cosmological and the teleological arguments for the existence of God, see chapter 7 pp. 187–188, 191–194 below.

[13] Pope John Paul II, *Crossing the Threshold of Hope*, ed. V. Messori (New York: Alfred A. Knopf, 1994), p. 38.

[14] R. Descartes, *Discourse on the Method*, Part 4 in *The Philosophical Works of Descartes* edited and translated by E. S. Haldane and G. R. T. Ross (Cambridge: University Press, 1972), vol. 1, p. 101.

[15] See St Thomas Aquinas, *Summa Theologiae*, I, q. 16, a. 1, where he indicates that truth is 'the equation of thought and thing', 'veritas est adaequatio rei et intellectus.'

[16] Pope John Paul II, *Crossing the Threshold of Hope*, p. 51; Cf. Idem, *Fides et Ratio* 81.

[17] R. Descartes, *Discourse on the Method*, Part 6 in *The Philosophical Works of Descartes*, vol. 1, p. 119.

[18] See R. Descartes, *The Seventh Set of Objections* in *The Philosophical Works of Descartes*, edited and translated by E. S. Haldane and G. R. T. Ross (Cambridge: University Press, 1972) vol. 2, pp. 325–344. See also Idem, *Discourse on the Method*, Part 3 in *The Philosophical Works of Descartes*, vol. 1, p. 99.

[19] R. Descartes, *Meditations on First Philosophy*, III in *The Philosophical Works of Descartes*, vol. 1, p. 170.

[20] S. L. Jaki, *The Road of Science and the Ways to God* (Edinburgh: Scottish Academic Press, 1978), pp. 68–69.

[21] Occasionalism maintains that all relations between physical things, or between human minds and physical things, which in a realist perspective are supposed to be causal, are in fact not causal. Instead, the relations are occasions for God to cause separately various events and link them together. For example, when our body perceives an given object, our mind is simultaneously endowed by God with the idea of that object.

[22] See B. Pascal, *Pensées* translated by W. F. Trotter (New York: E. P. Dutton, 1958), #72.

[23] Pascal, *Pensées*, #72. Pascal's view of the limitations of reason is also graphically portrayed in Thought 267: 'The last proceeding of reason is to recognise that there is an infinity of things which are beyond it. It is but feeble if it does not see so far as to know this. But if natural things are beyond it, what will be said of supernatural?'

[24] See Pascal, *Pensées*, #242.

[25] Pascal, *Pensées*, #273.

[26] Pascal, *Pensées*, #556.

[27] Pascal, *Pensées*, #588.

[28] In French *Siècle de Lumières* and in German *Aufklärung*.

29 For Gödel's theorems of incompletenesss see chapter 7, pp. 190, 215 below.

30 See S. L. Jaki, Introduction to his translation of I. Kant, *Universal Natural History and Theory of the Heavens* (Edinburgh: Scottish Academic Press, 1981), p. 70: 'Perhaps this translation will be helpful in showing that the apriorism (and subjectivism) of the Critique is already raising its bewitching head in the Allgemeine Naturgeschichte.'

31 *Ibid.*, p. 71.

32 Cf. Jaki, *The Road of Science and the Ways to God*, p. 120.

33 See Pope John Paul II, *Fides et Ratio* 46.

34 Jaki, *The Road of Science and the Ways to God*, p. 252.

35 The error attributed to A. Rosmini Serbati was condemned in the year 1887 by the Holy Office and which can be found in DS 3201. English translation from ND (141). See also Congregation for the Doctrine of the Faith, *Note on the Force of the Doctrinal Decrees Concerning the Thought and Work of Fr Antonio Rosmini Serbati* (1 July 2001) §7, which indicated that the meaning of the proposition, 'as understood and condemned by the Decree, does not belong to the authentic position of Rosmini, but to conclusions that may possibly have been drawn from the reading of his works.' At the same time 'the objective validity of the Decree *Post obitum* referring to the previously condemned propositions, remains for whoever reads them, outside of the Rosminian system, in an idealist, ontologist point of view and with a meaning contrary to Catholic faith and doctrine.'

36 One exponent of fideism was Huet, Bishop of Avranches, in his work *De imbecillitate mentis humanae* (Amsterdam, 1748).

37 L. G. A de Bonald, *Législation primitive considérée dans les derniers temps par les seules lumières de la raison*, I in L. G. A. de Bonald, *Oeuvres* vol. 2 (Paris: Le Clere, 1817), pp. 336–337.

38 Cf. Idem, *Recherches philosophiques sur les premiers objets des connoissances morales*, I in L. G. A. de Bonald, *Oeuvres* vol. 8 (Paris: Le Clere, 1817), pp. 94, 100, 119–240.

39 Cf. ibid., pp. 409–416.

40 Cf. F. de Lamennais, *Défense de l'Essai sur l'Indifférence en matière de Religion*, chapter xi in *Oeuvres Complètes de F. de la Mennais*, vol. 1 (Paris: Paul Daubrée et Cailleux, 1836–1837), p. 371.

41 F. de Lamennais, *Défense de l'Essai sur l'Indifférence*, chapter xi, in *Oeuvres Complètes de F. de la Mennais*, vol. 5 (Paris: Paul Daubrée et Cailleux, 1836–1837), pp. 112–113.

42 J. H. Newman, 'The Theory of Developments in Religious Doctrine, 1843', in J. H. Newman, *Conscience, Consensus and the Development of Doctrine: Revolutionary Texts by John Henry Cardinal Newman*, ed. J. Gaffney, (New York: Image/Doubleday, 1992), pp. 6–30; §2.

43 Ibid., §3
44 Ibid.
45 Ibid., §5.
46 Ibid..
47 Ibid., §7.
48 Ibid..
49 Ibid..
50 K. Adam, *The Spirit of Catholicism* (London: Sheed & Ward, 1952), p. 10.
51 Ibid., p. 11.
52 Ibid., pp. 12–13. Karl Adam cites Tertullian's judgement on the divisions among the heretics of his time: 'Nihil enim interest illis, licet diversa tractantibus, dum ad unius veritatis expugnationem conspirent .... Schisma est enim unitas ipsa.' (*De praescriptionibus adversus haereticos* chapters 41, 42 in *PL* 2, 56–58). Similarly St Augustine: 'Dissentiunt inter se, contra unitatem omnes consentiunt' (*Sermo* 47, chapter 15, n. 27 in *PL* 38, 313).
53 Note the comment by M. Schlick (of the Vienna Circle): 'The act of verification in which the path to the solution finally ends is always of the same sort: it is the occurrence of a definite fact that is confirmed by observation, by means of immediate experience. In this manner the truth (or falsity) of every statement, of daily life or science, is determined. There is thus no other testing and corroboration of truths except through observation and empirical science. Every science (in so far as we take this word to refer to the content and not to the human arrangements for arriving at it) is a system of cognitions, that is, of true experimental statements.' From M. Schlick, 'The Turning Point in Philosophy' in A. J. Ayer, editor, *Logical Positivism* (Glencoe, Illinois: The Free Press, 1960), p. 56.
54 S. Freud, *The Future of an Illusion* (New York: Norton, 1961), p. 30.
55 Idem, *Leonardo da Vinci* (New York: Random, 1947), p. 98.
56 K. Marx, *Contribution to the Critique of Hegel's Philosophy of Law*, in K. Marx and F. Engels, *Collected Works*, vol. 3: (Moscow: Progress Publishers, 1975). pp. 175–176.
57 Amoralism is understood to be the notion that moral distinctions are invalid.
58 See what was said about nihilism in chapter 1, pp. 17–18 above.
59 Pope John Paul II, *Fides et Ratio* 90.
60 For this idea see R. Laurentin, *Dio esiste ecco le prove* (Casale Monferrato: Piemme, 2001), p. 9.
61 For an interesting analysis of the challenge to Christian theism presented by Nietzsche's thought see D. D'Alessio, *Ecce Homo. Il dramma dell'umanesimo cristiano* (Milano: Edizioni Glossa, 2000), pp. 95–158.
62 See S. L. Jaki, *Science and Creation: From Eternal Cycles to an*

Oscillating Universe (Edinburgh: Scottish Academic Press, 1986²), pp. 318–329, who cites K. Löwith, *Nietzsches Philosophie der Ewigen Wiederkunft des Gleichen* (Berlin: Verlag Die Runde, 1935).

[63] E. Gilson, *L'esprit de la philosophie médiévale* (Paris: Vrin, 1944) pp. 32–33.

[64] Pope John Paul II, *Fides et Ratio* 76.

[65] G. K. Chesterton, *St Thomas Aquinas*, pp. 32–33.

[66] Cf. ibid., p. 38.

[67] See G. K. Chesterton, *The Catholic Church and Conversion* (New York: MacMillan, 1928), pp. 21–22.

[68] See ibid., p. 80.

[69] Ibid., p. 83.

[70] Ibid., p. 97.

[71] See Pope John Paul II, *Fides et Ratio* 47.

[72] See Pope John Paul II, *Discourse to Participants in a Congress on Environment and Health*, 24 March 1997, 4.

[73] See Pope John Paul II, *Fides et Ratio* 48.

CHAPTER 6

SCIENTIFIC SCHEMING

For these three reasons-the medieval birth of modern science in terms of a Christian dogma, the indispensability of a realist metaphysics in creative scientific method, and the reality of the universe as witnessed by modern scientific technology-the Catholic must feel on home ground when facing up to science.
Stanley Jaki, 'Science for Catholics'

The colours of the world are in our eyes;
The music of the world is in our ears;
And only when the microcosmic mind
Of man has made its own swift synthesis,
Does it reflect, in moments of strange light,
Whether in art or science, beauty or truth,
The macrocosmic harmonies of God.
Alfred Noyes, *The Torch-Bearers, The Last Voyage*

Now that the year 2000 has turned, one tends to look back over the past century and the past millennium. During the last hundred years in particular, life on our planet has progressed a great deal. Electricity has completely changed our lives, as well as the invention and development of motor cars and aeroplanes. In the medical realm, the discovery of antibiotics and anti-viral agents has meant that diseases which once were often fatal, like pneumonia, can now be cured. In the realm of daily living vast progress has been made in the last thirty years, particularly in computer science and technology bringing speedier and more efficient communications. However, our understanding of the universe has also developed greatly. About one hundred years ago, scientists thought that their understanding of the world was practically complete. But then, early in the twentieth century, the discovery of relativity theory and the development of quantum mechanics once again opened new frontiers in the physical world. The atom which seemed like a tiny billiard ball was then split, thus revealing hitherto unknown subatomic particles and forces. Our journey into the cosmos as a whole has also revealed the vastness, complexity and yet beauty of a universe which we are still uncovering. Similarly, the journey of discovery into the biological realm has also involved the breaking of new frontiers. The father of modern genetics was really an Augustinian priest, Gregor Mendel, from the latter part of the nineteenth century, whose studies into the laws of heredity in plants paved the way for great advances in the twentieth century. Now the human genome project has mapped the genetic profile of the human being in such a way that many diseases which up to now have been incurable may one day be cured. Clearly this remarkable scientific progress has not been without its problems. Technology has not always applied scientific discoveries for the best, and applications have not always been shared with humanity in such a way that the less fortunate could have also benefited from these developments.

The Birth of Science and the Science of its Stillbirths

An interesting question about this great scientific development over the past century concerns how it all came about in the first place. It is true that one discovery builds upon another. For example, the invention of computers is inconceivable without the prior discovery of electricity. Many scholars would say that the early moves, the 'baby steps' as they would say in America, in the development of modern science go all the way back to the Middle Ages. It is considered that the first pioneer physicist was John Buridan, professor at the Sorbonne in Paris around the year 1330. Buridan's vision of the universe was steeped in the Christian doctrine of the creation; in particular, he rejected the Aristotelian idea of a cosmos existing from all eternity. The Judaeo-Christian world-picture involves a cosmos which has a beginning, and this mentality encouraged scientific creativity to look for beginnings within cosmic processes. Thus Buridan developed the idea of impetus in which God was seen as responsible for the initial setting in motion of heavenly bodies, which then remained in motion without the necessity of a direct action on the part of God. This concept was different from Aristotle's approach, in which the motion of heavenly bodies had no beginning and would also have no end. His disciple, Nicholas Oresme, around the year 1370 continued Buridan's work; impetus theory anticipated Newton's first law of motion.[1] Modern natural science therefore had its unique viable birth in the medieval, Christian West. Underlying this viable birth is a metaphysics, related both to belief in God the Creator and to modern science. In an examination of the stillbirths and unique viable birth of science, there is a truth to be uncovered: '... one must show readiness to look for a lesson in all its phases, in the most developed as well in the most embryonic, and in particular to try to see whether a consistent lesson can be found in the entirety of the historical process.'[2] The stillbirths of science in all ancient cultures and its one viable birth in the Middle Ages constitute the fundamental paradigm of the history of science.[3]

Many great civilizations of antiquity possessed the preconditions for the growth of science. There were always people who had the time, technical skills, intelligence and the systems of writing and mathematics. Clearly all this was by itself insufficient. A suitably positive approach to the material world was lacking and this factor was necessary so that science could flourish. As Stanley Jaki recounts, although some scientific elements were first in evidence a little before 2000 BC, the subsequent three thousand years of scientific endeavour were marked by a pattern of repeated historical blind alleys. Science came to 'an aborted birth in seven great cultures: Chinese, Hindu, Maya, Egyptian, Babylonian, Greek and Arabic.'[4] The biologist Joseph Needham, despite his Marxism, observed that the failure of the Chinese in science resulted from a deterioration in their theology and world view. Early Chinese science had drawn strength from the belief in a personal Creator and in a universe with laws, but science was undermined in the pantheistic, organismic, cyclic world-view which eventually prevailed. In the Confucian view of the cosmos, a strong parallel was drawn between the parts of man's body and the parts of the universe; the latter was conceived as cyclic with respect to time. In the Taoist view of reality, nature was an all-encompassing living entity animated by impersonal volitions, and man was a ripple on the great rhythmic undulations of the *yin* and the *yang* (the two basic forces of the cosmos), with little sense of purpose. There were endless returns in nature, no real beginning, and the universe was essentially unfathomable. In the second century after Christ, Buddhism from India came into China and further reinforced an 'already strong preoccupation with cycles dominating the cosmos.'[5] The Chinese possessed some raw materials of science in printing, gunpowder and magnets, and yet there was no intellectual ferment and no real scientific progress. The cyclic conception of reality inhibited this growth, as the awareness of the causal connection between events was stymied for the Chinese. As Jaki notes: '... the ensuing resignation of the Chinese into practical mediocrity, though not into despair and despondency, was a matching counterpart of their moderate preoccupation with the exact period of the great cosmic cycle, the Great Year.'[6]

Insights into science among the Chinese of old were

eclipsed by those of ancient India, the birthplace, among other things, of the decimal notation. Despite these insights, there was an inability to develop them into a self-sustaining system of scientific investigation. The Hindus were greatly taken up with their cyclic notion of the cosmos, to assign an exact figure to the length of the Great Year, and they suffered from a strong despair resulting from their perception that 'the eternal recurrence was a treadmill out of which there was no point in trying to escape.'[7] The cosmos was also seen as a great living organism, whose movements were arbitrary. Therefore the very soul of science, consisting in 'theoretical generalisation leading to the formulation of quantitative laws and systems of laws,'[8] could not be achieved in the Hindu culture of old.

Despite the paucity of records, evidence can also be seen of a hopeless world-view in the culture of the pre-Columbian Americas. The Aztec gods were personifications of various periodically-changing forces and phenomena in nature. Organismic and cyclic notions ousted a reliable notion of space, time and causality. Nature was a source of fear and fatalism. The Incas could not break out of a cyclic cosmic view. Although the Maya had arithmetic, they failed to get beyond addition and subtraction. Again, the Maya held a cyclic notion of time, in which the universe had no beginning: they failed to go forward and interpret nature in a truly scientific way. The fact 'that they had not been successful in this respect illustrates that the emergence of science is a more extraordinary event than many children of the atomic age would imagine.'[9]

The Egyptians lived under the spell of a cyclic notion of time, and the whole world was considered as an animal, yielding an organismic, animistic, rhythmic cosmos. Even Akhenaton's (Amenophis IV's) 'monotheism' (around 1370 BC) could not change that world-view, trapped as it was in the morass of a pantheistic, animistic matrix. In some practical areas, such as the listing of certain drugs and their attention to the pulse-beat, the Egyptians failed to produce a coherent scientific enterprise owing to a superstitious and magical view of man and the cosmos. The stillbirth in Egyptian science is all the more striking because of such great technical achievements as the pyramids. The lack of development of scientific and historical reflections is no coincidence, for 'science and historiography are but different types of a causal and rationally confident probing into the space-time matrix in which external events, physical and human, run their irrevocable courses'. Instead, the Egyptians of old espoused an animistic cyclical world-view resting on the 'watery-abyss' as the ultimate entity: 'From its dark, pantheistic depths and from its utterly unpredictable stirrings there could not emerge an unambiguous and effective pointer suggesting the presence of clear, rational laws in the universe.' [10]

The Babylonians were also trapped in an animistic and cyclic world-view which was not a fertile soil for the development of scientific enterprise. Their gods, representing various forces in nature, were unpredictable, capricious and violent. Every part of nature had a will of its own, according to the Sumerians, Babylonians and Assyrians. The Babylonians observed the heavens in order to find out about the course of human events on earth. In the organismic and cyclic Babylonian cosmology, there was no true beginning or first principle: all lacked consistent explanation and exuded pessimism, as exemplified in the classic Babylonian cosmology, *Enumah Elish*. Babylon and Assur enjoyed a long period of peace, the Sumerians and Assyro-Babylonians experienced intellectual strength, industrial power, curiosity and patience; yet their culture did not yield science. The reasons are these: ancient Mesopotamia suffered a culture lacking confidence in the ability to investigate, predict, influence or control a world which was a wilful, animistic struggle between order and chaos; hence there was no self-sustaining scientific activity.

In ancient Greece, science came much closer to a viable birth than it did in other ancient cultures. Astronomy, algebra and geometry were better developed than in other ancient civilizations. Ancient Greek science went beyond the phase of description, observation and classification (this stage being exemplified by Aristotle's biology or Galen's medicine) and 'moved up to the stage where the entire body of knowledge was a derivative of some fundamental postulates.'[11] Yet a curious progression in Greek science can be observed: a very creative, yet short, period (450–350 BC), followed by an extended period of elaboration (350 BC–AD 150) and then a long stagnation coming to an end around AD 600. The fundamental reason for the stillbirth of science in ancient Greece was a world view 'steeped in the idea of eternal cycles.'[12] According to Aristotle, everything general, including ideas, recurred cyclically, and this undermined the concept of time. Aristotle's vision of the cosmos also bespoke necessity: this discouraged *a posteriori* investigation of the cosmos.

The Stoics tried to escape the clutches of the prospect of eternal recurrences, yet their belief in these remained alive even in the Hellenistic centuries: in their world-view, *process* rather than *being* dominated. However, the foundation of knowledge is the stability of reality rather than its flux. The Great Year was a circular barrier for the Greek mind and deprived it of insights and aspirations which were necessary for the growth of science. Calculus could not develop in ancient Greece because, for this development, it was necessary that time be 'no longer considered as a mirror image of eternal recurrences, but rather as an uninterrupted one-dimensional flow of events.'[13]

For Epicurus, the gods were not subject to cycles, so that the stars did not rigidly rule human events, yet he retained a cyclic view for the world as such. In trying to escape the absolutely necessary nature of Aristotle's cosmology, he made chance a basic factor, which, as a counterpart of atomism, deprived the Epicurean universe of rationality and consistency. The cyclic notion is 'the very foundation of the three main cosmologies developed by the Greeks, the Aristotelian, the Stoic and the Epicurean (atomistic).'[14] In this cyclic, and often pantheistic universe, matter and processes were eternal. This encouraged the view that 'man was merely a bubble on the inexorable sea of events whose ebb and flow followed one another with fateful regularity,'[15] and hardly stimulated a confidence in the experimental investigation of the universe. Jaki thus rejects the Marxist view that the stillbirth in science in ancient Greece arose from purely socio-political factors.[16]

Despite the fact that by the early ninth century the Arabs had acquired all of the available Greek learning, they were nevertheless unable to carry this scientific endeavour forward. According to Jaki, there were two essential reasons for this. First, there was 'the Koran's over-emphasis on divine will in relation to divine rationality.' For the orthodox school of Muslim thought (the Mutakallimun, exemplified by Al-Ashari and Al-Ghazzali), 'the notion of a consistent physical law was not acceptable because it seemed to derogate from Allah's sovereign will, which appears rather capricious in not a few pages of the Koran.'[17] The laws of nature were downplayed, since God's will was seen as so omnipotent as to amount to arbitrariness or mere capriciousness. Only in fields such as optics or mathematics (where there was need for little empirical investigation of events or processes) did the Arabs make some progress. Their chemistry, a field which deals with processes, was laced with superstition. Yet there is a second reason why science failed to take off in the Arab world. Those who were not such orthodox Muslims (the Mutazalite school represented by such figures as Avicenna and Averroës) followed Aristotle to such an extent that they took on board the pantheism and necessitarianism involved in the ancient Greek world-picture. Hence there was a schizophrenic split between their belief in God and their philosophy. Being so wholeheartedly Aristotelian, these Mutazalites had cast away the belief in the Creator 'that could have helped them to steer clear of the pantheistic shallows of the Greek world-view including the notion of the Great Year.'[18]

Modern science, a self-sustaining enterprise in which one step follows another, did not come to birth in the Muslim world; the Newtonian science of mechanics was not devised among the Arabs. Avicenna (who died in 1037) was the Muslim scholar who came potentially closest in the Arab world to a theory of impetus; yet it was Buridan who was to formulate this, 'for the crucial insight in Buridan's discussion of impetus is a theological point which is completely alien to Avicenna's thinking.' Even a devout Muslim like Al-Biruni was ambivalent about a world finite in time with a beginning and an end, and did not affirm creation out of nothing or the rationality of the cosmos. In short, the Muslim notion of the Creator was insufficient to overcome cyclic, pantheistic, animistic, organismic and magical elements. Jaki notes, however, that 'much of the Greek scientific and philosophical corpus reached the Latin West through Muslim mediation.'[19]

That science suffered stillbirths in many ancient cultures and that these stillbirths can be linked with world-pictures inadequate for the stimulation of scientific growth implies that, since science is now a self-sustaining enterprise, the conditions for its growth must be found in the relatively recent past. In fact, the period of the viable birth of science can be regarded as 1250–1650 in Europe. Pierre Duhem's monumental work, *Le système du monde*, first showed that the medieval period was not a dark age for science but rather its very cradle.[20] The accepted view had been, for three hundred years prior to Duhem, that the Renaissance was the important period for the rise of modern science. This derived 'partly from the reformer's scorn for medieval Catholicism and partly from the hostility of the leaders of the French Enlightenment to anything Christian.'[21] Instead, it is emphatically not 'a freak happening of history that science was born in a Europe that was living through its centuries of faith.'[22]

In the Middle Ages, ideas about the created universe had developed which were greatly conducive to scientific enterprise. This world vision included the idea that the cosmos is good, and therefore attractive to study. Also the universe was considered to be a single entity with inner coherence and order, and not a gigantic animal which would behave in an arbitrary fashion, as was often believed in antiquity. The world was deemed to be endowed with its own laws which could be tested and verified; it was not magical or divine. Further, the cosmos was seen to be rational and consistent, so that what was investigated one day would also hold true the next. The world picture also involved the tenet that cosmic order is accessible to the human mind, and can be investigated experimentally, not just by pure thought. In addition to these ideas, medieval Christendom also was imbued with the concept that it was worthwhile to share knowledge for the common good. It turned out that during this fertile period of scientific growth, there was a harmonious relationship between science and Christianity, and indeed many of the earliest scientists were devout believers, like Saint Albert the Great, renowned for his investigations in the physical and chemical realms, and Blessed Hildegard of Bingen, known for her pioneering work in the biological and ecological areas. Other unknown early scientists worked on such areas as the development of clocks. Before the rise of science, human activity followed biological time and solar time, regulated by the natural succession of night and day. In contrast, scientific time involves high numerical accuracy. Monasteries needed to have a way of measuring time with reasonable accuracy so as to regularize the hours of prayer, work and study and while they followed biological time at first, gradually they developed sand and water clocks. By the twelfth century, highly sophisticated mechanical clocks had been built, and these produced a profound effect on civil society as well. At the heart of scientific activity lies the measurement of time.

Therefore, harmony between faith and science preceded

disharmony. For instance, the Galileo affair, which took place after science had been born in a Christian setting, is sometimes used to obscure the many examples of harmonious and fruitful collaboration between the Church and science. In fact, Galileo himself was an example of a devout Christian and a great scientist. Moreover, even in the Galileo case 'the agreements between religion and science are more numerous and above all more important than the incomprehension which led to the bitter and painful conflict that continued in the course of the following centuries.'[23] It is true that in the Galileo affair, as in other misunderstandings, a healing of memories is needed. What can be learned from the Galileo situation is the necessity to delineate with increasing clarity the respective fields of competence, methods and value of the conclusions of science and theology, according to their respective nature. In particular, the Holy Scriptures do not teach us scientific details about the physical world but rather the fact that it was created.[24]

Church authorities have often expressed the essential and basic harmony between science and religion. Over one hundred years ago, the First Vatican Council put it this way: 'Truth cannot contradict truth.'[25] In 1936, Pope Pius XI enunciated what must be the first principle of relations between science and religion when he wrote 'science as a true understanding of reality can never contradict the truths of the Christian faith.'[26] Fifty years later, at the celebration of the fiftieth anniversary of the Pontifical Academy of Sciences, Pope John Paul II stated that 'there is no contradiction between science and religion'.[27]

While science and religion enjoy their own fields of competence, there can be fruitful collaboration between them. Scientific discovery uncovers more and more of the material cosmos, both in the realm of the very small atomic world and the very large astrophysical universe. More and more can be seen and is understood in the biological sphere. The complexity, beauty and intricacy of the universe thus unveiled are a stimulus towards adoration of the Creator who made this cosmos, and who guides it in His Providence. Scientific progress has helped to exorcise superstition, another service for which religion is grateful. At the same time, religion can assist science not to close its eyes to a larger canvas. At this present time, it can guide scientists and technologists to use their discoveries for the real good of mankind. Such guidance is needed so that the right decisions are made regarding the applications of advances in genetics, and other matters which touch the beginning and end of human life, so that the immense value of human life is always respected and never manipulated or damaged. Religion can assist in the sharing of scientific progress with all sectors of the community, especially with the less fortunate ones. Science and technology have brought untold benefits to mankind, for which we should be thankful and which we must use for the best. In Christ's words: 'When someone is given a great deal, a great deal will be demanded of that person; when someone is entrusted with a great deal, of that person even more will be expected' (Luke 12:48). Much has been entrusted to humanity through scientific growth, and thus more will be expected in loving response to the Creator.

The opponents of theism, on the other hand, often base their ideologies upon certain misinterpretations of science. For instance some interpret ideologically modern cosmology with a casual idea of quantum mechanics, so undermining the principle of *efficient causality* in the universe. Others approach the theory of evolution in such a way that chance undermines the idea of *final causality* in the cosmos.

Big Bang Cosmology

The Big Bang theory is a series of models and corrections to those models which constitute an attempt to reconstruct the early history of the physical universe. Some scientists attempt to use cosmology as way of denying the existence of the Creator, a denial which has become increasingly easy since the Enlightenment. The oscillating model of the universe has often used by those who wish to assert its everlasting duration, for they posit an infinite number of cycles. However, since all physical processes in a closed system are subject to the law of entropy, each successive cycle should be smaller. It is possible to calculate, tentatively, the number of cycles which would bring the universe back to vanishing point. There is thus no danger to a proper notion of creation in this finite oscillation model (which has a finite energy reservoir) because it is again highly specific. Also it stands in contradistinction to a universe oscillating for ever, the eternal treadmill of pagan civilisations in which worlds 'follow one another in endless sequence.'[28]

The cosmologist Stephen Hawking attempts to exclude God from His own cosmos. His first step is to give an ontological status to the uncertainty principle, which he says 'is a fundamental, inescapable property of the world'.[29] In this way, it becomes easier to make the cosmos come into being through a quantum mechanical quirk of nature. At first, Hawking thought that there was an initial singularity of the cosmos, and then in 1981 he used quantum gravity considerations to propose the idea that time and space together form a surface of finite dimensions, but without any edge or boundary. In Hawking's words:

> There would be no singularities at which the laws of science would break down and no edge of space-time at which one would have to appeal to God or some new law to set the boundary conditions for space-time. One could say: 'The boundary condition of the universe is that it has no boundary.' The universe would be completely self-contained and not affected by anything outside itself. It would be neither created or destroyed. It would just BE.[30]

Significantly, Hawking admits that 'this idea that space and time could be finite without boundary is just a *proposal*: it cannot be deduced from any other principle. Like any other scientific theory, it may initially be put forward for aesthetic or metaphysical reasons, but the real test is whether it makes predictions that agree with observation. This, however, is difficult to determine in the case of quantum gravity'.[31] It would seem that Hawking departs from the sphere of competence of science saying that a theory may be put forward for aesthetic or metaphysical reasons. We would say that a hypothesis should be proposed on the basis of an already existing hypothesis and some empirical data, however remote. It seems that Hawking eliminates God with an *a priori* hypothesis, which makes his argument circular. His conclusion is:

> So long as the universe had a beginning, we could suppose it had a creator. But if the universe is really self-contained, having no boundary or edge, it would have neither beginning or end: it would simply be. What place, then, for a creator?[32]

Hawking seems to limit God's action to an initial singularity in a deistic approach, resulting in a 'God of the gaps.' The proposition that the universe gave birth to itself in a type of quantum fluctuation is but one example of an illegitimate extrapolation of science outside its own sphere. Physical science has to be related to real or possible experiments, and this cannot be the case in the consideration of the absolute origin of the whole universe from nothing. Science is radically incapable of measuring the boundary of the *whole* universe in space or time, because a scientist cannot get outside the cosmos. Atheism based on scientific misinterpretation or upon ideologies constructed around scientific theories consists of an irrational leap of reason which runs against reason; it is the gravest form of intellectual suicide. Once the reference to God has been excluded, it is not surprising that the understanding of reality then becomes profoundly deformed.[33]

It is also a misuse of scientific cosmology to identify the Big Bang with the moment of creation. The reason for this is that science can only trace one physical stage of the physical universe back to another physical stage of it.[34] The method of physics always means an inference from one observable state to another.[35] Scientific cosmology is thus radically incapable of measuring the 'nothing' which preceded the creation. Nevertheless, cosmology contains pointers to philosophy, and thence to God. The connection between science and metaphysics is important and the axiom that the existence of beings grounds knowledge is crucial.[36] Modern science indicates that the universe is a most 'specifically constructed entity, a machine if you wish, tuned with extreme precision for a very specific purpose.' [37] In the reconstruction of the early phases of the universe, there was an interaction between matter and antimatter resulting in the production of one part in ten billion (10^{10}) more matter than antimatter. Later, the lighter elements could only be produced from a mixture, after the end of the first three minutes of cosmic expansion, in which '1 proton, 1 neutron, and 1 electron had to interact with a little less than 40 billion photons at a most specific temperature and pressure.'[38] The universe thus had a very narrow escape to become what it now is. These examples suggest one choice among a great number of possibilities, which means that the cosmos is specific; this specificity discourages any sober mind from thinking that such is its only conceivable and necessary form; this line of argument leads to the idea that the universe should be regarded as contingent.

The physical development of the universe took place within very specific limits. If the ratio of photons to baryons had been slightly different, then much of the hydrogen would have turned into helium, so forestalling the formation of most other elements, all indispensable for the rise of organic life in the universe. Also, if the total mass of the original matter had been different, the universe could not have developed into its present form. The cosmos seems indeed to have been made for man. That the cosmos has been on a path which made possible the later appearance of man is referred to as the 'anthropic principle.'

A further point is that modern cosmology reinforces the concept of the totality of the cosmos. Stanley Jaki defines the cosmos as the *totality of consistently and most specifically interacting contingent but rationally coherent and ordered beings*.[39] In a sense, all science is cosmology: each basic scientific law 'reveals something all-encompassing about the universe.'[40] Science of itself cannot 'provide a demonstration that there is a Universe.'[41] Nevertheless the affirmation of the cosmos is possible through philosophy. The import of general relativity lies in its ability to give, for the first time in scientific history, a consistent treatment of the universe as the totality of gravitationally interacting entities. Therefore, from the viewpoint of science, the notion of the universe is a valid one, a point of utmost importance with respect to Kant's criticism of the cosmological argument.[42] The general theory of relativity also provides further support for the notion of the cosmos as specific. The cosmology of the theory of general relativity cannot tell us whether the total mass of the universe is finite or not, nor whether it is contracting or expanding, nor how old it is; rather, it concerns the value of the space-time curvature valid for the entire universe. This value is very specific whether it is a small positive number, which signifies the closed spherical net of permissible paths of motion, or a small negative number standing for a hyperbolic space or a saddle with no edges, but with very well-defined slopes. 'The only possibility which is excluded is Euclidean infinity whose curvature is 0, an age-old symbol of non-existence.'[43] The universe therefore looks no less specific than a garment on the tailor's rack, carrying a tag on which one could read if not its price at least its main measurements.[44] Just as there is no need for the garment to be of that particular size, there is no scientific reason why the universe has to have the singular or specific value of the curvature. Again, singularity in the sense of specificity is a pointer to cosmic contingency, which in turn indicates the Creator. This singularity and contingency of the universe imply that the cosmos cannot be fathomed by *a priori* introspection, but must be investigated by an empirical and experimental approach. Not only is the universe at the heart of coherent philosophical and scientific discussion, it is also that ground through which the mind can rise to the existence of the Creator.

Four essential properties of the universe make scientific endeavour possible, and these properties are also connected with a philosophy linked to Christian theism; they are stepping stones to the Creator. First, the cosmos has an objective existence and reality independent of the observer. 'Man through his consciousness is always in touch with a reality existing independently of him.'[45] This is the way of a moderate epistemological and metaphysical realism, a 'middle ground.' If this were not the case, man would not be seeing the world but only his own footprints. Similarly to be rejected here is a multi-world theory according to which there are as many universes as there are observers, for how then can one observer get out of his own world to communicate with another observer? Second, the material entities in the universe must have a *coherent rationality* and hence be capable of investigation; these entities must be subject to laws which can be expressed in a quantitative framework, 'and they must have a validity which transcends the limits of any time and location.'[46] Third, for science there can be only one universe, the cosmos. Thus the entities in the universe form a coherent whole, being subject to a consistent set of interactions. Even if the interactions are not all discovered or interrelated by the science of one particular epoch, this very coherence lies waiting to be further uncovered. Fourth, the very specific way in which the coherent wholeness occurs cannot be considered as a necessary form of existence. The mental road to the extracosmic Absolute remains therefore fully open.[47]

Evolutionary Tactics

Evolution may be defined in terms of a series of theories through which scientists seek to explain how present-day living organisms may have successively developed from simpler life-forms in the course of a process which lasted hundreds of millions of years. The process of evolution, as will be seen, poses two kinds of problems which hitherto have not been completely solved. First, the status of its proofs and second the mechanisms under which evolution was brought about. In a manner analogous to the study of the development of the material cosmos, the science of evolution seeks to uncover the secrets of the world of living creatures from its earliest phases in the remotest past. The scientific theories of evolution are based on various strands of empirical data. From paleontology, which studies the fossils and other remains of ancient organisms buried in earth and ice, is obtained the only direct evidence of evolution. There are, however, many theories regarding the passage from one species to another, attempting to explain how the various transitions took place.[48] Comparative anatomy and physiology have indicated relations between living beings and have also uncovered evidence of evolutionary adaptation. Comparisons between the genetic make-up of different species of living organisms have demonstrated a link between various living beings, even between plants and animals. The geographical distribution of various species yields evidence concerning evolution, if continental drift is taken into account. From all the data, it has been possible to draw up evolutionary trees, to show how some living organisms have developed from more primitive species. The various strands of evidence corroborate each other, converging to the view that evolution played a part in the development of life upon this planet. Nevertheless, in the scientific domain, several empirical links are missing in the various chains of evidence needed to prove evolution at every stage in the biological developmental process. It is necessary to distinguish this scientific process from *ideologies* constructed around evolution.

A Darwinist ideology of evolution is firmly present within present-day society. A brief history of the Darwinist approach shows how this state of affairs has come about.   From the scientific point of view, evolutionary theory was spread by J. B. de Monet, Chevalier de Lamarck (1744–1829), who propounded a mechanism of inheritance of new acquired characteristics. Darwin (1809–1882), in his works *The Origin of Species* (1859) and *The Descent of Man* (1871), proposed a different mechanism for evolution, namely natural selection. The latter theory contained the notions of random variations, the struggle for survival and the survival of the fittest. Initially, Darwin was an Anglican, but gradually he lost his faith in a personal Creator God, and sought to eliminate any divine rôle in evolution, substituting for Divine Providence his theory of natural selection as the guiding force. When Darwin set out on his epic voyage aboard H. M. S. *Beagle* in 1831, he was a graduate of Cambridge University with a degree in theology, and wished to seek ministry in the Church of England. His notebooks give ample evidence of a mind itself going through a process of transformation. He described the change much later in the pages of his *Autobiography*:

> I had gradually come, by this time, to see that the Old Testament from its manifestly false history of the world, with the Tower of Babel, the rainbow as a sign, ..., and from its attributing to God the feelings of a revengeful tyrant, was no more to be trusted than the sacred books of the Hindoos, or the beliefs of any barbarian .... I gradually came to disbelieve in Christianity as a divine revelation .... Thus disbelief crept over me at a very slow rate, but was at last complete.[49]

He ended his career in a state of total confusion about one key problem, namely, how to explain the origin and evolution of life in scientific terms without an appeal to religion.

As he confided in a letter to his friend and colleague, Asa Gray:

> I am conscious that I am in an utterly hopeless muddle. I cannot think that the world, as we see it, is the result of chance; and yet I cannot look at each separate thing as the result of Design.[50]

The central pillar of Darwin's system was the idea of natural selection; here he depicts nature as a 'power, acting during long ages and rigidly scrutinising the whole constitution, structure, and habits of each creature, favouring the good and rejecting the bad.'[51] Similarly Darwin wrote:

> It may metaphorically be said that natural selection is daily and hourly scrutinising, throughout the world, the slightest variations; rejecting those that are bad, preserving and adding up all that are good; silently and insensibly working, whenever and wherever opportunity offers, at the improvement of each organic being.[52]

At times, Darwin himself maintained that natural selection, even as it furthered science, seemingly could also advance our understanding of God:

> To my mind it accords better with what we know of the laws impressed on matter by the Creator, that the production and extinction of the past and present inhabitants of the world should have been due to secondary causes .... There is grandeur in this view of life, with its several powers, having been originally breathed into a few forms or into one; and that, whilst this planet has gone cycling on according to the fixed law of gravity, from so simple a beginning endless forms most beautiful and most wonderful have been, and are being, evolved.[53]

Yet Darwin expressed a blind optimism rather akin to that of Hegel when he proposed a grand design in the silent and invisible work of natural selection. 'We may look with some confidence to a secure future of great length. And as natural selection works solely by and for the good of each being, all corporeal and mental endowments will tend to progress toward perfection.'[54] Darwin's view of man seems materialist: 'Why is thought, being a secretion of the brain, more wonderful than gravity, a property of matter?'[55] Having deprived man of the spiritual side of his nature, Darwin's norm became an allegiance to the absence of all norms. This system 'beckoned toward unfathomable whirls in which one was no more than flotsam hurled round and round by the blindest of blind fates.'[56]

A contemporary of Darwin, St George Jackson Mivart (1827–1900), a Catholic, pointed out that there was no contradiction between evolution and belief. He distinguished between primary and secondary causality in creation:

> In the strictest and highest sense 'creation' is the absolute origination of any thing by God without pre-existing means or material, and is a supernatural act. In the secondary and lower sense, 'creation' is the formation of any thing by God derivatively; that is, that the preceding matter has been created with the potentiality to evolve from it, under suitable conditions, all the various forms it subsequently assumes.

He proposed that God is not excluded from concurring in the processes of evolution. In this concurrence, which he terms 'derivative creation' God acts in and through natural laws, and physical science, if unable to demonstrate such action, is at least as impotent to disprove it. Indeed the evidence from physical facts agrees well with the overruling, concurrent action of God in the order of nature; this is no miraculous action, but the operation of laws which owe their foundation, institution and maintenance, to the omniscient Creator. St George Mivart in effect indicated that Darwinism is more of an ideology than a science: 'Certain of Mr. Darwin's objections, however, are not physical, but metaphysical, and really attack the dogma of secondary or derivative creation, though to some perhaps they may appear to be directed against absolute creation only.'[57]

Darwin's disciples, especially E. Haeckel (1834–1919) and T. H. Huxley (1825–1895) propounded evolutionary theory as a materialist and atheist ideology and as an instrument of anti-religious propaganda. Molecular biology revealed that the mechanisms of inheritance are located at the microscopic genetic level and neo-Darwinism sought to extend Darwin's approach by considering evolution as a combination of casual genetic changes with natural selection. Richard Dawkins exemplifies the neo-Darwinist ideology, in which chance is 'tamed' and endowed with the metaphysical properties of a creative force:

> The essence of life is statistical improbability on a colossal scale. Whatever is the explanation of life, therefore, it cannot be chance. The true explanation for the existence of life must embody the very antithesis of chance. The antithesis of chance is nonrandom survival, properly understood .... We have sought a way of taming chance .... 'Untamed chance', pure, naked chance, means ordered design springing into existence from nothing, in a single leap .... To 'tame' chance means to break down the very improbable into less improbable small components arranged in a series .... And provided we postulate a sufficiently large series of sufficiently finely graded intermediates, we shall be able to derive anything from anything else.[58]

This constitutes a negation of the idea of any extra-cosmic causality, which is lost in a web of infinitesimal quantities. Chance is neither able to explain the presence of beauty in the universe nor the human capacity for appreciating such cosmic beauty. In Stanley Jaki's words, 'Darwinism is among all major scientific theories the one that claims the most on the basis of relatively the least.'[59] For many secular scientists natural selection functions as a substitute for God. For if natural selection does everything that God is supposed to do, don't we simply have God by another name?

Therefore, evolutionism must be distinguished from Darwinism, so that the Christian does not throw out the evolutionary baby with the materialistic bathwater. It is necessary for the Christian to distinguish the 'gold from the straw in the evolutionary theory.'[60] Time has a special dignity within the framework of Christian faith, because Christ came in time. Hence, in itself, the attempt to understand the biological realm in relation to its time-development should pose no problem. Nevertheless, Christian thinkers have often failed to notice the 'huge piles of straw' in evolutionary theory. This failure lies in not noticing that Darwinian ideology effectively turns time into a hopeless treadmill. Nor did Darwin notice that Christian faith liberated man from a pessimistic imprison-ment within a world-picture based on inexorable cycles in time. It is rather tragic that, having been freed from the bondage of ancient pagan visions, man should once again fall into another cyclic world-picture, this time modern.[61] Huxley conjured up 'the vision of a meaningless evolution in which higher and lower were indistinguishable precisely because moving into the future was not, in the Darwinian perspective, different from receding into the past.'[62] The confrontation with Darwinism once again brought to the fore the relation between human nature and time within Christian theology, as had already been seen in the great clash involving 'nascent Christianity and Hellenistic culture over the question whether life, includ-ing the redeeming life of Christ, was a once-and-for-all proposition, or whether life was mere flotsam on the unfathomable cyclic currents of blind cosmic force.'[63]

There is no opposition between creation and evolution: the clash with Darwinism arises because the latter is a materialist position which excludes creation. Further, the basic problem in the Darwinian perspective on evolution is the blindness towards purpose and mind in a philosophy of 'ultimate meaninglessness, in which the partial aspects are found meaningful, but never the whole'.[64] An analogical relationship exists between various types of proof, be they legal, scientific, mathematical, philosophical, or theological. In a legal case, it is clear that it is harder to prosecute a criminal for an offence committed a long time in the past, because some of the key witnesses may no longer be available. Moreover distortion of the facts can occur over the years, and even tampering with the evidence. Definite criteria are required in order to admit a body of evidence from some time in the distant past. In scientific proof, which differs from legal proof, there are nevertheless some extrapolations which are made in the discussion of the development of the early cosmos and the evolution of early life-forms. While micro-evolution (the study of transitions between very similar organisms) can in some cases be clearly documented, macro-evolution (which studies a larger picture of relations between very different living organisms) is a much more difficult proposition.

The empirical data cannot justify the proposition of some evolutionists that genetic mutations came about by chance. Care must be taken to distinguish between hard scientific fact (obtained in an *a posteriori* manner) in the theory of evolution and an unjustified *a priori* extrapolation of this theory to form an atheist ideology. The fact that materialistic views of evolution easily lend themselves to ideology is illustrated in the connection between a Darwinist perspective and the most repressive totalitarian politics of last century:

> The enthusiasm for Darwinism of the advocates of the dictatorship of the proletariat and of a master race is all too understandable. Marx was quick to notice the usefulness of Darwinist theory for promoting class struggle, and Hitler volubly echoed Darwinist views very popular among German military leaders prior to the First World War as a justification of their and his plans.[65]

The real danger to man and society is presented by those philosophies which deny the true nature of man and therefore deprive society of its foundation. As Stanley Jaki stated: 'The real enemies of open society are not societies based on absolute and even on supernatural revealed truths, but the ideas of intellectual circles that opted for chance as the ultimate .... Ideas are more dangerous than weapons.' Western society has been thriving on an inherited corpus of absolute beliefs which are implicitly held. Since the reason and background for these beliefs, Christian Revelation, is not acknowledged, secular society thrives on these implicitly Christian truths as a 'parasite.'[66] In modern democratic thought, truth is often reduced to popular or social consensus. In one particular such approach, conventionalism,[67] truth is based on freely chosen conventions, which may be maintained in the face of apparent counter-evidence. A convention is a principle or proposal which is adopted by a group of people, either by explicit choice, as in a country's decision about the colour of their postage stamps, or as a matter of custom, whose origins are unknown and unplanned, as in the convention of driving on the left or on the right. The crucial point, though, is that conventions are not forced on us by nature and could, if we collectively wished, be changed. If we desire to move to a new theory, it will not in the final analysis be because the evidence forces us to do so, but because the new theory (or 'convention') is accepted by the majority, is simpler, easier to apply, more aesthetic, or is supported by some other reason which is not based on metaphysics. Within this perspective, it is difficult to encourage an access to God through reason, as this is often confined within the bounds of a purely pragmatic approach to truth and is not underpinned by metaphysics.

A complete understanding of the evolution of living beings should take into account not only the effects of the environment or genetic modifications, but above all should be open to considering the power of Providence guiding created beings through the laws inscribed upon them. Chance cannot be responsible for directed and coordinated developments which gave rise to complex biological structures like the eye or the ear. Making chance responsible for the evolution of living beings is more ridiculous than proposing that all the phrases in Shakespeare's complete works could be put on a computer at random, and then assembled at random into the Bard's prose and poetry. Evolution cannot be seen as a means to exclude the Creator but rather presupposes creation. Evolutionist ideology can replace neither creation nor Providence. Indeed creation can be seen in the light of evolution as an event which is extended in time, like a continuous creation, in which God is clearly seen as the Creator of heaven and earth.[68] The theory of natural evolution, understood in a sense that does not exclude divine causality, does not necessarily contradict the truth which the Book of Genesis presents concerning the creation of the visible world.[69] Evolution may be envisaged as a kind of programmed creation, in which God has written into creation the laws for its evolution; in this way a clear link can be seen between God's action at the beginning of the cosmos and His constant Providence which guides its constant development. The evidence for design in living beings can be proposed as evidence pointing towards the Creator.[70]

As soon as one casts doubt on the true nature of man, one closes off a road to affirming God the Creator. By denying the distinction between spirit and matter, either all becomes matter which exists on its own without the need for a Creator, or else all becomes a mind closed within its *a priori* presuppositions; as a product of such a mind, the material world is no longer a privileged realm which reveals itself as the work of the Creator. In the next chapter we turn to how reason may rather be employed in the service of God by demonstrating His existence.

Notes

1   See S. L. Jaki, *The Savior of Science* (Washington, D.C.: Regnery Gateway, 1988), pp. 46–54.

2   S. L. Jaki, *The Road of Science and the Ways to God* (Edinburgh: Scottish Academic Press, 1978), p. 319.

3   Cf. ibid., p. 243. Although Jaki uses the term 'paradigm,' also used by T. S. Kuhn, his position differs from Kuhn's; for this difference, see ibid., p. 241, where Jaki states: 'Kuhn's is a heavily tilting balance when he acknowledges that world views and metaphysical beliefs are essential ingredients in any paradigm constitutive of science and pays no further attention to them.'

4   S. L. Jaki, 'The Last Century of Science: Progress, Problems and Prospects' in *Proceedings of the Second International Humanistic Symposium* (Athens: Hellenic Society for Humanistic Studies, 1973), p. 259. See also chapters 1–6 and 9 of S. L. Jaki, *Science and Creation: From Eternal Cycles to an Oscillating Universe* (Edinburgh: Scottish Academic Press, 1986²).

5   Jaki, *Science and Creation*, p. 33.

6   S. L. Jaki, 'The History of Science and the Idea of an Oscillating Universe' in *The Center Journal* 4 (1984), p. 140. The Great Year is the length of time in years for an entire cosmic cycle to elapse, analogous with the time period of an oscillation in physics.

7   Jaki, 'The History of Science and the Idea of an Oscillating Universe', p. 141.

8   Jaki, *Science and Creation*, p. 14.

9   Ibid., p. 62.

10   Ibid., p. 80.

11   S. L. Jaki, 'The Greeks of Old and the Novelty of Science' in *Arete Mneme: Konst Vourveris. Vourveris Festschrift*. (Athens: Hellenic Humanistic Society, 1983), p. 267.

12   Jaki, 'The History of Science and the Idea of an Oscillating Universe', p. 243.

13   Jaki, *Science and Creation*, p. 118.

14   Jaki, 'The History of Science and the Idea of an Oscillating Universe', p. 144.

15   Jaki, *Science and Creation*, p. 130.

16   Jaki, 'The Greeks of Old and the Novelty of Science', p. 267.

17   S. L. Jaki, 'Science and Christian Theism: A Mutual Witness' in *Scottish Journal of Theology* 32 (1979), p. 567.

18   Jaki, 'The History of Science and the Idea of an Oscillating Universe', p. 145.

19   S. L. Jaki, 'The Physics of Impetus and the Impetus of the Koran' in *Modern Age* 29 (1985), pp. 155, 157.

20   See P. Duhem, *Le système du monde. Histoire des doctrines*

cosmologiques de Platon à Copernic. 10 vols. (Paris: Hermann 1913–1959).

21   S. L. Jaki, 'On Whose Side is History?' in *National Review* (23 August 1985), pp. 43–44.

22   S. L. Jaki, 'The Role of Faith in Physics' in *Zygon* 2 (1967), p. 195.

23   Pope John Paul II, *Discourse to the Plenary Session of the Pontifical Academy of Sciences to commemorate the centenary of the birth of Albert Einstein*, 10 November 1979, in *DP* p. 154. Referring in a note to the life and works of Galileo, the Pastoral Constitution of Vatican II *Gaudium et spes* 36.1 stated: 'We cannot but deplore certain attitudes (not unknown among Christians) deriving from a shortsighted view of the rightful autonomy of science; they have occasioned conflict and controversy and have misled many into opposing faith and science.'

24   See Pope John Paul II, *Discourse to the Plenary Session of the Pontifical Academy of Sciences*, 31 October 1992, paragraphs 6 and 12. In particular, the Pope cited the adage of Cardinal Baronius: 'Spiritui Sancto mentem fuisse nos docere quomodo ad caelum eatur, non quomodo caelum gradiatur.' (The Holy Spirit wishes to teach us how to go to heaven, but not how the heavens move).

25   First Vatican Council, Dogmatic Constitution *Dei Filius* on the Catholic Faith, chapter IV in *DS* 3017.

26   Pius XI, Motu Proprio *In multis solaciis* in *AAS* 28 (1936), p. 421.

27   Pope John Paul II, *Discourse on the occasion of the Fiftieth Anniversary of the Pontifical Academy of Sciences*, 28 October 1986, §3 in *DP* p. 194.

28   S. L. Jaki, 'God and Man's Science: A View of Creation' in *The Christian Vision: Man in Society*. (Hillsdale, Michigan: Hillsdale College Press, 1984), p. 49.

29   S. W. Hawking, *A Brief History of Time* (London: Bantam Press, 1988), p. 55.

30   Ibid., p. 136.

31   Ibid., pp. 136–137.

32   Ibid., pp. 140–141.

33   See Pope John Paul II, Encyclical *Evangelium Vitae* 22.3.

34   See S. L. Jaki, 'The Intelligent Christian's Guide to Scientific Cosmology' in *Catholic Essays* (Front Royal: Christendom Press, 1990), p. 148.

35   S. L. Jaki, *God and the Cosmologists* (Washington, D.C./Edinburgh: Gateway Editions/Scottish Academic Press, 1989), p. 81.

36   Cf. St Thomas Aquinas, *Summa Theologiae*, I, q. 16, a. 1.

37   S. L. Jaki, 'Religion and Science: The Cosmic Connection' in J. A. Howard (ed.) *Belief, Faith and Reason* (Belfast: Christian Journals, 1981), p. 21.

38   S. L. Jaki, 'Physics and the Ultimate' in *Ultimate Reality and Meaning* 11/1 (March 1988), p. 70.

39 This composite definition has been put together from S. L. Jaki, *The Road of Science and the Ways to God*, pp. 38, 122; Idem, *Chesterton: A Seer of Science* (Urbana/Chicago: University of Illinois Press, 1986), p. 112. It appears in a large number of Jaki's books and articles in some shape or form. See St Thomas Aquinas, *Summa Theologiae*, I, q. 47 a.3.

40 Jaki, 'God and Man's Science', p. 44. In *Chesterton, A Seer of Science*, pp. 96, 153, Jaki notes that Popper uses the expression 'all science is cosmology'; see K. R. Popper, *Conjectures and Refutations* (New York: Harper and Row, 1968) p. 136. Jaki makes it clear that Popper did not invent this expression nor, in Jaki's opinion, does Popper hold the truths implied by this expression.

41 S. L. Jaki, *Means to Message. A Treatise on Truth*, (Grand Rapids, MI; Cambridge: Eerdmans, 1999), p. 146.

42 Jaki insists on this in *The Road of Science and the Ways to God*, p. 122; *The Savior of Science*, p. 107; and *God and the Cosmologists*, pp. 9–20.

43 S. L. Jaki, 'The University and the Universe' in J. R. Wilburn (ed.) *Freedom, Order and the University* (Malibu, California: Pepperdine University Press, 1982), pp. 52–53.

44 See Jaki, *The Road of Science and the Ways to God*, p. 269.

45 S. L. Jaki, 'From Subjective Scientists to Objective Science' in *Proceedings of the Third International Humanistic Symposium* (Athens: Hellenic Society for Humanistic Studies, 1977), p. 328.

46 S. L. Jaki, *Cosmos and Creator* (Edinburgh: Scottish Academic Press, 1980), p. 54.

47 See chapter 7, pp. 189–190 below, for a discussion of a proof of the existence of God based on contingency. See also, S. L. Jaki, 'The Absolute Beneath the Relative: Reflections on Einstein's Theories' in *Intercollegiate Review* 20 (Spring/Summer 1985), p. 36.

48 See Pope John Paul II, *Message to the Pontifical Academy of Sciences*, 22 October 1996, §4, where he stated: 'rather than *the* theory of evolution, we should speak of *several* theories of evolution.'

49 C. Darwin, *The Autobiography of Charles Darwin*, ed. N. Barlow (London: Collins, 1958), pp. 85–87.

50 As quoted in N. C. Gillespie, *Charles Darwin and the Problem of Creation* (Chicago: University of Chicago, 1979), p. 87.

51 C. Darwin, *The Origin of Species* (New York: Collier and Son, 1909), p. 487.

52 Ibid., p. 91.

53 Ibid, pp. 505–506.

54 Ibid., p. 506.

55 *Darwin's Early and Unpublished Notebooks* transcribed and annotated by P. H. Barrett, with a foreword by J. Piaget (New York: E. P. Dutton, 1974), C notebook, p. 451.

[56] S. L. Jaki, *Angels, Apes and Men* (La Salle, Illinois: Sherwood Sugden and Company, 1983), p. 55.

[57] See St George J. Mivart, *On the Genesis of Species* (New York: D. Appleton and Company, 1871), pp. 269–283, 294–305.

[58] R. Dawkins, *The Blind Watchmaker* (Harlow: Longmans, 1986), p. 317.

[59] S. L. Jaki, *The Purpose of It All* (Edinburgh: Scottish Academic Press, 1990), p. 32.

[60] Jaki, *Angels, Apes and Men*, p. 66.

[61] For an account of how the Christian linear vision of the cosmos freed man from cyclic, pantheistic and eternalist pagan notions, see S. L. Jaki, *Science and Creation* (Edinburgh: Scottish Academic Press, 1986²).

[62] Jaki, *Angels, Apes and Men*, p. 67.

[63] Ibid.

[64] Ibid., p. 70.

[65] S. L. Jaki, *Cosmos and Creator*, p. 114 and notes 5 and 6 on p. 160.

[66] S. L. Jaki, 'Order in Nature and Society: Open or Specific' in G. W. Carey (ed.) *Order, Freedom and the Polity (Critical Essays on the Open Society)* (Lanham, Maryland/London: University Press of America: 1986), pp. 100–101.

[67] Conventionalism was developed in the context of the philosophy of science, in the first instance by J. H. Poincaré (1854–1912), especially in his work *Science and Hypothesis* of 1905. See *La science et l'hypothèse* (Paris: Flammarion, 1927). Linked to instrumentalism and positivism, it urges us to regard deep-level theories about the nature of the world as chosen by us from among many possible alternative ways of explaining the observable phenomena.

[68] See Pope John Paul II, *Discourse to participants in an international symposium on «Christian faith and the theory of evolution»*, 26 April 1985 in *IG* 8/1 (1985), p. 1129.

[69] See Idem, *Discourse at General Audience*, 29 January 1986, in *IG* 9/1 (1986), p. 212.

[70] More will be said about this in chapter 7, pp. 191–194 below in regard to the teleological argument.

CHAPTER 7

PROOFS FOR THE EXISTENCE OF GOD

The God of Christians is not a God who is simply the author of mathematical truths, or of the order of the elements; that is the view of heathens and Epicureans. He is not merely a God who exercises His providence over the life and fortunes of men, to bestow on those who worship Him a long and happy life. That was the portion of the Jews. But the God of Abraham, the God of Isaac, the God of Jacob, the God of Christians, is a God of love and of comfort, a God who fills the soul and heart of those whom He possesses, a God who makes them conscious of their inward wretchedness, and His infinite mercy, who unites Himself to their inmost soul, who fills it with humility and joy, with confidence and love, who renders them incapable of any other end than Himself. All who seek God without Jesus Christ, and who rest in nature, either find no light to satisfy them, or come to form for themselves a means of knowing God and serving Him without a mediator .... Without Jesus Christ the world would not exist.

Blaise Pascal, *Pensée* 556

With the stars and the clouds I have clothed Myself here for
    your eyes
To behold That which Is. I have set forth the strength of the
    skies
As one draweth a picture before you to make your hearts wise;
That the infinite souls I have fashioned may know as I know,
Visibly revealed

In the flowers of the field,
Yea, declared by the stars in their courses, the tides in their
flow,
And the clash of the world's wide battle as it sways to and fro,
Flashing forth as a flame
The unnameable Name,
The ineffable Word,
I am the Lord.

Alfred Noyes, 'The Paradox'

In the eighteenth century, the famous mathematician Leonard Euler reputedly was capable of solving any problem which was set before him. At the court of Catherine the Great of Russia he was faced with the French philosopher Denis Diderot, who was an atheist. Catherine the Great did not want Diderot to turn the Russians into atheists, and so asked Euler to help her. The mathematician thought about this and came up with an algebriac proof of the existence of God. Euler and Diderot were convened to the palace of the Empress Catherine, where Euler stood before the assembly and simply stated:

$$\text{'Sir,} \quad \frac{a + b^n}{n} = x, \quad \text{hence God exists; reply!'}$$

Diderot had no special understanding of algebra and so was unable to discuss the point with Euler. Diderot left St Petersburg and returned to France apparently defeated.[1] Clearly this is not the type of proof we are proposing in support of God's existence, because it confuses mathematical proof with philosophical proof. It reduces philosophical demonstration to a mathematical formula.

In everyday life, three types of proof are commonly encountered. First, scientific proof, where the tools used are measurement, controlled testing environments, repeatability of observations, statistical methods, and various others. However, scientific endeavour makes a set of hidden assumptions which *may* be valid, but which we cannot prove. For example, we assume that an experiment which has the same result five thousand times will always have the same result. We assume that the laws of nature that we observe today will be the same tomorrow. We assume that these laws are uniform across the universe. None of these assumptions can be proven. The second kind of proof is mathematical proof, where every step in reasoning must be cautious and precise and justified according to rules that are specific and fixed. Many consider this to be probably the best and purest form of human reasoning. A drawback to this kind of proof is that it works 'on paper,' in a highly abstract world of manipulated symbols. Its principles spill over into science and even into everyday life, and they are useful; but their usefulness in 'real life' is limited because of the extreme complexity of the universe in which we live. The third major kind of proof is termed legal and historical proof. This is the kind of reasoning used, for example, by detectives, lawyers, judges, and historians. It is frequently confused with scientific proof, because the methods and tools of science are sometimes used as forensic aids. Legal proof is concerned with the gathering and analysis of physical evidence, but it is also concerned with eyewitness testimony and the reliability of those witnesses, with alibis, with circumstantial evidence, and the analysis of motives and human psychology. It is the most useful in everyday life, but by the same token, it is also fallible and inexact. These three types of proof should be distinguished from and related to philosophical proof, which involves a greater degree of abstraction.

Actually, centuries before Euler, the Fathers of the Church had come up with rational ways of demonstrating God's existence, based on the fact that in creating the cosmos and the human person God has left a seal, an imprint or a trade mark upon His creation. Saint Augustine, in a Platonic key, opened a new way in the West for a rational demonstration of the existence of God, based on the value of truth. According to this great Doctor of the Church, nothing within man is superior to reason. However, truth, which is eternal, necessary and immutable, forms the basis upon which reason makes its judgement; this truth is above reason and transcends it. Therefore God, who is in Himself absolute Truth, exists. 'God exists, and on a supreme and absolute level: this truth is not only the object of our unshakeable faith, but is also received by us through a process of rational knowing.'[2] In the East, St Basil explained that God 'has left a clear and evident mark of His immense wisdom' even in a little creature like the sea-urchin, which seamen use as an indication of fine or stormy weather.[3] St John Damascene, another Greek Father paved the way for the medieval proofs for the existence of God, this time in an Aristotelian framework. He furnished three demonstrations of God's existence, the first based on the mutability and contingence of the cosmos, the second upon the conservation and government of the universe, and the third from the ordered arrangement of beings, which cannot be the result of chance.[4]

While the demonstrations of the Church Fathers often sustained an apologetic rôle in order to convince pagans and non-believers, the thinkers of the Middle Ages developed proofs of God's existence not so much to confute atheistic ideas, but rather to illustrate the marvellous harmony between faith and reason.[5] The medieval Scholastics proposed two essential ways to prove the existence of God. These two ways are classified according to the distinction between an *a priori*, or deductive process, and an *a posteriori*, or inductive process. While all admit the validity and sufficiency of the latter method, opinion is divided in regard to the former. Some maintain that a valid *a priori* proof (usually called the ontological argument) is possible; others deny this completely; while some others maintain an attitude of compromise or neutrality. This difference of opinion applies only to the question of proving God's actual existence; since, once His self-existence has been affirmed, it is necessary to employ *a priori* or deductive inference in order to arrive at a knowledge of His nature and attributes, and as it is impossible to develop the arguments for His existence without some working concept of His nature, it is necessary to some extent to anticipate the deductive stage and combine the *a priori* with the *a posteriori* method. The *a posteriori* approach of demonstrating God's existence from his creation, can be subdivided according to a twofold point of departure: the physical world, and the human person.

The Ontological Argument

The deductive way starts from a reflection upon God as being an object of 'thought' in order to arrive at His reality as an 'existing' being. This approach, which had its origin in Platonic and Augustinian thought, was principally expounded by St Anselm of Canterbury (1033–1109), and later accepted by Alexander of Hales (died 1245) and St Bonaventure (1217–1274). As propounded by St Anselm, the ontological argument runs as follows. The idea of God as the Infinite means the greatest Being that can be thought of. However, unless actual existence outside the mind is included in this idea, God would not be the greatest conceivable Being since a Being that exists both in the mind as an object of thought, and outside the mind or objectively, would be greater than a Being that exists in the mind only. This presupposes that existence in reality is greater than mere existence in the understanding. Therefore, God must exist in reality, not just in the understanding.[6] Further, Anselm pointed out that it is impossible to imagine that God does not exist. If a mind could imagine a being greater than God, 'the creature would rise above the Creator; and this is most absurd.'[7] So, then, no one who truly understands what God is can conceive that God does not exist. For God is that than which nothing greater can be imagined.[8] Gaunilo, a contemporary monk of Anselm, wrote an attack on

Anselm's argument in which he offered several criticisms. The most well known of these is a parody on Anselm's argument in which he proves the existence of the greatest possible island. If instead of using the expression 'something than which nothing greater can be conceived' one used 'an island than which none greater can be conceived' then we would prove the existence of that island.[9] Gaunilo's point was that we could prove the existence of almost anything using Anselm's style of argument. St Anselm replied to Gaunilo's critique, and stated that it is not possible to infer the real existence of a lost island from the fact of its being conceived. For the real existence of a being which is said to be *greater than all other beings* cannot be demonstrated in the same way as the real existence of one that is said to be *a being than which a greater cannot be conceived*.[10] Gaunilo overlooked the fact that the argument was not intended to apply to finite ideals but only to the strictly infinite; and if it is admitted that we possess a true idea of the infinite, and that this idea is not self-contradictory, it does not seem possible to find any flaw in the argument.

Later, Descartes proposed the ontological argument in a slightly different form as follows. Whatever is contained in a clear and distinct idea of a thing must be predicated of that thing; but a clear and distinct idea of an absolutely perfect Being contains the notion of actual existence; therefore since we have the idea of an absolutely perfect Being, such a Being must really exist. In a third form of the ontological demonstration of the existence of God, Leibniz affirmed: God is at least possible since the concept of Him as the Infinite implies no contradiction; but if He is possible He must exist because the concept of Him involves existence. Actual existence is certainly included in any true concept of the Infinite, and the person who admits that he has a concept of an Infinite Being cannot deny that he conceives it as actually existing. However, the difficulty lies in this preliminary proposition of conceiving an actually existing Infinite Being, which requires to be justified by recurring to the *a posteriori* argument, namely to an inference by way of causality from contingency to necessarily existing Being and thence by way of deduction to infinity. Hence the great majority of philosophers have rejected the ontological argument as propounded by St Anselm, Descartes and Leibniz.

In particular, when St Thomas Aquinas indicated that the existence of God is not self-evident, he illustrated the weakness of the ontological argument. He argued that even if everyone understands the word 'God' to signify something than which nothing greater can be thought, nevertheless, it does not therefore follow that he understands that what the word signifies exists actually, but only that it exists mentally. Nor can it be argued that it actually exists, unless it be admitted that there actually exists something than which nothing greater can be thought; and precisely this is not admitted by those who hold that God does not exist.[11] St Thomas preferred the *a posteriori* approach to the demonstration of God's existence, preceding from the effects to the Cause, because the effects are better known to us than the Cause.[12] Although God transcends sense and the objects of sense, nevertheless sensible effects are the basis of rational demonstration of the existence of God.[13]

The Five Ways

St Thomas advanced the five following arguments to prove the existence of God. The first is the argument from motion, by which he meant passing from potency to act. When this takes place in the universe it implies a first unmoved Mover (*primum movens immobile*), who is God; otherwise it would be necessary to postulate an infinite series of movers, which is inconceivable.[14] The second way proposed by the Angelic Doctor involves the idea of efficient causality. Efficient causes, as they are seen to operate in the universe, imply the existence of a First Cause that is uncaused, a Cause that possesses in itself the sufficient reason for its existence; and this is God.[15] The third way is based on contingency, whereby the fact that contingent beings exist (namely beings whose non-existence is recognised as possible) implies the existence of a necessary being, who is God.[16] The fourth way of St Thomas involves the consideration that the gradated perfections of being actually existing in the universe can be understood only by comparison with an absolute standard that is also actual, namely the infinitely perfect Being who is God.[17] In the fifth way, St Thomas suggested that the marvellous order in the cosmos is evidence of intelligent design within the universe. This design implies the existence of a Designer beyond the cosmos, who is God Himself.[18]

Blessed John Duns Scotus adopted both of the two processes in his proofs of God's existence. The first process is an entirely *a posteriori* approach, which resembled the first three ways of St Thomas. The objects of our experience are changing realities, or are beings in the course of 'becoming.' Now that which changes possesses in itself neither the sufficient reason for its existence nor for its activity. Hence we are led to admit the existence of a Being, namely God, that is outside the chain of succession and change, and that justifies the existence and action of beings in various stages of becoming. Scotus' second process consists in a development of the argument of St Anselm. To supply validity to this *a priori* argument, Scotus inserts *a posteriori* elements, namely the analysis of the possibility (contingency) that is affirmed by our experience. For Scotus, to say that God is 'a being than which a greater cannot be conceived' is to say that God is infinite. Now, according to Scotus, the weakness of St Anselm's argument does not rest with the transition from possibility to real existence, but in this: that St Anselm did not prove that the concept of the infinite is possible. Scotus proves this possibility negatively by showing that the concept of an infinite being involves no contradiction. If it did involve a contradiction, our mind, which has for its object 'being as being', would notice it. Positively, Scotus begins with the data of experience, which tells us that many things are possible. However, all possible series of beings are related to the Uncaused Being, which, since it is uncaused, is infinite Perfection. Hence an infinite being not only is possible, but actually exists. 'Thus, absolutely speaking, the primary efficient cause can exist in its own right; hence it exists by itself.'[19]

The Cosmological Argument

The first two of St Thomas' ways can be developed into the Cosmological Argument for God's existence, also known as the argument from general causality. It is so called because it assumes as a starting point the objective validity of the principle of causality, an assumption upon which the procedure of the physical sciences in particular, and of human knowledge in general, is based.[20] To question its objective certainty, as did Kant, and represent it as a mere mental *a priori*, or possessing only subjective validity, would open the door to subjectivism and universal scepticism. It is impossible to prove the principle of causality, just as it is impossible to prove the principle of non-contradiction; but it is not difficult to see that if the former is denied the latter may also be denied and the whole edifice of human reasoning crumbles. In the universe, certain things are observed to be effects, as they depend for their existence on other things, and these again on others; but, however far back this series of effects and dependent causes be extended, we must, if human reason is to be taken seriously, come ultimately to a cause that is not itself an effect, in other words to an uncaused cause or self-existent being which is the ground and cause of all being. Thus there cannot be an infinite number of regressions of causes to things that exist, but a final uncaused Cause of all things. This uncaused Cause is asserted to be God. The Cosmological Argument takes several forms but is basically represented as follows. Things exist, but it is possible for those things not to exist. Whatever has the possibility of non-existence, yet exists, has been caused to exist. Something cannot bring itself into existence, since it must exist to bring itself into existence, which is illogical. There cannot be an infinite number of causes to bring something into existence, because an infinite regression of causes ultimately has no initial cause which means there is no cause of existence. Since the universe exists, it must have a cause. Therefore, there must be an uncaused Cause of all things, who is God.

Pantheism is the view that God is identical with the world or is completely immanent within it.[21] The pantheist critique of the cosmological argument is fallacious, namely that the world, whether of matter or of mind or of both, contains within itself the sufficient reason of its own existence. A self-existing world would exist of absolute necessity and would be infinite in every kind of perfection; but we are certain from experience that the universe as we know it, in its totality as well as in its parts, actualises only finite degrees of perfection. It is simply a contradiction in terms, however much one may try to conceal the contradiction by an ambiguous use of language, to predicate infinity of matter or of the human mind, and the pantheist holds one or the other or both to be infinite. In other words for the pantheist the distinction between the finite and the infinite must be abolished and the principle of non-contradiction denied. While theism safeguards certain primary truths like the reality of human personality, freedom, and moral responsibility, pantheism tends to sacrifice all these, to deny the existence of evil, whether physical or moral, to destroy the rational basis of religion, and, under the pretence of making man his own God, to rob him of nearly all his plain, common sense convictions and of all his highest incentives to good conduct. The philosophy which leads to such results must be radically flawed.

The Argument from Contingency

The third way of St Thomas has been developed into the *argument from contingency*. For Avery Dulles, contingency means that the whole of reality is made up of dependent beings, things that do not exist by their own intrinsic powers. 'If A depends on B, and B is also dependent, there must be a C to account for the existence of B.' Dulles points out that the chain of dependency cannot extend endlessly, or else 'there would be no sufficient reason why anything exists.'[22] He illustrates the impossibility of an infinite regress with an amusing example:

> A student can get a good mark by copying a paper from another student who got the right answers. That student, in turn, could have copied from a third. But it is absurd to argue that all the students were copying from other students, even in an infinite series. There must be at least one student who got the right answers by personal knowledge. A chain of dependent causes, even if infinitely long, does not explain the effect.[23]

Thus we are led to the one Necessary Being, who must be the absolute fullness of reality and power, and be endowed with every positive perfection, that does not of itself bespeak limitation. The Necessary Being is life, intelligence, and freedom, and is therefore personal.[24]

Stanley Jaki defines the meaning of the word 'contingent' as 'dependent on a factor outside the set of parameters that determine the scientific handling of the problem or configuration. In the case of the universe as a whole, the factor in question can only be a metaphysical factor. Such a meaning of "contingent" is essentially different from its being taken equivalent to "accidental".'[25] Jaki states that a 'contingent universe and a created universe are two sides of the same philosophical coin.'[26] For Jaki, the concept of contingency is related to the notion of boundary conditions which make the whole of the universe coherent. They are given, are not derivable from laws, and all exist in relation to the overall boundary conditions which make nature a totality of beings. The 'explanation of a given set of boundary conditions can only be done in terms of a more general set', but in such a procedure there can be no regress to infinity. The overall boundary condition of the universe cannot therefore be self-explaining: it depends upon an explanation outside the universe which is therefore contingent. This link between contingency and createdness implies that, for Jaki, Aquinas' five ways are essentially one way, 'the way from contingency.'[27]

The description of the physical universe is highly mathematical. Every mathematical structure is constructed from a series of axioms. The theorems within that structure are then derived from those axioms. Within that given mathematical structure it can be shown how the theorems are derived logically from the axioms. However, the original choice of axioms cannot be justified from within the system. This kind of justification has to be provided from outside the system. This relates to what Kurt Gödel demonstrated in 1931, namely that it is impossible to prove, using mathematical methods, that the axioms are consistent. By consistent is meant that the conclusions drawn from such axioms are always contradiction free. Even if it were possible to prove the consistency of a given system, that system would never be complete within itself. In other words, from within a given system it is impossible to prove the truth of all the true statements contained within it.[28] Thus within mathematical descriptions of reality there lies an inherent incompleteness. So within the universe each system depends on a broader system to demonstrate its validity. For the universe as a whole, the proof of its consistency must lie outside it, in its Creator. The cosmos, imbued with intelligibility, is then penultimate, the ultimate in intelligibility being God the Creator, Who alone is above all things.[29]

The Teleological Argument

St Thomas Aquinas' fifth way has been developed by many thinkers under the name of the Teleological Argument, also known as the argument from design. In its basic form, it states that a Designer must exist since the universe and living things display marks of design in their order, consistency, unity, and pattern. One form of this argument was the image of the Watchmaker offered by William Paley (1743–1805). The argument runs as follows:

> In crossing a heath, suppose I pitched my foot against a stone, and were asked how the stone came to be there; I might possibly answer, that, for anything I knew to the contrary, it had lain there forever: nor would it perhaps be very easy to show the absurdity of this answer. But suppose I had found a watch upon the ground, and it should be inquired how the watch happened to be in that place; I should hardly think of the answer which I had before given, that, for anything I knew, the watch might have always been there. Yet why should not this answer serve for the watch as well as the stone?[30]

Paley then states that a simple examination of the watch leads the mind inexorably forward to affirm that the watch must have had a maker; that there must have existed, at some time, and at some place or other, an artificer or artificers, who formed it for the purpose which we find it actually to answer; who understood its construction, and designed its use.[31] The logical conclusion is that it was designed and not the product of random formation. Paley extends his argument to all the works of nature, every organised natural body whether plant or animal, simple or complex, which also must have a Maker. Paley argues not only as a theologian but also as a scientist, where he compares the human eye and the telescope. Both manifest similar principles of design and construction; both are modelled according to the same laws of optics; the eye differs only in being more versatile and more subtle in its operations. As the telescope is inconceivable apart from its designers, so too is the eye. The eye is an amazing organ, for in order for it to work there must be many different convergent parts that individually have no function but have value only in a designed whole. Only in the organic whole does each part carry out its function for the whole, indicating design and purpose.

Paley's work is open to the criticism that he espoused a rather mechanical view of the cosmos, in vogue during his time. Paley also mistakenly proposed that God has sacrificed omnipotence, allowing the creative process to proceed according to clearly discernible laws of nature; in and through the very laws of nature, God has accomplished the creation of life. 'It is this', concludes Paley, 'which constitutes the order and beauty of the universe. God, therefore, has been pleased to prescribe limits to his own power, and to work his ends within those limits. The general laws of matter have perhaps the nature of these limits.'[32] At the same time, Paley's natural theology was a stimulus for science, for his natural theology was imbued with a really concrete interaction between the phenomena of nature and its Creator: 'The world thenceforth becomes a temple, and life itself one continued act of adoration.'[33]

The evolutionary perspective, far from diminishing the value of design and purpose in the cosmos as pointers to its Creator, only serves to strengthen the argument. The evidence for design which the universe manifests is even more impressive when viewed from the evolutionary standpoint. The eye, for example, as an organ of sight is a clear embodiment of intelligent purpose, even more so when viewed as the product of God's providence in an evolutionary process rather than the immediate handiwork of the Creator. The eye is only one of the countless examples of adaptation to particular ends discernible in every part of the universe, inorganic as well as organic; for the atom as well as the cell contributes to the evidence in favour of design. Another example lies in the incredible complexity of the human genetic code. The word 'code' itself implies an Intelligence who designed it; human intelligence has then deciphered the human genome. The only alternative to an Intelligence is 'chance'; however the chances of the genome coming together by accident are nil, even less than the probability of throwing all the parts of a computer together and hoping that, one day, all these parts will come together by themselves in the right order to make the computer. Nor is the argument weakened by our inability in many cases to explain the particular purpose of certain structures or organisms. Furthermore, in the search for particular instances of design, evidence supplied by the harmonious unity of nature as a whole must not be overlooked. The universe as we know it is a cosmos.[34] This is a vastly complex system of correlated and interdependent parts, each subject to particular laws, and all together subject to a common law or a combination of laws, as the result of which the pursuit of particular ends is made to contribute in a marvellous way to the attainment of a common purpose. It is simply unimaginable that this cosmic unity should be the product of chance or accident. If it be objected that there is another side to the picture, that the universe abounds in imperfections, such as disfunctionality, failures, seemingly purposeless waste, at least one reply is possible. The existing world is not the best of all possible ones, and it is only on the supposition of its being so that the imperfections referred to would be excluded. Admitting the existence of physical evil, but without exaggerating its reality, there still remains a large balance on the side of order and harmony, and to account for this there is required not only an intelligent mind but one that is good and benevolent. The full sweep of cosmic design cannot be comprehended, for it is not a static universe in question, but a universe that is progressively developing and moving towards the fulfilment of an ultimate purpose under the guidance of a master Mind. The imperfect as well as the perfect, apparent evil and discord as well as obvious good order, may contribute towards that purpose in ways which can only be dimly discerned.

The humble and balanced investigator of nature is aware of his or her own limitations in the presence of the Designer of the universe, not claiming that every detail of that Designer's purpose should at present be plain, but rather is happy to await the final solution of enigmas which the hereafter promises to furnish.

The Aesthetic Argument

Related to the argument from design and to Aquinas' fourth way, is the argument from beauty in the cosmos, also termed the *Aesthetic Argument* for the existence of God. St Augustine was perhaps one of the first exponents of this approach:

> Question the beauty of the earth, question the beauty of the sea, question the beauty of the air distending and diffusing itself, question the beauty of the sky .... question all these realities. All respond: 'See, we are beautiful.' Their beauty is a profession. These beauties are subject to change. Who made them if not the Beautiful One who is not subject to change?[35]

St Thomas Aquinas defined beauty in the clearest terms: 'Beauty includes three conditions, integrity or perfection; due proportion or harmony; and lastly, brightness, or clarity.'[36] Man is capable of seeing that creation is good, notwithstanding original sin. He can also perceive that there is a unity within creation. Noting the different forms of truth, goodness, and unity of the cosmos, man appreciates beauty within the universe in the various wonders of nature. Man does not create all this beauty but rather he receives and unveils it and thus co-operates in its revelation. However, more than this, man can arrive, via a reflection upon creation, at the fact that beauty is not able to explain its own existence, it is not here by chance, it is not chaotic, but rather it is created. Furthermore, the human person enjoys the capacity to appreciate beauty which also cannot be a chance link with the cosmos, but this connatural connection between the harmony of the universe and man the perceiver must be the result of a supreme design. Kant made beauty a subjective quality (purely in the eye of the beholder) once he made it non-conceptual: 'The beautiful is that which pleases universally without a concept.'[37] Clearly this is false, there must be objective criteria for beauty. Otherwise how could one explain that the beauty of St Peter's Square in Rome attracts many non-Christians, that beauty spots in the countryside get very crowded at the weekend, that famous fashion models, actresses and actors can make a good living. We realise that there is always something more beautiful than what we have experienced or uncovered, and so we are led by degrees to Uncreated Beauty. It is as if God has left a kind of metaphysical trademark upon creation which can thus be traced back to its Creator. Hence, man fully discovers and admires beauty only when he refers it back to its source, the transcendent beauty of God.

St John of the Cross offered a stark reminder of the inadequacy of the beauty of creatures as a road to God, a sharp *via negativa* in proceeding to God:

> All the being of creation, then, compared with the infinite Being of God, is nothing. And therefore the soul that sets its affection upon the being of creation is likewise nothing in the eyes of God, and less than nothing; for, as we have said, love makes equality and similitude, and even sets the lover below the object of his love .... And, coming down in detail to some examples, all the beauty of the creatures, compared with the infinite beauty of God, is the height of deformity even as Solomon says in the Proverbs: 'Favour is deceitful and beauty is vain.' And thus the soul that is affectioned to the beauty of any creature is the height of deformity in the eyes of God. And therefore this soul that is deformed will be unable to become transformed in beauty, which is God, since deformity cannot attain to beauty; and all the grace and beauty of the creatures,

compared with the grace of God, is the height of misery and of uncomeliness.[38]

At the same time this great saint and mystic nuances his position elsewhere by referring to the grove from the Song of Songs:

> The grove, because it contains many plants and animals, signifies God as the Creator and Giver of life to all creatures, which have their being and origin from Him, reveal Him and make Him known as the Creator. The beauty of the grove, which the soul prays for, is not only the grace, wisdom, and loveliness which flow from God over all created things, whether in heaven or on earth, but also the beauty of the mutual harmony and wise arrangement of the inferior creation, and the higher also, and of the mutual relations of both. The knowledge of this gives the soul great joy and delight.[39]

Anthropological Arguments

Many of the arguments above dealt with demonstrations of God's existence based upon a reflection upon the physical world. It is also possible to adopt arguments drawn from the nature and dignity of the human person, which can be termed anthropological arguments for God's existence. Many of these arguments run in the following manner. The human being is open to truth and beauty, possesses a sense of moral goodness, experiences freedom and the voice of his or her conscience. Man and woman bear longings for the infinite and for happiness, and ask questions about God's existence. In all this man and woman discern signs of their spiritual soul. The soul, the 'seed of eternity we bear in ourselves, irreducible to the merely material'[40] can have its origin only in God.[41] Some of these arguments can now be examined in more detail.

The Argument from Conscience

The moral argument for the existence of God was developed by the eighteenth-century German philosopher Immanuel Kant, who maintained that the highest good includes moral virtue, with happiness as its appropriate reward. He held that it is the duty of humanity to seek this highest good and that it must therefore be possible to realise it. Furthermore, Kant claimed that this highest good cannot be realised unless there is 'a supreme cause of nature,' one that has the power to bring about harmony between happiness and virtue. Such a cause could only be God. Critics of the moral argument counter that it is by no means clear that the highest good is what Kant supposed. To Newman and others, the argument from conscience, or the sense of moral responsibility, has seemed the most deeply persuasive of all the arguments for God's existence. Newman stated that while some people think that there is a moral obligation because God exists, rather the contrary is true, namely that God exists because we can perceive a moral law.[42] The existence within of a sense which is termed conscience indicates the concept of a Father or Judge, of One who sees my heart. For Newman, the conscience enables man to make the right choices. In a sense it transcends the human person; man did not make it, nor can he destroy it. Because conscience is an authoritative voice, there necessarily arises in our mind the idea of a Being who completely transcends us as the source of moral obligation. The voice of conscience impels us to avoid evil and do good. Now the absolute quality of doing good is not founded only within man, but rather outside him upon the absolute Good, Who is the End of man.[43] It is not that conscience, as such, contains a direct revelation or intuition of God as the author of the moral law, but that, taking man's sense of moral responsibility as a phenomenon to be explained, no ultimate explanation can be given except by supposing the existence of a Superior and Lawgiver whom man is bound to obey. And just as the argument from design evokes prominently the attribute of intelligence, so the argument from conscience brings out the attribute of holiness in the First Cause and self-existent Personal Being with whom we must ultimately identify the Designer and the Lawgiver. 'Thus conscience is a connecting principle between the creature and his Creator.'[44]

The Argument from Universal Consent

An example of this argument was provided by William Rees-Mogg:

> I would endeavour to show that religious experience is very widely distributed, virtually universal in terms of history, region, faith and culture. I would argue that a majority of people report some type of religious experience, but that this ranges up to a group of higher mystics who have known something close to the direct perception of God. They now constitute for us what St Paul called 'a cloud of witnesses'.
>
> I would go on to argue that these witnesses could not be dismissed as weak-minded or mentally disturbed; on the contrary, they include many of the wisest, most self-sacrificing and most admired of human beings. In a world which often seems to be crazy, they seem exceptionally sane. Such figures have been recorded in all periods, and have not ceased to exist. To mention only a few, we have lived in the time of Yehudi Menuhin, Mother Teresa and Basil Hume, people almost universally admired.[45]

The confirmatory argument based on the consent of mankind may be stated briefly as follows: mankind as a whole has at all times and everywhere believed and continues to believe in the existence of some superior being on whom the material world and man himself are dependent, and this fact cannot be accounted for except by admitting that this belief is true or at least contains a germ of truth. It is admitted of course that polytheism, dualism, pantheism, and other forms of error and superstition have mingled with and disfigured this universal belief of mankind, but this does not destroy the force of the argument under consideration. For at least the seminal truth which consists in the recognition of some kind of deity is common to every form of religion and can therefore claim in its support the universal consent of mankind. This consent seems best explained as a result of people's perception of the evidence for the existence of deity. Discussion of the various theories that have been proposed to account in some other way for the origin and universality of religion is beyond the scope of this work. This consent of mankind speaks ultimately in favour of theism. It is clear from history that religion is liable to degenerate, and has in many instances degenerated instead of progressing; nevertheless, there is a good deal of positive evidence supporting the idea that monotheism was the primitive historical religion. If this be the true reading of history, it is correct to interpret the universality of religion as witnessing implicitly to an original truth which could never be entirely extinguished. Even if the history of religion is to be read as a record of progressive development one ought in all fairness, to seek its true meaning and significance not at the lowest but at the highest point of development; and it cannot be denied that theism in the strict sense is the ultimate form which religion naturally tends to assume.

The Argument from Human Restlessness

St Augustine provided the foundation for this approach when he wrote: 'Despite everything, man, though but a small a part of Your creation, wants to praise You. You Yourself encourage him to delight in Your praise, for You have made us for Yourself, and our heart is restless until it rests in You.'[46] According to Avery Dulles, within the human person is a great capacity to love, to worship, and to serve. The nature of the human spirit is such that it starts from the double experience of knowing and willing. On the one hand, we experience a deep desire for happiness and fulfilment; on the other hand we know that no finite reality can satisfy this desire. From this contrast, the aspiration towards the Infinite is born. The basis for this aspiration lies in the fact that the human intelligence and the will cannot be fulfilled in finite being, so that they are launched towards the Infinite. Actually, human intelligence is never satisfied with what it knows but always wants to go further, and the human will is never really gratified by a partial good, but tends towards the Infinite Good. This dynamism of the human intellect and will is an indication of the existence of God in Whom alone are found the total Truth and the total Good. Man and woman are constantly on the lookout for some reality, some Person, to whom they can dedicate their full energies and who commands their full devotion. Unless we find God, we are likely to idolise creatures and eventually be disillusioned. Either we must live with a void of meaning, which leaves us spiritually famished, or we must turn to God as the supreme object of our love.[47]

Pascal's Wager

In the seventeenth century, Blaise Pascal affirmed that it was essentially by faith that we know of God's existence.[48] Thus he developed an argument not so much for the *existence* of God but for the *value* of believing in God. He claimed that even if there was no satisfactory evidence for believing God existed, it is still better for us to believe in God rather than not. Pascal's argument was proposed in the form of a bet or wager. People have more to lose by not believing in God than by believing in Him. If we 'wager' on God existing (theism), yet when we die there is no God, we have lost nothing, except maybe a few hours a week at church and other religious activities. If we 'bet' on God not existing (atheism), yet when we die there is a God, we will have lost everything.[49] Thus according to Pascal it is better to be a theist rather than an atheist. Apart from the philosophical difficulties of assigning probabilities to such a weighty matter as God's existence, the argument smacks of a pragmatist or utilitarian approach. It would be more praiseworthy to weigh up the evidence carefully and make an honest and open-hearted search for God.

It would be quite mistaken therefore to maintain that faith ultimately rests on an accumulation of probabilities.[50] Newman adopted the expression 'an *accumulation* of various probabilities'[51] and pointed out that from probabilities we may construct legitimate proof. Here, Newman refers solely to the proof of faith afforded by the motives of credibility, and he rightly concluded that, since these are not demonstrative, this line of proof may be termed 'an accumulation of probabilities'. Therefore, Newman did not base the final assent of faith on this accumulation, for here he was not examining the act of faith, but only the grounds for faith. His analysis of the accumulation of probabilities does not undermine authority.

Motives for Credibility

Another type of proof for the existence of God lies in demonstrating the cogency of Christianity in an historical perspective. One approach seeks to indicate that the Church has flourished in the face of adversity, another that the Scriptures are credible historical documents, another again indicates the historical existence of Christ in non-Christian sources, and a fourth demonstrates the positive influence of Christianity upon human society.

The Survival of the Church

Despite the ebb and flow of her fortunes seen from a human perspective, the Catholic Church has not only survived but flourished. This argument is to be found, for example, in the well-known passage of the non-Catholic historian Macauley:

> There is not, and there never was on this earth, a work of human policy so well deserving of examination as the Roman Catholic Church. The history of that Church joins together the two great ages of human civilisation. No other institution is left standing which carries the mind back to the times when the smoke of sacrifice rose from the Pantheon, and when camelopards and tigers bounded in the Flavian amphitheatre. The proudest royal houses are but of yesterday, when compared with the line of the Supreme Pontiffs. That line we trace back in an unbroken series, from the Pope who crowned Napoleon in the nineteenth century to the Pope who crowned Pepin in the eighth; and far beyond the time of Pepin the august dynasty extends, till it is lost in the twilight of fable. The republic of Venice came next in antiquity. But the republic of Venice was modern when compared with the Papacy; and the republic of Venice is gone, and the Papacy remains. The Papacy remains, not in decay, not a mere antique, but full of life and youthful vigour. The Catholic Church is still sending forth to the farthest ends of the world missionaries as zealous as those who landed in Kent with Augustine, and still confronting hostile kings with the same spirit with which she confronted Attila .... Nor do we see any sign which indicates that the term of her long dominion is approaching. She saw the commencement of all the governments and of all the ecclesiastical establishments that now exist in the world; and we feel no assurance that she is not destined to see the end of them all. She was great and respected before the Saxon had set foot on Britain, before the Frank had passed the Rhine, when Grecian eloquence still flourished at Antioch, when idols were still worshipped in the temple of Mecca. And she

may still exist in undiminished vigour when some traveller from New Zealand shall, in the midst of a vast solitude, take his stand on a broken arch of London Bridge to sketch the ruins of St Paul's.[52]

Karl Adam illustrated that the growth of the Catholic Church from a tiny seed sown by Christ her Founder depended specifically on the divine power of the Holy Spirit guiding her through the ups and downs of history:

The Gospel of Christ would have been no living gospel, and the seed which He scattered no living seed, if it had remained ever the tiny seed of AD 33, and had not struck root, and had not assimilated foreign matter, and had not by the help of this foreign matter grown up into a tree, so that the birds of the air dwell in its branches. So we are far from begrudging the religious historian the pleasure of reading off the inner growth of Catholicism by means of the annual rings of its trunk, and of specifying all those elements which its living force has appropriated from foreign sources. But we refuse to see in these elements thus enumerated the essence of Catholicism, or even to grant that they are 'structural elements of Catholicism' in the sense that Catholicism did not achieve historical importance save through them. For the Catholic is intimately conscious that Catholicism is ever the same, yesterday and today, that its essential nature was already present and manifest when it began its journey through the world, that Christ Himself breathed into it the breath of life, and that He Himself at the same time gave the young organism those germinal aptitudes which have unfolded themselves in the course of the centuries in regular adaptation to the needs and requirements of its environment. Catholicism recognises in itself no element that is inwardly foreign to it, that is not itself, that does not derive from its original nature.[53]

Newman also pointed out how the growth of Christianity, which Christ predicted, into a great power which filled the earth was not achieved by force or worldly means, but by the 'novel expedient of sanctity and suffering'.[54] Newman concluded that this growth must derive from a Divine Power and cannot be reduced simply to 'the ordinary operation of moral, social, or political causes.'[55]

Credibility of the Scriptures

The uniqueness of the Bible in many ways points to the fact that it is not simply a work of human literature but that its composition was guided by a divine Hand. It bears witness to great continuity, since despite the fact that many and various authors, languages, and cultures are to be found within it, there is only one clear and basic message which it proposes, namely God revealing Himself in creation, in history and above all in His only Son. The Scriptures have a massive circulation. The Bible was the first major book ever printed, in 1450, in the form of the Latin vulgate on the Gutenberg press. Since then, it has been read by more people than any other book ever written. It is noteworthy that now the Bible has been translated into almost four thousand languages. It has survived many persecutions, not least that of Diocletian who decreed in the year 303 that every Bible be destroyed.

Since the original Biblical writings are no longer existent, the question of the accuracy of the copies arises. The certainty that we actually have reliable copies of the originals comes from four main areas. First, there are a massive number of *copies* of the original manuscripts, five thousand complete copies of the New Testament, far greater than those of other ancient works, religious and secular. These copies, upon comparison with one another, show by their uniformity how carefully and accurately they must have been transcribed from the originals. Second, the time period between the writing of the original and their transcription is extremely small. With the works of Plato, the time elapsed between the originals and the copies is estimated at 1000 years; with books of the New Testament, the corresponding period would be around 100 years at the most. Does this mean that the works of Plato are of questionable accuracy? Of course not. However, if one chooses to discount the Bible because of the time lag between the writing of its original manuscripts and its copies, one should, on the same basis, discount the accuracy and truthfulness of every other literary work of the ancient world. The shorter this period is, the smaller the possibility of any tampering. The New Testament books were massively and rapidly copied and distributed throughout the quickly expanding Christendom. Third, the New Testament documents were translated into several other languages at an early date; translation was rare in the ancient world, so this is an added proof of authenticity for the New Testament. The Greek New Testament was translated into Syrian, Egyptian, Coptic, Latin and other languages during the first century. Again, translation into a new language insures the originals from being tampered with. Fourth, apart from these manuscripts, much of the New Testament is reflected in the early Patristic writings of the first and second centuries. Therefore, to tamper with the New Testament, one would have to have made an addition or deletion to the original before any copies were produced, originals which the Church Fathers would have guarded with their lives. Or, it would have been necessary to obtain all the copies, and correct them, including all those copies translated into new languages, as well as any work quoting a New Testament book. The conclusion is that the Bible has far stronger manuscript support than any other work of ancient literature, including the works of Plato, Aristotle, Caesar and Tacitus.

The reliability of Scripture is also confirmed through the eyewitness credentials of the authors. Moses, for example, participated in and was an eyewitness to some remarkable events: Israel's captivity in Egypt, the Exodus, the Forty Years in the Desert, and Israel's final encampment before entering the Promised Land, all of which are accurately chronicled in the Old Testament. Even sceptical authorities grudgingly agree that the Old Testament is a remarkably accurate historical document. The New Testament possesses the same kind of eyewitness authenticity, but in an even stronger form. Matthew and John were with Jesus during His ministry, being two of the original twelve Apostles called by Jesus. Mark, according to early Church Fathers wrote his gospel, as delivered to him by another eyewitness, the Apostle Peter. Luke, though not an eyewitness of Christ, gathered the testimonies of numerous eyewitnesses and all available records, then sifted through the data, 'carefully investigating everything' regarding the life of Jesus (Lk 1:1–3). The New Testament Letters too, were written by eyewitnesses like Paul, Peter, John, James. This testimony provided bedrock confidence to the hearers and writers that their teaching was reliable. Peter, for example, reminded his readers that the disciples 'did not follow cleverly invented stories' but were 'eyewitnesses of His majesty' (2 Pt 1:16). Many New Testament authors later died for refusing to deny their testimonies, illustrating their certainty that what they wrote was the Truth.

Unlike any other book in the world, the Bible is the only one to offer specific predictions hundreds of years in advance of their literal fulfilment. The Bible contains nearly two thousand individual prophecies. The Bible is about thirty percent prophecy, and for this reason alone it is absolutely unique. There are no fulfilled prophecies in the Koran, in the Hindu Vedas or the Bhagavad-Gita, in the sayings of Buddha or Confucius, in the Book of Mormon, or anywhere else but in the Bible. Nor are there any prophecies concerning the coming of Buddha, Krishna, Mohammed, Zoroaster, Confucius, or any other founder or leader of a world religion. The Messiah is absolutely unique in this respect. His coming was foretold in many specific prophecies which were fulfilled in the minutest detail in the Life, Death, and Resurrection of Jesus Christ.[56] The best explanation for the fulfilment of such predictions, made hundreds of years earlier, is the existence of a transcendent God who knows all things, including 'the beginning from the end' (Is 46:10). Sceptics sometimes claim equal authority for predictions from psychics. However, there is a quantum leap between the fallible human soothsayers and the unerring prophets of the Bible.

Non-Christian Corroboration

Despite the fact that the Incarnation of the Son of God took place in the greatest humility, nevertheless secular historians, caught up by more stirring events and by famous personages, made passing but significant references to Him.[57] Such references to Christ are found for example in *The Antiquities of the Jews*, a work compiled in Rome between the years 93 and 94 by the historian Flavius Josephus (AD 37–110), a Jewish historian, who was well disposed to the Romans, and served Vespasian and his son Titus, who both became emperors. He wrote various historical works in Greek, including *The Antiquities of the Jews*, which describes Jewish history from Abraham until the time of Flavius himself. A significant passage is to be found in book eighteen, which is cited also by St Eusebius of Caesarea:

> Now there was about this time (AD 30) Jesus, a wise man, if it be lawful to call him a man; for he was a doer of wonderful works, a teacher of such men as receive the truth with pleasure. He drew over to him both many of the Jews and many of the Gentiles. He was [the] Christ. And when Pilate, at the suggestion of the principal men amongst us, had condemned him to the cross, those that loved him at the first did not forsake him; for he appeared to them alive again the third day; as the divine prophets had foretold these and ten thousand other wonderful things concerning him. And the tribe of Christians, so named from him, are not extinct at this day.[58]

In his *Annals,* written between the years AD 115 and 120, Tacitus reports the burning of Rome in the year 64, falsely attributed by Nero to the Christians, and makes explicit reference to Christ:

> Yet no human effort, no princely largesse nor offerings to the gods could make that infamous rumour disappear that Nero had somehow ordered the fire. Therefore, in order to abolish that rumour, Nero falsely accused and executed with the most exquisite punishments those people called Christians, who were infamous for their abominations. The originator of the name, Christ, was executed as a criminal by the procurator Pontius Pilate during the reign of Tiberius.[59]

Suetonius also, in his biography of the Emperor Claudius, written around AD 121, informs us that the Jews were expelled from Rome because 'under the instigation of a certain Chrestus they stirred up frequent riots.'[60] This passage is generally interpreted as referring to Jesus Christ, who had become a source of contention within Jewish circles in Rome. To understand why the form *Chrestus* was used, it is necessary to know that in the first century, the Greek words *christòs* (meaning anointed) and *chrestòs* (meaning the best) were pronounced in the same way. Thus Suetonius probably made a mistake and thought that the head of this 'new sect' was called 'the best' rather than 'the anointed one.' Also of importance as proof of the rapid spread of Christianity is the testimony of Pliny the Younger, the Governor of Bithynia, in his report to the Emperor Trajan, between the years 111 and 113: 'especially on account of the number of those that are in danger; for there are many of every age, of every rank, and of both sexes, who are now and hereafter likely to be called to account, and to be in danger; for this superstition is spread like a contagion, not only into cities and towns, but into country villages also, which yet there is reason to hope may be stopped and corrected.' Pliny the Younger said that the Christians themselves affirmed that 'they were wont, on a stated day, to meet together before it was light, and to sing a hymn to Christ, as to a god, alternately; and to oblige themselves by a sacrament [or oath], not to do anything that was ill: but that they would commit no theft, or pilfering, or adultery; that they would not break their promises, or deny what was deposited with them, when it was required back again; after which it was their custom to depart, and to meet again at a common but innocent meal.'[61]

Positive Impact of Christianity

A final argument is based on the positive impact of Christianity upon humanity in terms of the development of the arts and sciences, political progress and social justice. The birth of science from the philosophical consequences of a Christian world picture is a particular pointer to the positive impact of Christianity.[62] The Second Vatican Council effectively affirmed this when it stated: 'even in the secular history of mankind the Gospel has acted as a leaven in the interests of liberty and progress.'[63] Because the existence of God is also a truth of reason, other truths of reason then follow, such as the nature of man, the natural law, and the grounding of the socio-political order. Newman explained that this benefit took place despite the human weaknesses and sins of individual Christians. This benefit was based upon 'an intelligent notion about the Supreme God' and the effects of the Christian religion have included the raising of moral awareness. The Christian message 'has abolished great social anomalies and miseries, has elevated the female sex to its proper dignity, has protected the poorer classes, has destroyed slavery, encouraged literature and philosophy, and had a principal part in that civilisation of human kind.' For Newman, the impact of Christianity is an accumulation of coincidences which comes close to being a miracle 'as being impossible without the Hand of God directly and immediately in them.'[64]

Finally, the convergence of all of the demonstrations of the existence of God is in itself a further proof. All the individual proofs are as many pointers conspiring to demonstrate God's existence, Who is the Ultimate Truth able to explain the otherwise unexplainable. The various proofs of God's existence can encourage a predisposition to faith and help people to see that faith is not opposed to reason.[65] This reasonable nature of Christian faith will be examined in more detail in the next chapter.

Notes

[1]   See S. Singh, *Fermat's Last Theorem* (London: Fourth Estate, 1998), p. 82.

[2]   St Augustine, *De libero arbitrio*, Book 2, chapter 15, n. 39 in *PL* 32, 1262.

[3]   St Basil, *Sermon 7 on the Hexaemeron*, chapter 5 in *PG* 29, 159–160.

[4]   See St John Damascene, *De fide orthodoxa*, Book 1, chapter 3 in *PG* 94, 795–798.

[5]   See Editorial, 'Prove dell'esistenza di Dio' in *La Civiltà Cattolica* 147/II (1996), p. 7.

[6]   See St Anselm, *Proslogion*, chapter 2 in *PL* 158, 227–228: 'For, it is one thing for an object to be in the understanding, and another to understand that the object exists. When a painter first conceives of what he will afterwards perform, he has it in his understanding, but he does not yet understand it to be, because he has not yet performed it. But after he has made the painting, he both has it in his understanding, and he understands that it exists, because he has made it . . . .

    Therefore, if that, than which nothing greater can be conceived, exists in the understanding alone, the very being, than which nothing greater can be conceived, is one than which a greater can be conceived. But obviously this is impossible. Hence, there is no doubt that there exists a being, than which nothing greater can be conceived, and it exists both in the understanding and in reality.'

[7]   Ibid., chapter 3 in *PL* 158, 228.

[8]   See Ibid., chapter 4 in *PL* 158, 229.

[9]   See Gaunilo, *On behalf of the fool*, n. 6 in *PL* 158, 246–247: 'For example: it is said that somewhere in the ocean is an island, which, because of the difficulty, or rather the impossibility, of discovering what does not exist, is called the lost island. And they say that this island has an inestimable wealth of all manner of riches and delicacies in greater abundance than is told of the Islands of the Blest; and

that having no owner or inhabitant, it is more excellent than all other countries, which are inhabited by mankind, in the abundance with which it is endowed.

Now if some one should tell me that there is such an island, I should easily understand his words, in which there is no difficulty. But suppose that he went on to say, as if by a logical inference: "You can no longer doubt that this island which is more excellent than all lands exists somewhere, since you have no doubt that it is in your understanding. And since it is more excellent not to be in the under-standing alone, but to exist both in the understanding and in reality, for this reason it must exist. For if it does not exist, any land which really exists will be more excellent than it; and so the island already understood by you to be more excellent will not be more excellent."

If a man should try to prove to me by such reasoning that this island truly exists, and that its existence should no longer be doubted, either I should believe that he was jesting, or I know not which I ought to regard as the greater fool: myself, supposing that I should allow this proof; or him, if he should suppose that he had established with any certainty the existence of this island. For he ought to show first that the hypothetical excellence of this island exists as a real and indubitable fact, and in no wise as any unreal object, or one whose existence is uncertain, in my understanding.'

10 See St Anselm, *In reply to Gaunilo's answer in behalf of the fool*, chap-ters 3 and 5 in *PL* 158, 252 and 255–256.

11 See St Thomas Aquinas, *Summa Theologiae*, I, q. 2, a. 1.

12 See St Thomas Aquinas, *Summa Theologiae*, I, q. 2, a. 2.

13 See St Thomas Aquinas, *Summa Contra Gentiles*, Book 1, chapter 12. Here, St Thomas also remarked that 'our knowledge, even of things which transcend the senses, originates from the senses.'

14 See St Thomas Aquinas, *Summa Theologiae*, I, q. 2, a. 3: 'The first and more manifest way is the argument from motion. It is certain, and evident to our senses, that in the world some things are in motion. Now whatever is in motion is put in motion by another, for nothing can be in motion except it is in potentiality to that towards which it is in motion; whereas a thing moves inasmuch as it is in act. For motion is nothing else than the reduction of something from poten-tiality to actuality. But nothing can be reduced from potentiality to actuality, except by something in a state of actuality. Thus that which is actually hot, as fire, makes wood, which is potentially hot, to be actually hot, and thereby moves and changes it. Now it is not possible that the same thing should be at once in actuality and potentiality in the same respect, but only in different respects. For what is actually hot cannot simultaneously be potentially hot; but it is simultaneously potentially cold. It is therefore impossible that in the same respect and in the same way a thing should be both mover

and moved, i.e. that it should move itself. Therefore, whatever is in motion must be put in motion by another. If that by which it is put in motion be itself put in motion, then this also must needs be put in motion by another, and that by another again. But this cannot go on to infinity, because then there would be no first mover, and, consequently, no other mover; seeing that subsequent movers move only inasmuch as they are put in motion by the first mover; as the staff moves only because it is put in motion by the hand. Therefore it is necessary to arrive at a first mover, put in motion by no other; and this everyone understands to be God.'

See also Idem, *Summa Contra Gentiles*, Book 1, chapter 13: 'Whatever is in motion is moved by another: and it is clear to the sense that something, the sun for instance, is in motion. Therefore it is set in motion by something else moving it. Now that which moves it is itself either moved or not. If it be not moved, then the point is proved that we must needs postulate an immovable mover: and this we call God. If, however, it be moved, it is moved by another mover. Either, therefore, we must proceed to infinity, or we must come to an immovable mover. But it is not possible to proceed to infinity. Therefore it is necessary to postulate an immovable mover.'

15   See St Thomas Aquinas, *Summa Theologiae*, I, q. 2, a. 3: 'The second way is from the nature of the efficient cause. In the world of sense we find there is an order of efficient causes. There is no case known (neither is it, indeed, possible) in which a thing is found to be the efficient cause of itself; for so it would be prior to itself, which is impossible. Now in efficient causes it is not possible to go on to infinity, because in all efficient causes following in order, the first is the cause of the intermediate cause, and the intermediate is the cause of the ultimate cause, whether the intermediate cause be several, or only one. Now to take away the cause is to take away the effect. Therefore, if there be no first cause among efficient causes, there will be no ultimate, nor any intermediate cause. But if in efficient causes it is possible to go on to infinity, there will be no first efficient cause, neither will there be an ultimate effect, nor any intermediate efficient causes; all of which is plainly false. Therefore it is necessary to admit a first efficient cause, to which everyone gives the name of God.'

16   See St Thomas Aquinas, *Summa Theologiae*, I, q. 2, a. 3: 'The third way is taken from possibility and necessity, and runs thus. We find in nature things that are possible to be and not to be, since they are found to be generated, and to corrupt, and consequently, they are possible to be and not to be. But it is impossible for these always to exist, for that which is possible not to be at some time is not. Therefore, if everything is possible not to be, then at one time there

could have been nothing in existence. Now if this were true, even now there would be nothing in existence, because that which does not exist only begins to exist by something already existing. Therefore, if at one time nothing was in existence, it would have been impossible for anything to have begun to exist; and thus even now nothing would be in existence – which is absurd. Therefore, not all beings are merely possible, but there must exist something the existence of which is necessary. But every necessary thing either has its necessity caused by another, or not. Now it is impossible to go on to infinity in necessary things which have their necessity caused by another, as has been already proved in regard to efficient causes. Therefore we cannot but postulate the existence of some being having of itself its own necessity, and not receiving it from another, but rather causing in others their necessity. This all men speak of as God.'

[17] See St Thomas Aquinas, *Summa Theologiae*, I, q. 2, a. 3: 'The fourth way is taken from the gradation to be found in things. Among beings there are some more and some less good, true, noble and the like. But "more" and "less" are predicated of different things, according as they resemble in their different ways something which is the maximum, as a thing is said to be hotter according as it more nearly resembles that which is hottest; so that there is something which is truest, something best, something noblest and, consequently, something which is uttermost being; for those things that are greatest in truth are greatest in being .... Now the maximum in any genus is the cause of all in that genus; as fire, which is the maximum heat, is the cause of all hot things. Therefore there must also be something which is to all beings the cause of their being, goodness, and every other perfection; and this we call God.'

[18] See St Thomas Aquinas, *Summa Theologiae*, I, q. 2, a. 3: 'The fifth way is taken from the governance of the world. We see that things which lack intelligence, such as natural bodies, act for an end, and this is evident from their acting always, or nearly always, in the same way, so as to obtain the best result. Hence it is plain that not fortuitously, but designedly, do they achieve their end. Now whatever lacks intelligence cannot move towards an end, unless it be directed by some being endowed with knowledge and intelligence; as the arrow is shot to its mark by the archer. Therefore some intelligent being exists by whom all natural things are directed to their end; and this being we call God.'

[19] J. Duns Scotus, *Opus Oxoniense*, n. 16.

[20] See chapter 1, pp. 23–25 above for an explanation of the principle of causality.

[21] For more on pantheism, see my *Mystery of Creation* (Leominster: Gracewing, 1995), pp. 49–50, 91–92.

22   A. Dulles, *The New World of Faith* (Huntington, IN: Our Sunday Visitor, 2000), p. 31.

23   Ibid., p. 32. For a further amusing illustration of the impossibility of an infinite regress see the exposition of Hilbert's Hotel in W.L. Craig, 'The Existence of God and the Beginning of the Universe' in *Truth: A Journal of Modern Thought* 3 (1991), pp. 85–96: 'Let us imagine a hotel with a finite number of rooms. Suppose, furthermore, that *all the rooms are full*. When a new guest arrives asking for a room, the proprietor apologizes, "Sorry, all the rooms are full." But now let us imagine a hotel with an infinite number of rooms and suppose once more that all the rooms are full. There is not a single vacant room throughout the entire infinite hotel. Now suppose a new guest shows up, asking for a room. "But of course!" says the proprietor, and he immediately shifts the person in room #1 into room #2, the person in room #2 into room #3, the person in room #3 into room #4 and so on, out to infinity. As a result of these room changes, room #1 now becomes vacant and the new guest gratefully checks in. But remember, before he arrived, all the rooms were full! Equally curious, according to the mathematicians, there are now no more persons in the hotel than there were before: the number is just infinite. But how can this be? The proprietor just added the new guest's name to the register and gave him his keys – how can there not be one more person in the hotel than before? But the situation becomes even stranger. For suppose an infinity of new guests show up the desk, asking for a room. "Of course, of course!" says the proprietor, and he proceeds to shift the person in room #1 into room #2, the person in room #2 into room #4, the person in room #3 into room #6, and so on out to infinity, always putting each former occupant into the room number twice his own. As a result, all the odd numbered rooms become vacant, and the infinity of new guests is easily accommodated. And yet, before they came, all the rooms were full! And again, strangely enough, the number of guests in the hotel is the same after the infinity of new guests check in as before, even though there were as many new guests as old guests. In fact, the proprietor could repeat this process *infinitely many times* and yet there would never be one single person more in the hotel than before.

But Hilbert's Hotel is even stranger than the German mathematician gave it out to be. For suppose some of the guests start to check out. Suppose the guest in room #1 departs. Is there not now one less person in the hotel? Not according to the mathematicians – but just ask the woman who makes the beds! Suppose the guests in room numbers 1, 3, 5, ... check out. In this case an infinite number of people have left the hotel, but according to the mathematicians there are no less people in the hotel – but don't talk to that laundry woman! In fact, we could have every other guest check out of the hotel and repeat this process infinitely many times, and yet there would never be any less people in the hotel. But suppose instead the persons in room number 4, 5, 6, ... checked out. At a single stroke the hotel would be virtually emptied, the guest register reduced to three names, and the infinite converted to finitude. And yet it would remain true that the *same number* of guests checked out this time as when the guests in room numbers 1, 3, 5, ... checked out. Can anyone sincerely believe that such a hotel could exist in reality? These sorts of absurdities illustrate the impossibility of the existence of an actually infinite number of things. If the universe never began to exist, then prior to the present event there have existed an actually infinite number of previous events. Hence, a beginningless series of events in time entails the existence of an actually infinite number of things, namely, past events.'

[24] Dulles, *The New World of Faith*, p. 32.

[25] S. L. Jaki, 'The History of Science and the Idea of an Oscillating Universe' in *The Center Journal* 4 (1984), p. 164, footnote 50.

[26] Ibid., p. 159.

[27] S. L. Jaki, *The Road of Science and the Ways to God* (Edinburgh: Scottish Academic Press, 1978), p. 292.

[28] See R. Stannard, 'God's Purpose in and Beyond Time' in J. M. Templeton (ed.) *Evidence of Purpose* (New York: Continuum, 1994), p. 43.

[29] S. L. Jaki was the first to offer the extension of Gödel's theorem to cosmology in his seminal work *The Relevance of Physics* (Edinburgh: Scottish Academic Press, 1992²), pp. 127–130; this treatment has been articulated in greater detail in his *Cosmos and Creator* (Edinburgh: Scottish Academic Press, 1980), pp. 49–51, 54, 108; *The Savior of Science* (Washington, DC: Regnery Gateway, 1988), pp. 108–109, 198; 'From Scientific Cosmology to a Created Universe' in *Irish Astronomical Journal* 15 (1982), pp. 257–258; *God and the Cosmologists* (Washington, D.C./Edinburgh: Gateway Editions/ Scottish Academic Press, 1989), pp. 103–109. For the explanation of the universe as penultimate and God as the Ultimate in intelligibility, see S. L. Jaki, 'Physics and the Ultimate' in *Ultimate Reality and Meaning* 11/1 (March 1988), pp. 68–72.

[30] W. Paley, *Natural Theology: or, Evidences of the Existence and Attributes and of the Deity, Collected from the Appearances of Nature* (Boston: Gould, Kendall and Lincoln, 1849), p. 6.

[31] Cf. ibid., p. 6.

[32] Ibid., p. 26.

[33] Ibid., pp. 293–94.

[34] See S. L. Jaki's definition of the cosmos in chapter 6, p. 164 above.

35   St Augustine, *Sermon 241*, chapter 2, 2 in *PL* 38, 1134. See also St Hilary's approach on pp. 60–61 above.

36   St Thomas Aquinas, *Summa Theologiae*, I, q. 39, a. 8.

37   I. Kant, *Critique of Judgment* §9, trans. J. H. Bernard (New York: Hafner Publications, 1966), p. 54.

38   St John of the Cross, *Ascent of Mount Carmel*, Book I, Chapter 4, 4.

39   St John of the Cross, *A Spiritual Canticle of the Soul*, Stanza XXXIX, 14.

40   Vatican II, *Gaudium et Spes* 18.1; cf. 14.2.

41   See *CCC* 33.

42   See J. H. Newman, *The Grammar of Assent* (London: Burns, Oates and Company, 1870) p. 101: 'As from a multitude of instinctive perceptions, acting in particular instances, of something beyond the senses, we generalize the notion of an external world, and then picture that world in and according to those particular phenomena from which we started, so from the perceptive power which identifies the intimations of conscience with the reverberations or echoes (so to say) of an external admonition, we proceed on to the notion of a Supreme Ruler and Judge, and then again we image Him and His attributes in those recurring intimations, out of which, as mental phenomena, our recognition of His existence was originally gained. And, if the impressions which His creatures make on us through our senses oblige us to regard those creatures as *sui generis* respectively, it is not wonderful that the notices, which He indirectly gives us through our conscience, of His own nature are such as to make us understand that He is like Himself and like nothing else.'

43   See Newman, *The Grammar of Assent*, pp. 110–111.

44   Newman, *The Grammar of Assent*, pp. 113.

45   W. Rees-Mogg, 'Opinion' in *The Times*, 28 August 2000.

46   St Augustine, *Confessions* Book 1, Chapter 1, n. 1 in *PL* 32, 661.

47   Dulles, *The New World of Faith*, p. 34.

48   See B. Pascal, *Pensées* translated by W. F. Trotter (New York: E. P. Dutton, 1958), # 233.

49   See ibid. The proof runs as follows: '"God is, or He is not." But to which side shall we incline? Reason can decide nothing here. There is an infinite chaos which separated us. A game is being played at the extremity of this infinite distance where heads or tails will turn up ... Which will you choose then? Let us see. Since you must choose, let us see which interests you least. You have two things to lose, the true and the good; and two things to stake, your reason and your will, you knowledge and your happiness; and your nature has two things to shun, error and misery. Your reason is no more shocked in choosing one rather than the other, since you must of necessity choose ... But your happiness? Let us weigh the gain and

the loss in wagering that God is ... If you gain, you gain all; if you lose, you lose nothing. Wager, then, without hesitation that He is .... Since there is an equal risk of gain and of loss, if you had only to gain two lives, instead of one, you might still wager. But if there were three lives to gain, you would have to play (since you are under the necessity of playing), and you would be imprudent, when you are forced to play, not to chance your life to gain three at a game where there is an equal risk of loss and gain. But there is an eternity of life and happiness. And this being so, if there were an infinity of chances, of which one only would be for you, you would still be right in wagering one to win two, and you would act stupidly, being obliged to play, by refusing to stake one life against three at a game in which out of an infinity of chances there is one for you, if there were an infinity of an infinitely happy life to gain. But there is here an infinity of an infinitely happy life to gain, a chance of gain against a finite number of chances of loss, and what you stake is finite. It is all divided; wherever the infinite is and there is not an infinity of chances of loss against that of gain, there is no time to hesitate, you must give all ....'

50   The proposition, 'The assent of supernatural faith ... is consistent with merely probable knowledge of revelation' was a laxist error condemned by Pope Innocent XI in 1679, as noted in DS 2121. The Decree *Lamentabili sane* in 1907 condemned the proposition (see DS 3425) 'the assent of faith rests ultimately on an accumulation of probabilities.'

51   J. H. Newman, *The Grammar of Assent*, p. 406.

52   T. B. Macauley, Essay on L. von Ranke's *History of the Popes* in *Edinburgh Review* 72 (1840), pp. 227–228.

53   K. Adam, *The Spirit of Catholicism* (London: Sheed & Ward, 1952), pp. 3–4.

54   Newman, *The Grammar of Assent*, p. 450.

55   Ibid., p. 451.

56   There are many prophecies concerning the Messiah that were fulfilled in Jesus Christ. Since the coming of the Messiah is the theme of the Old Testament, the predictions fulfilled in Jesus Christ outnumber all others. These Old Testament prophecies, and their fulfilment as recorded in the New Testament, include the following predictions concerning Christ the Messiah:

   1) He would be a descendent of Abraham (Genesis 12:3 and 17:9→Matthew 1:1, Galatians 3:16).
   2) He would be of the tribe of Judah (Genesis 49:10→Luke 3:33, Hebrews 7:14).
   3) He would be of the house of David (2 Samuel 7:12→Matthew 1:1).

4) He would be born of a Virgin (Isaiah 7:14→Matthew 1:21).

5) He would be born in Bethlehem (Micah 5:1–2→Matthew 2:1, Luke 2:4–7).

6) A messenger would go before Him (Isaiah 40:3, Malachi 3:1→, Matthew 3:3, Mark 1:2–4).

7) His ministry to begin in Galilee (Isaiah 8:23–9:1→ Matthew 4:13–16).

8) His zeal for God would carry Him away (Psalm 69:9→John 2:17).

9) He would perform miracles (Isaiah 35:5–6→Matthew 9:35).

10) He would be rejected by the Jewish leaders (Psalm 118:22. →1 Peter 2:7).

11) He would be rejected by His own people (Isaiah 53:3→John 1:10–11; 7:5, 48).

12) He would enter Jerusalem on a donkey (Zechariah 9:9→John 12:14–15).

13) He would be betrayed for thirty pieces of silver (Zechariah 11:12–13→Matthew 26:14–15).

14) The money used in His betrayal would be thrown into the temple, and the Potter's field bought with it (Zechariah 11:13→Matthew 27:3–10).

15) He would be silent before His accusers (Isaiah 53:7→Matthew 27:12–19).

16) He would be mocked (Psalm 22:7–8. →Matthew 27:39–40).

17) His back would be struck (Isaiah 50:6→Mark 15:15).

18) His face would be spat upon (Isaiah 50:6→Matthew 26:67; 27:30).

19) He would be crucified, and the effects were described in the Old Testament centuries before the Romans adopted this method of execution (Psalm 22:13–15→Matthew 27:32–44; John 19:28–30).

20) He would be put to death with criminals (Isaiah 53:12→Luke 23:33).

21) He would pray for His persecutors (Isaiah 53:12→Luke 23:34).

22) People would gamble for His clothes (Psalm 22:18→John 19:23–24).

23) His side would be pierced and His bones would not be broken (Zechariah 12:10, Psalm 34:20→John 19:33–34).

24) His Passion would be redemptive (Isaiah 53:5→1 Peter 2:24).

25) He would be buried in a rich man's tomb (Isaiah 53:9→Matthew 27:57–60).

26) He would rise from the dead on the third day (Hosea 6:1–3; Isaiah 26:19; Psalm 16:10–11; Jonah 2:1→Luke 24:46; Matthew 12:40).

Several features are unique about these prophecies, in contrast to all other examples of attempted predictions today. First, unlike the predictions of Nostradamus, these prophecies were very specific and detailed. For example, they gave the very name of the tribe, city, and other circumstances of Christ's coming. Second, none of these predictions failed, unlike those of the Jehovah's Witnesses, and other sects, concerning the date of the end of the world. Third, these prophecies were written hundreds of years before Jesus was born. It was not a question of reading the trends of the times or simply making intelligent guesses. Fourth, many of these predictions were beyond human ability to arrange a fulfilment. For example, if Jesus were a mere human being, he would have had absolutely no control over when, where, or how he would be born, how he would die (especially since a foreign power, Rome, was to be the instrument of his death), or whether he would rise from the dead.

57 See Pope John Paul II, *Tertio Millenio Adveniente*, 5.

58 Flavius Josephus, *The Antiquities of the Jews* Book 18, 63–64. See also Eusebius of Caesarea, *Ecclesiastical History* Book 1, chapter 11 in *PG* 20, 115–118 and De *demonstratione evangelica* Book 3, n. 5 in *PG* 22, 221–222.

59 Tacitus, *Annales* 15, 44.

60 Suetonius, *Vita Claudii*, 25, 4. The expulsion took place in the year AD 49. See also Acts 18:42.

61 Pliny the Younger, *Epistle* 1, 96.

62 As regards the development of science from a Christian matrix see my *Creation and Scientific Creativity. A Study in the Thought of S. L. Jaki* (Front Royal, VA: Christendom Press, 1991) and chapter 6 above, pp. 150–160.

63 Vatican II, *Ad Gentes Divinitus* 8.

64 Newman, *Grammar of Assent*, p. 439.

65 See CCC 35.

CHAPTER 8

FAITH IS REASONABLE

Now God forbid that Faith be blind assent,
Grasping what others know; else Faith were nought
But learning, as of some far continent
Which others sought,
And carried thence, better the tale to teach,
Pebbles and shells, poor fragments of the beach.

Now God forbid that Faith be built on dates,
Cursive or uncial letters, scribe or gloss,
What one conjectures, proves, or demonstrates:
This were the loss
Of all to which God bids that man aspire,
This were the death of life, quenching of fire.
            Robert Hugh Benson, 'Christian Evidences'

Christian Revelation is the true lodestar of men and women as
they strive to make their way amid the pressures of an imma-
nentist habit of mind and the constrictions of a technocratic
logic. It is the ultimate possibility offered by God for the human
being to know in all its fullness the seminal plan of love which
began with creation. To those wishing to know the truth, if they
can look beyond themselves and their own concerns, there is
given the possibility of taking full and harmonious possession of
their lives, precisely by following the path of truth.
                John Paul II, *Fides et Ratio* 15

Mutual Impact

The fact that faith is reasonable is exemplified in the fruitful mutual relations between faith and reason. These effects of faith and reason upon one another were summarised in a neat axiom by Hugh of St Victor (died 1141): 'faith is aided by reason and reason is perfected by faith.'[1] Now, there are two basic dimensions to faith, the truth in which we believe and the act by which we believe.[2] The doctrinal element grounds the living act of faith. While belief here obviously includes the sense of a response in obedience, nevertheless the content aspect is more objective and easier to pin down in a historical and cultural perspective. In the doctrinal aspect of faith as taught by the Magisterium, reflected upon by theologians and interiorized by the entire people of God, one can readily trace the effect of an objective content of belief upon reason and vice versa. It is the content aspect of Christian belief in God which can best be seen in relation to reason considered as an objective content and process. However, it must be remembered that faith does not stop at the propositions but in the realities which they express.[3] In the New Testament, sometimes the faith is referred to as a content or deposit (see 1 Tm 4:1; 2 Tm 1:13); it is a knowledge of Jesus Christ and of His work (1 Pt 1:12, 25; 2 Th 2:13). In other parts of the New Testament, faith refers to the act of the believer responding to what God has revealed, as found for example in chapter eleven of the Letter to the Hebrews. St Thomas Aquinas defined the act of supernatural faith as 'the act of the intellect assenting to a Divine truth owing to the movement of the will, which is itself moved by the grace of God.'[4] The act of faith is the assent of the intellect to a truth which is beyond its comprehension, but which it accepts under the influence of the will moved by grace and so the virtue of faith is a supernatural habit by which we firmly believe those things to be true which God has revealed. Generally, every virtue is the perfection of some faculty, but faith results from the combined action of two faculties, namely, the intellect which elicits the act, and the will which moves the intellect to do so; consequently, the perfection of faith will depend upon the perfection with which each of these faculties performs its allotted task; the intellect must assent unhesitatingly, the will must promptly and readily move it to do so. Just as the light of faith is a gift supernaturally bestowed upon the understanding, so also divine grace moving the will is, as its name implies, an equally supernatural and an absolutely gratuitous gift. Neither gift is due to previous study and neither of them can be acquired by human efforts, but they are gratuitous gifts which can be asked for.

The unhesitating assent of the intellect is not simply derived from an intellectual conviction of the reasonableness of faith, whether with regard to the grounds on which it rests or to the actual truths we believe, for 'only faith can guarantee the blessings that we hope for, or prove the existence of realities that are unseen' (Heb 11:1). The basis for the act of faith is that that these truths are revealed on the authority and divine infallible testimony of God Himself, who can 'neither err nor deceive.'[5] Although faith deals essentially with what is unseen, the particular function of the light of faith does not provide vision, but rather an instinctive appreciation of the truths which are declared to be revealed. In every act of faith this unhesitating assent of the intellect is due to the motion of the will as its efficient cause, and the same must be said of the theological virtue of faith when we consider it as a habit or as a moral virtue, for, as St Thomas insists, there is no virtue, in the strict sense, in the intellect except in so far as it is subject to the will.[6] Thus the habitual readiness of the will in moving the intellect to assent to the truths of faith is not only the efficient cause of the intellect's assent, but is precisely what gives to this assent its virtuous, and consequently meritorious, character. Lastly, this readiness of the will can only come from its unswerving tendency to the Supreme Good.

Since faith is a virtue, it follows that a man's readiness

in believing will stimulate him to love the truths he believes, and he will therefore study them, not in a spirit of doubting inquiry, but rather seeking to grasp them better as far as human reason will allow. Such inquiry will be meritorious and will render his faith more robust, because sometimes he will have to grapple with the intellectual difficulties which are involved, and will have to employ his faith more keenly. Thus in the case of a person who already believes, reason helps faith to deepen its understanding. As St Augustine affirmed:

> Our intellect therefore is of use to understand whatever things it believes, and faith is of use to believe whatever it understands; and in order that these same things may be more and more understood, the thinking faculty is of use in the intellect. But this is not brought about as by our own natural powers but by the gift and the aid of God.[7]

The assent of faith is not a 'blind impulse of the mind,'[8] for God wished that the response of faith be in harmony with reason, hence it was God's will that, linked to the *internal assistance* of the Holy Spirit, there should be *external indications* of His revelation, such as miracles and prophecies, which demonstrate the omnipotence and infinite knowledge of God, and are suited to the understanding of all as the most certain signs of revelation.[9] St Thomas Aquinas explained that external signs are helpful in this context: 'A man would not believe unless he saw the things he had to believe, either by the evidence of miracles or of something similar.'[10]

These signs which God, in His providence, offers to assist faith in its birth and growth are in a sense evidence that the matters asserted are revealed truths. In other words, the credibility of the statements made is correlative with and proportionate to the credentials of the authority who makes them. Now the credentials of God are indubitable, for the very idea of God involves that of omniscience and of the Supreme Truth. Hence, what God reveals is supremely credible, though not necessarily supremely intelligible to us. The motives for credibility which have been mentioned in the last chapter are convergent, namely they point in one direction, that of God who reveals.[11] The Old Testament outlines the marvellous dealings of God with the people of Israel to whom He repeatedly reveals Himself; it speaks of miracles wrought in their favour and as proofs of the truth of the revelation He makes; it offers the most sublime teaching and the repeated announcement of God's desire to save the world from sin and its consequences. Moreover, throughout the pages of this book are found a series of hints, sometimes obscure, sometimes clear, of the wondrous Person who is to come as the world's Saviour. It is asserted sometimes that He is man, at others that He is God Himself. The New Testament immortalises the birth, life, and death of One Who, while clearly man, also claimed to be God, and Who proved the truth of His claim by His whole life, miracles, teachings, and death, and finally by His glorious resurrection. Moreover He founded a Church which should, according to Him, continue until He come again the end of time, which should serve as the treasure house of His teaching, and should be the means of applying to all people the sacramental fruits of His redemption. In subsequent history, this Church was to spread rapidly everywhere, despite its humble origin, its unworldly teaching, and the cruel persecution which it experienced at the hands of the princes of this world. As centuries passed, this Church battled against heresies and schisms, and the scandal of the sins of her own people and of her own rulers. Nevertheless she continued the same, proclaiming the same Gospel, and setting before men and women the same mysteries of the life, death and resurrection of Christ, Who had gone before to prepare a home for those who while on earth should have believed in Him and loved Him. So since the history of the Church from New Testament times confirms the New Testament itself, and the New Testament completes the Old Testament, these books must really contain what they claim to contain, namely Divine revelation. Above all, that Person Whose life and death were foretold in such detail in the Old Testament, and Whose narrative, as told in the New Testament, so perfectly corresponds with its prophetic portrayal in the Old Testament, must be what He claimed to be, namely the Son of God. His work, therefore, must be Divine.[12] The Church which He founded must also be Divine and thus be the guardian and deposit of His teaching. Therefore, for every truth of Christianity which we believe, Christ Himself is our testimony, and we believe in Him because the Divinity He claimed rests upon the concurrent testimony of His miracles, His prophecies, His personal character, the nature of His doctrine, the marvellous propagation of His teaching in spite of its running counter to flesh and blood, the united testimony of thousands of martyrs, the stories of countless saints who for His sake have led heroic lives, the history of the Church herself since the Crucifixion, and, perhaps more remarkable than any, the history of the papacy from St Peter to Pope John Paul II. The Church herself 'by reason of her astonishing *propagation*, her outstanding *holiness* and her inexhaustible *fertility* in every kind of *goodness*, by her catholic *unity* and her unconquerable *stability*, is a kind of great and perpetual *motive of credibility* and an incontrovertible evidence of her own divine mission.'[13] Thus from belief in the Church we can arrive at belief in Christ, her divine Founder, and vice versa: 'The Apostles saw the Head and believed in the Body; we see the Body let us believe in the Head.'[14]

However, the meaning and nature of the motives of credibility need to be clarified. In the first place, they yield definite and certain knowledge of Divine revelation. This knowledge precedes faith, but is not the final motive for our assent to the truths of faith, since as St Thomas says: 'Faith has the character of a virtue, not because of the things it believes, for faith is of things that appear not, but because it adheres to the testimony of one in whom truth is infallibly found.'[15] This knowledge of revealed truth which precedes faith can only generate human faith, and it is not even the cause of Divine faith, but is rather to be considered a remote disposition to it. Hence faith is not to be regarded as practically a necessary consequence of a careful study of the motives of credibility, a view which the First Vatican Council expressly condemns:

> If anyone says that the assent to Christian faith is not free, but is produced with necessity by arguments of human reason; or that the grace of God is necessary only for that living faith which works by charity: let him be anathema.[16]

Furthermore, the motives of credibility cannot make the mysteries of faith clear in themselves, for the signs and arguments which induce us to believe do not prove the faith itself, but only the truthfulness of Him who declares it to us, and consequently they do not beget knowledge of faith's mysteries, but only faith.[17] On the other hand, the genuine probative power of the motives of credibility within their true domain must not be undermined: 'Reason declares that from the very outset the Gospel teaching was rendered conspicuous by signs and wonders which gave, as it were, definite proof of a definite truth.'[18]

The act of assenting to supernatural truth is to be distinguished from the act of purely human faith. Nevertheless human faith can be a powerful analogy for supernatural faith as R. H. Benson graphically illustrated:

> A scientist, let us say, proposes to make observations upon the structure of a fly's leg. He catches his fly, dissects, prepares, places it in his microscope, observes, and records. Now here, it would seem, is Pure Science at its purest and Reason in its most reasonable aspect. Yet the acts of faith in this very simple process are, if we consider closely, simply numberless. The scientist must make acts of faith, certainly reasonable acts, yet none the less of faith, for all that: first, that his fly is not a freak of nature; next, that his lens is symmetrically ground; then that his observation is adequate; then that his memory has not played

him false between his observing and his recording that which he has seen. These acts are so reasonable that we forget that they are acts of faith. They are justified by reason before they are made, and they are usually, though not invariably, verified by Reason afterwards. Yet they are, in their essence, Faith and not Reason.

So, too, when a child learns a foreign language. Reason justifies him in making one act of faith that his teacher is competent, another that his grammar is correct, a third that he hears and sees and understands correctly the information given him, a fourth that such a language actually exists. And when he visits France afterwards he can, within limits, again verify by his reason the acts of faith which he has previously made. Yet none the less they were acts of faith, though they were reasonable.[19]

The supernatural truths of faith, however they may transcend our reason, cannot be opposed to it, for 'truth cannot contradict truth,'[20] and the same God Who gave us the powers of reason by which we assent to natural truths is Himself the cause of those truths, which are but a reflection of His own Divine truth. When He chose to reveal to us further truths concerning Himself, the fact that these latter are beyond the grasp of the natural light which He has bestowed upon us does not mean that they are against our reason.

While it is clear that God cannot deny Himself, nor can truth ever be in opposition to truth, sometimes there appears to be a contradiction between truths of the faith and those of reason. One particular example of this was the Galileo affair, a problem concerning the relations between faith and science, about which the Second Vatican Council remarked:

> For by the very circumstance of their having been created, all things are endowed with their own stability, truth, goodness, proper laws and order. Man must respect these as he isolates them by the appropriate methods of the individual sciences or arts. Therefore if methodical investigation within every branch of learning is carried out in a

genuinely scientific manner and in accord with moral norms, it never truly conflicts with faith, for earthly matters and the concerns of faith derive from the same God. Indeed whoever labours to penetrate the secrets of reality with a humble and steady mind, even though he is unaware of the fact, is nevertheless being led by the hand of God, who holds all things in existence, and gives them their identity. Consequently, we cannot but deplore certain habits of mind, which are sometimes found too among Christians, which do not sufficiently attend to the rightful independence of science and which, from the arguments and controversies they spark, lead many minds to conclude that faith and science are mutually opposed.[21]

This apparent contradiction can occur when the dogmas of faith are not understood and explained in accordance with the mind of the Church, or when mere opinions are taken to be absolute truth at the level of reason. Not only are faith and reason never basically at odds with one another but rather they mutually support each other. The works produced by man's own talent and energy are not in opposition to God's power, and man and woman as rational creatures are not to be seen as a kind of rival to the Creator; rather Christians are convinced that the triumphs of the human race are 'a sign of God's grace and the flowering of His own mysterious design.'[22] On the one hand right reason can establish the foundations of the faith, and, illuminated by its light, can develop theological understanding. On the other hand, faith frees and purifies reason from errors and protects it, providing it with further knowledge of many kinds.[23] The guiding star of faith also helps reason to discern between that which lies beyond reason at present, but will later be known in this way, and that which is absolutely beyond the powers of reason and must be divinely revealed in order to be humanly known.

In certain formulations of mystics or particular expressions of spiritual masters, faith may sometimes appear to be paradoxical. This at least can be said of St Ignatius of Loyola when he wrote:

To arrive at complete certainty, this is the attitude of mind we should maintain: I will believe that the white object I see is black if that should be the decision of the hierarchical Church, for I believe that linking Christ our Lord the Bridegroom and His Bride the Church, there is one and the same Spirit, ruling and guiding us for our souls' good. For our Holy Mother the Church is guided and ruled by the same Spirit, the Lord who gave the Ten Commandments.[24]

Nevertheless, Ignatius is not in favour of an irrational universe. He adopts the contrast between 'being' and 'seeming' to favour faith, because there are limitations in human knowing. The testimony of the whole Church is preferred to the witness of the senses, which can be misled, and to the argumentation of reason, which can be erroneous. 'Black' and 'white' are categories employed as an illustration of the contrast between what appears to me and what is, as the Church tells me. Obviously the Church does not pontificate on the colour of material objects, which does not fall within the competence of the Magisterium, whose ambit lies in faith, morals and philosophical themes needed to support faith and morals. However, what the Church tells me is true, such as the real and substantial presence of Christ in the Eucharist, even when it does not appear that way to the senses or to natural reason. Supernatural truths which the natural mind cannot fathom are higher than natural truths, and we have greater certitude about them. So if the Church proposes supernatural truths we must accept them and believe them, even when all natural reasonings and appearances cannot reach them, as in the case of transubstantiation. Nevertheless transubstantiation, while it is a truth beyond reason, is not against reason. There is a divine logic to it. When the Eternal Word made Man left us and ascended to the Father, He left us Himself in His sacrifice veiled under the appearances of bread and wine. This act of love clearly lies within His divine power. It would have been merely human to leave us symbols of His presence, but since He is Divine He gave us His very

Self. After all, which human being in love with another would choose a merely symbolic contact instead of a flesh and blood relationship, if it lay within their power? Thus since it lies within God's power to change bread and wine into the Body and Blood of His Son, and mindful of His Son's promise 'I am with you always; yes, to the end of time' (Mt 28:20), it is in harmony with God's same power that He entrusted to His Church the power of consecrating the Body and Blood of His Son. In the *kenosis* of the Incarnation, the Word took flesh and dwelt among us. This self-emptying continued in the Redemption, when Christ's sufferings hid his divine beauty and finally in the Eucharist, where Christ further veils His glory under the appearances of bread and wine.[25] Hence what St Ignatius stated does not contradict the idea of St Thomas Aquinas, that those things which are received by faith from divine revelation cannot be contrary to our natural knowledge.[26]

In the present and actual historical conditions of humanity, however, men and women experience many difficulties in coming to know God by the light of reason alone. Human reason is, strictly speaking, truly capable by its own natural power and light of attaining to a true, real and certain knowledge of the one personal God, who watches over and controls the world by His providence; reason is also technically able to perceive the natural law written in our hearts by the Creator. However, there are many obstacles which prevent reason from the effective and fruitful use of this inborn faculty. The truths that concern the relations between God and man wholly transcend the visible order of things, and also, when one looks at the consequences and impact of this upon human choice and action, self-surrender and abnegation are called for, which may not be so very attractive. The human mind is hampered in the attaining of such truths, not only by the impact of the senses and the imagination, but also by disordered appetites which are the consequences of original sin. So it happens that people in such matters easily persuade themselves that what they would not like to be true is false or at least doubtful.[27] Human intelligence also sometimes experiences difficulties in forming a judgement about the credibility of Christianity, despite the many wonderful external signs God has given and continues to give, which are sufficient to prove with certitude by the natural light of reason alone the divine origin of the Christian religion. People are free and so can, whether from prejudice or confusion or even bad intentions, refuse, resist and reject not only the evidence of the external proofs, but also the impulses of actual grace.[28] Thus, the human person needs to be enlightened by God's revelation, not only about those things that exceed his understanding, but also concerning those religious and moral truths which of themselves can be grasped by human reason, so that 'even in the present condition of the human race, they can be known by all men with ease, with firm certainty and with no admixture of error.'[29] Reason is like a cup which is open and receptive to receive the wine of the faith.

As regards the effects of faith upon reason, these can be summarised in the Thomistic axiom that just as grace builds on nature and brings it to fulfilment, so faith builds upon and perfects reason.[30] Faith is not proud, it is not a cruel tyrant that dominates reason, nor does it contradict it: 'the stamp of truth is placed by God both on faith and on reason.'[31] As R. H. Benson pointed out, faith does not silence reason:

> Is Reason, then, to be silent henceforth? Why, the whole of theology gives the answer. Did Newman cease to think when he became a Catholic? Did Thomas Aquinas resign his intellect when he devoted himself to study? Not for one instant is Reason silent. On the contrary, she is active as never before. Certainly she is no longer occupied in examining as to whether the Church is divine, but instead she is busied, with incredible labours, in examining what follows from that fact, in sorting the new treasures that are opened to her with the dawn of Revelation upon her eyes, in arranging, deducting, and understanding the details and

structure of the astonishing Vision of Truth. And more, she is as inviolate as ever. For never can there be presented to her one article of Faith that gives the lie to her own nature, since Revelation and Reason cannot contradict one the other. She has learned, indeed, that the mysteries of God often transcend her powers, that she cannot fathom the infinite with the finite; yet never for one moment is she bidden to evacuate her own position or believe that which she perceives to be untrue. She has learned her limitations, and with that has come to understand her inviolable rights.[32]

The torch of faith radiates its light, a light which does not humiliate the intellect, and when it makes it kneel down in reverence, rather 'exalts it before the truth and truthfulness of God.'[33] Illumined by faith, reason is liberated from the fallenness and limitations deriving from the disobedience of sin and finds the strength required to rise to the knowledge of the Triune God. In a sense the act of faith possesses a sacramental property, it is an outward sign of inward grace. Revelation heals, elevates and perfects reason.

As has already been mentioned, the will also has a place in the act of faith. Faith is an act of the intellect assenting to a truth which is beyond its grasp, such as the mystery of the Holy Trinity. However, the intellect only assents to a statement for one of two reasons: either because that statement is immediately or mediately evident in itself, for example a first principle or a conclusion from premises, or because the will moves it to do so. Extrinsic evidence clearly comes into play when intrinsic evidence is wanting. Although it would be unreasonable, without weighty evidence in its support, to assent to a truth which we do not grasp, nevertheless no amount of this evidence can make us assent. It could only show that the statement in question was credible, and so our ultimate actual assent could only be due to the intrinsic evidence which the statement itself offered, or, failing that, due to the will. Therefore St Thomas repeatedly defines the act of faith as the assent of the intellect determined by the will.[34] The reason, then, why people cling to certain beliefs more tenaciously than the arguments in their favour would warrant, is to be sought in the will rather than in the intellect. Authorities are to be found on both sides, the intrinsic evidence is not convincing, but something is to be gained by assenting to one view rather than the other, and this appeals to the will, which therefore determines the intellect to assent to the view which promises the most. Similarly, in Divine faith the credentials of the authority which tells us that God has made certain revelations are strong, but they are always extrinsic to the proposition, 'God has revealed this or that', and consequently they cannot compel our assent; they merely show us that this statement is credible. The free assent can only be offered to any particular statement in the first place if there be strong extrinsic evidence in its favour, for to believe a thing merely because we wished to do so would be absurd. Second, the proposition itself does not compel our assent, since it is not intrinsically evident, but there remains the fact that only on condition of our assent to it shall we have what the human soul naturally yearns for, namely the possession of God, Who is, as both reason and authority declare, our ultimate End.

Just as the intellect needs a new and special light in order to assent to the supernatural truths of faith, so also the will needs a special grace from God in order that it may tend to that supernatural good which is eternal life. The light of faith, then, illumines the understanding, though the truth still remains obscure, since it is beyond the intellect's grasp; but supernatural grace moves the will, which, having now a supernatural good put before it, moves the intellect to assent to what it does not understand. Hence it is that faith is described as bringing 'every thought into captivity and obedience to Christ' (2 Co 10:5). In this way, grace heals the intellect and the will in the supernatural act of faith. As the First Vatican Council taught, 'faith is a supernatural virtue, by means of which, with the grace of God inspiring and assisting us, we believe to be true what He has revealed, not because we perceive its intrinsic truth by the natural light of reason, but because of the authority of God Himself, who makes the revelation and can neither deceive nor be deceived.'[35] Divine faith is supernatural both in the principle which elicits the acts and in the objects or truths which it holds. The principle which elicits assent to a truth which is beyond the grasp of the human mind must be that same mind illumined by a light superior to the light of reason, namely the light of faith. Even with this light of faith, the intellect remains human, and the truth to be believed remains still obscure, so that the final assent of the intellect must come from the will assisted by Divine grace. However, both this Divine light and this Divine grace are pure, gratuitous gifts of God. It is at this point that the adventure of faith enters in; the power of reason will lead to the antechamber of faith but there it leaves us. At this point, we must echo the words 'I have faith. Help my lack of faith!' (Mk 9:24). Or, as St Augustine expresses it: 'Where reason fails there faith builds up.'[36]

Hilaire Belloc affirmed that the Catholic Church offers a backbone of philosophy to present-day thought:

> Intellectual Europe today is again aware of the one consistent philosophy upon this earth which explains our little passage through the daylight; which gives a purpose to things and which presents not a mere hodgepodge of stories and unfounded assertions, but a whole chain and body of cause and effect in the moral world. It is further becoming apparent that there is, as yet, no rival in this respect to the Catholic Church. There is now no full alternative system left.[37]

The fact that human reason has this capacity to know God gives Christians a confidence in the possibility of speaking about Him to all people and with all people, and therefore of dialogue with people of other religions, with philosophers and scientists, as well as with unbelievers and atheists.[38] In this case, a synthetic approach is very much to be encouraged.

Reason and Synthesis

St Thomas, following Pseudo-Dionysius and St Albert the Great, applied the theory of analogy to the faith.[39] This forms the basis of the so-called analogy of faith. The First Vatican Council stated that if reason enlightened by faith enquires persistently, piously and soberly, it can achieve by God's grace some fruitful understanding of the mysteries of faith, both from the analogy with the objects of its natural knowledge and from the connection of these mysteries with one another and with the final end of humanity.[40] Before Revelation has taken place, analogy is unable to discover the mysteries of faith, since reason can know of God only what is manifested of Him and is in necessary causal relation with Him in created things. In the process of Revelation, analogy is necessary, since God cannot reveal the mysteries to men except through conceptions intelligible to the human mind, and therefore analogical. After Revelation has taken place, analogy is useful to give us certain knowledge of these mysteries, either by comparison with natural things and truths, or by consideration of the mysteries in relation to one another and to the destiny of man and woman. This forms the basis for forming a synthesis in theology, one of the greatest services which reason can render to faith.

Just as the cosmos, in the order of nature, is a unified whole, so also, in the realm of grace, the several aspects of the Christian faith make up a single hymn of praise in response to God the Creator Who reveals Himself in Christ. Faith is a response to the content of what God reveals, an example being the profession that God created the whole cosmos out of nothing. Without faith and reason together in various aspects, it is not possible to mould Christian theology into a global or synthetic understanding. In this picture, theology is like a large castle in which each stone has a value in the whole edifice: indeed if one brick is removed, damage is done to the whole building. Theology can also be compared to a seamless garment of many colours forming a unified whole. In a world where intense specialisation leads to fragmentation in many disciplines, including theology, it is more necessary than ever to see the unitary nature of this sacred science. Although the theological mystery is examined here from many facets, it remains a seamless whole. We always analyse in order to synthesise. Just as by dismantling an aeroplane, a mechanic may better understand how it works, so also the analytic process in theology furnishes a clearer perspective of the unified whole.

The point of departure for a unified approach to theology is that, according to the analogy of faith, all truths or dogmas are intimately linked with each other and with the entire economy of the deposit of revelation. Moreover, the doctrine of creation is the logical and ontological basis of all other doctrines: 'Without Creation, and a Creation by God who is Father, there is no possibility of a discourse about Incarnation, Redemption, and final consummation in a New Heaven and Earth.'[41] Three types of synthesis can be specified. The first is the kind belonging to one particular natural science or the interdisciplinary relations between a group of such sciences. The aim here is to obtain a unified view of a particular science, and difficult though this is, it is the object of reason. The second type of synthesis is that existing between mysteries which are accessible to faith alone, where the synthesis is a gift from God, and the aim is the contemplation of God Himself. This is the privileged domain of the mystic. The third variety of synthesis is the one relating truths which are the object of faith with those which are the object of reason. This work is theological, in which faith and grace guide reason.

A synthetic theological picture has the clear advantage of assisting perception of the organic unity of all theology, so indicating the one mystery revealed by Christ: 'The individual theological disciplines are to be taught in such a way that, from their internal structure and from the proper object of each as well as from their connection with other disciplines, including philosophical ones and the sciences of man, the basic unity of theological instruction is clear, and in such a way that all the disciplines converge in a profound understanding of the mystery of Christ, so that this can be announced with greater effectiveness to the People of God and to all nations.'[42]

A unified approach also has the advantage that it is stimulating to student and scholar alike, furnishing them with a sense of the relatedness of all truth. A synthesis differs from a mere system, where theological truths are organised for convenience or pragmatic pedagogical reasons; it respects the nature of the theological truths in themselves and never forces *a priori* relations between them where they are not appropriate. *Syncretism* is markedly different from synthesis, in that the former mixes together with Christian theology elements which may be alien and even opposed to it. Indeed many types of philosophy are incompatible with Christian faith and thus cannot be used in a synthesis of Catholic theology.[43] In the light of faith, therefore, the Church can and must authoritatively exercise a critical discernment of opinions and philosophies which contradict Christian doctrine. In particular it is important to indicate which philosophical presuppositions and conclusions are incompatible with revealed truth, thus articulating the demands which faith's point of view makes of philosophy.[44] In fact, it is precisely the realist philosophy which has been mentioned above that constitutes the metaphysics and epistemology germane to the construction of an organic vision of Catholic theology.

These observations are very pertinent to the study of relations between faith and reason, where it is all too easy to mingle together many elements from various religions, philosophical systems and scientific opinions and thus end up with confusion. 'It is important to emphasise that when theology employs the elements and conceptual tools of philosophy or other disciplines, discernment is needed. The ultimate normative principle for such discernment is revealed doctrine which itself must furnish the criteria for the evaluation of these elements and conceptual tools and not vice versa.'[45]

Various erroneous philosophies in vogue during the present times represent an obstacle to a synthetic view. The first inadequate approach goes by the name of *eclecticism*, by which is meant the tendency to use individual ideas drawn from different philosophies, without concern for their internal coherence and consistency, or for their place within a system or their historical context. The danger here is the incapacity to distinguish the partial truth of a given doctrine from elements of it which may be erroneous or ill-suited to the task at hand.[46]

A further error is that of *historicism*, which claims that the truth of a philosophy is determined on the basis of its appropriateness to a certain period and a certain historical purpose. At least implicitly, therefore, the enduring validity of truth is denied. Thus history is sometimes seen as the haphazard succession of sundry paradigms. This undermines the ontological basis of history, in much the same way that for logical positivists there is no ontological underpinning to language. What was true in one period, historicists claim, may not be true in another. Thus for them the history of thought becomes little more than an archaeological resource useful for illustrating positions once held, but for the most part outmoded and meaningless now. The historicist approach tends to forget that, 'even if a formulation is bound in some way by time and culture, the truth or the error which it expresses can invariably be identified and evaluated as such despite the distance of space and time.'[47] In philosophical and theological thought, historicism appears for the most part under the guise of *modernism*. The modernists based their thought on Kantian subjectivism and upon an evolutionary concept of truth. The modernist tendency towards a subjectivist and an evolutionary concept of truth coupled with a liberal approach to biblical criticism, led to an attempt to undermine the doctrine of the divine institution and divine and supernatural aspects of the Church. Since one of the fundamental principles of modernism was historical development, this system proposed a development based on purely human and social factors.

An additional threat to a synthetic view of philosophical and theological reality lies in *scientism*. This is the obstinate attitude that wants every area of human experience and reflection to be interpreted by the quantitative, experimental method of physical science. Scientism is also spoken of as *physicalism*, or the conviction that the method and concepts of physics provide the model for any science which claims to be 'exact.'[48] Scientism refuses to admit the validity of forms of knowledge other than those of the positive sciences; and it relegates religious, theological, ethical and aesthetic knowledge to the realm of mere fantasy.[49] Positivism and neo-positivism, which considered metaphysical statements to be meaningless, can be considered as under the umbrella of scientism.

A further obstacle is *pragmatism*, a widespread attitude of mind which, in making its choices, sets aside theoretical considerations or judgements based on ethical principles. The practical consequences of this mode of thinking are significant. In particular there is growing support for a concept of democracy which is not grounded upon any reference to unchanging values: whether or not a course of action is admissible is decided by the vote of a parliamentary majority. The consequences of this are clear: in practice, the great moral decisions of humanity are subordinated to decisions taken one after another by institutional agencies.[50] All these errors undermine the real rationality and reasonableness of human experience and replace it with systems based on the vortex of anarchy or upon the trap of totalitarianism.

Faith and the Irrational

It has already been seen that after the Middle Ages, there was an increasing tendency towards irrationalism in philosophy, which culminated in nihilism.[51] This tendency left faith rather naked, like a leap in the dark, without the humanity which befits this act of the mind and the heart towards God. We may say that while faith is reasonable, it is not simply rational, it cannot be reduced to reason and logic. Thus faith is deemed to be supra-rational or above reason, but it is certainly not irrational or against reason.

Atheism[52] is the worst form of irrationalism, for it robs reason of its highest Reference Point. It steals from reason its greatest and most noble task, the affirmation of God. If the affirmation of God is the supremely reasonable act which the intellect can make, then the negation of God is the greatest wound that the intellect can inflict upon itself, the most unreasonable and irrational action of which it is capable. Atheism is irrational because a denial of God also damages the cause of reason. That is, atheism, or non-theism, destroys the ground of reason as well as that of faith. This is because the affirmation of God is a task of reason, not purely of faith, and thus if reason is deprived of this task, it is left worse off or handicapped. This most irrational action brings with it untold harm, for the denial of God brings in its wake the destruction of the human being, even on a large scale as happened in the communist Soviet Union. The men and women of the present age have fallen victim to a new kind of atheism: the atheism of indifference that distances humanity from God as much as the radical and militant atheism that opposes religion. Today people dispense with God and intellectuals label themselves agnostics because they have not even asked themselves about the choice they must make before God. The Protestant distrust of reason, and the general denial of the proofs of the existence of God, making the affirmation of God purely an act of faith, in some ways left the door open to atheism. As the Second Vatican Council put it, atheism is a poisonous doctrine which contradicts reason and the common experience of humanity, and dethrones man from his native excellence.[53] When God is forgotten, the creature itself grows unintelligible.[54] Alongside atheism, agnosticism is the next worst form of irrational behaviour, as it denies to reason the power to affirm the existence of God. It often derives from an exaggerated emphasis on one kind of knowledge at the expense of an another. For example today's progress in science and technology can foster a certain exclusive emphasis on observable data, and an agnosticism about everything else.[55]

The issue of the irrational is related to the problem of evil. The question is often framed in the following terms: 'If God the Father almighty, the Creator of the ordered and good world, cares for all His creatures, why does evil exist?' This question is urgent, as many ask it, and is thus unavoidable. It is painful as it challenges both faith and reason. Finally it is mysterious, and no quick answer will suffice to answer the problem of evil.[56] A further question is 'Why did God not create a world so perfect that no evil could exist in it?' One answer is that with infinite power God could always create something better.[57] However, with infinite wisdom and goodness, God freely willed to create a world 'in pilgrimage' towards its ultimate perfection. In God's plan this process of becoming involves the appearance of certain beings and the disappearance of others, the existence of the more perfect alongside the less perfect, both constructive and destructive forces of nature. This allows the possibility that alongside physical good there exists also *physical evil* as long as creation has not reached perfection.[58] Even worse than physical evil is the *moral evil* which arises from the sins of rational creatures. God is in no way, directly or indirectly, the cause of moral evil.[59] God permits it, however, because He respects the freedom of His creatures and, mysteriously, knows how to derive good from it. Almighty God, because He is supremely good, would never allow any evil whatsoever to exist in His works if He were not so all-powerful and good as to cause good to emerge from evil itself.[60] It is possible that physical evil, such as earthquakes and other natural disasters, could, as has been argued elsewhere also be a secondary consequence of original sin.[61] Diabolical action against God's creation is also not to be excluded. Thus the irrationality of sin may even lie behind apparent physical evil.

Now evil is a privation of good; 'there is no such thing as a nature of evil, because all nature, as nature is good.'[62] St Augustine was one of the first Christian thinkers to stress this fundamental point, that evil is the privation of good:

> In this universe, even what is called evil, when it is rightly ordered and kept in its place, commends the good more eminently, since good things yield greater pleasure and praise when compared to the bad things. For the Omnipotent God, whom even the heathen acknowledge as the Supreme Power over all, would not allow any evil in His works, unless in His omnipotence and goodness, as the Supreme Good, He is able to bring forth good out of evil. What, after all, is anything we call evil except the privation of good? In animal bodies, for instance, sickness and wounds are nothing but the privation of health. When a cure is effected, the evils which were present (namely the sickness and the wounds) do not retreat and go elsewhere. Rather, they simply do not exist any more. For such evil is not a substance; the wound or the disease is a defect of the bodily substance which, as a substance, is good. Evil, then, is an accident, namely a privation of that good which is called health. Thus, whatever defects there are in a soul are privations of a natural good.[63]

Evil, therefore, has its origin, not in nature, but in the will. Sin is an action which is against the right use of reason. An accumulation of sins, which leads to great evils, causes great difficulties as regards affirmation of God. The existence of evil is sometimes used as a counter argument against proofs of God's existence. Nevertheless, evil is connected with free choices of rational creatures, and without freedom it is impossible to love. Sometimes, to counter the argument of those who maintain that evil represents an obstacle to the affirmation of God, the reply could be that what we see is only part of the mosaic, and that within the whole picture God can bring a final good out of evil, the supreme example being the crucifixion of His Son as the source of human salvation. From the greatest moral evil ever committed, the rejection and murder of God's only Son, caused by the sins of all men, God, by His grace that 'abounded all the more'(Rm 5:20), brought the greatest of goods: the glorification of Christ and our redemption. Nevertheless, evil is not simply imaginary nor does it ever become a good.[64] The very human capacity of being able rationally to identify evil for what it is, to reject it, and to perceive its incongruity in a good world created by God, is in itself a pointer towards God. As Josef Pieper pointed out: 'The incomprehensibility of evil in the world becomes fully apparent only against the background of the indestructible happiness of God.'[65] This very fact that all evil is to some degree shocking and remarkable triggers an argument for God's real existence.[66] Or, in other words, if the universe were chaotic and absurd, we would not be able to identify evil as evil.

However, the problem of evil is one area where reason can only give a partial response to the question. Only Christian faith as a whole furnishes an answer to this issue: the goodness of creation, the drama of sin and the patient love of God who comes to meet man by His covenants, the redemptive Incarnation of His Son, His gift of the Holy Spirit, His institution of the Church, the power of the sacraments and His call to a blessed life to which free creatures are invited to consent in advance, but from which they can also turn away.[67]

The approach to the relation between reason and belief can be a benchmark for distinguishing between the true religion and false ones. Christianity at least in its Catholic expression insists on a rational basis for belief. World religions outside Judaism and Christianity contain many irrational elements – hence the difficulty of interreligious dialogue. Where a religion is irrational, there is also the danger that the view of creation will be irrational and vice-versa. Nowhere does this problem become more apparent than in the problem of sects, or false religions which are based on indoctrination. The characteristics of a sect or a cult can be summed up as follows. It adopts psychological coercion to recruit, indoctrinate and retain members, because its teaching has no internal rational coherence. It forms an elitist society, because it is doomed to be a minority interest as it goes against what is human. Often it features a self-appointed leader who appears messianic, dogmatic and unaccountable. A further aspect where reason is left aside is that the 'end justifies the means' in the approach to recruitment and fundraising, and most often members do not share in the wealth of this rascal organisation. Typical techniques employed by cults include hypnosis, peer group pressure, deprivation of food and drink, and 'love bombing', creating a sense of belonging through constant hugging and flattery. Leaders may also bombard the new recruit with complex lectures on incomprehensible doctrine, which can break down rational thought, and implant subliminal messages by repeating slogans. It is quite clear that what a cult or sect means by terms such as 'God' is radically different from the Christian concept. Hence the necessity for Christians to provide rational discourse concerning belief in God, in order to counter the danger of sects.

Superstition is defined by St Thomas as 'a vice opposed to religion by way of excess; not because in the worship of God it does more than true religion, but because it offers Divine worship to beings other than God or offers worship to God in an improper manner.' Superstition sins by excess of religion, and this differs from the vice of irreligion, which sins by defect. The theological virtue of religion stands midway between the two.[68] Superstition comes in many varied forms, all of which are against faith, because they involve putting a trust without any basis, in inferior beings, and they also belittle reason and natural science. Some examples are divination which consists in the attempt to extract from creatures, by means of religious rites, a knowledge of future events or of things known to God alone; astrology, the reading of the future and of man's destiny from the stars; charms and amulets, or objects worn as a protection or remedy against evils; palmistry, or divination by the lines of the hand; cartomancy, divination by playing cards; necromancy, the evocation of the dead, as old as history and perpetuated in modern spiritism; the use of potions or charms intended to arouse love; oneiromancy, the superstitious interpretation of dreams; lucky and unlucky days, numbers, persons, things, actions; the use of fortune-tellers and horoscopes to divine the future. Even more serious in terms of false religion are devil-worship, witchcraft and magic in all their ramifications. Widespread superstition was to a great extent eliminated by the preaching of Christianity and the rise of science. Nevertheless, it has returned in new forms in a post-Christian epoch.

The paradox is that in a highly developed scientific and technological age, more and more people seem to be turning to sects and superstition. It is strange but true that in a cultural climate where people believe in nothing, they are inclined to believe in anything. Perhaps the reason is that, experiencing a basic need for the spiritual, and having turned their back on the true faith, men and women of today try out false religions, esoteric cults and occult sciences to satisfy their hunger for God. In a sense, the world of religious experience has become a supermarket where commercial interest counts above all. These sects can easily flourish in a world in which the new cultural model proposes the rejection of reason in favor of emotions. In a society where there is information overload, and people receive an avalanche of stimulation from the media, many take the easy way of survival by drifting, without major worries, passing from idea to idea without any problem. Thus they fall victim to sects.

Thus in the present age, scientific and technical prowess exist cheek by jowl with superstition and astrology, the twin ancient enemies of both reason and of faith. They are indeed ancient, because they existed way back in the Patristic era, as St John Damascene testifies:

> So, then, it is the sun that makes the seasons, and through them the year: it likewise makes the days and nights, the days when it rises and is above the earth, and the nights when it sets below the earth: and it bestows on the other luminaries, both moon and stars, their power of giving forth light. Further, they say that there are in the heavens twelve signs made by the stars, and that these move in an opposite direction to the sun and moon, and the other five planets, and that the seven planets pass across these twelve signs. Further, the sun makes a complete month in each sign and traverses the twelve signs in the same number of months .... But the moon traverses the twelve signs each month, since it occupies a lower position and travels through the signs at a quicker rate. For if you draw one circle within another, the inner one will be found to be the lesser: and so it is that owing to the moon occupying a lower position its course is shorter and is sooner completed. Now the heathens declare that all our affairs are controlled by the rising and setting and interaction of these heavenly bodies: astrology deals with these matters. But we hold that we get from them signs of rain and drought, cold and heat, moisture and dryness, and of the various winds, and so forth, but no sign whatever as to our actions. For we have been created with free wills by our Creator and are masters over our own actions. Indeed, if all our actions depend on the courses of the stars, all we do is done of necessity: and necessity precludes either virtue or vice. But if we possess neither virtue nor vice, we do not deserve praise or punishment, and God, too, will turn out to be unjust, since He gives good things to some and afflicts others. Indeed, He will no longer continue to guide or provide for His own creatures, if all things are carried and swept along in the grip of necessity. And the faculty of reason will be superfluous to us: for if we are not masters of any of our actions, deliberation is quite superfluous.

Reason, indeed, is granted to us solely that we might take counsel, and hence all reason implies freedom of will.[69]

Modern neo-paganism also involves a flirting with the irrationality of eternal cycles and reincarnation, false notions which New Testament writers warned against.[70] The great remedy to irrational superstition is a faith informed by reason and by love, which will be examined in the next and final chapter.

Notes

1 Hugh of St Victor, *De sacramentis* I, III, 30 in *PL* 176, 232. The Latin expression is 'fides ratione adiuvetur et ratio fide perficitur.'

2 See chapter 4, pp. 91–92 above, where we discussed St Thomas Aquinas' doctrine on this subject.

3 See St Thomas Aquinas, *Summa Theologiae*, II–II, q. 1, a. 2.

4 St Thomas Aquinas, *Summa Theologiae*, II–II, q. 4, a. 2.

5 Vatican I, *Dei Filius*, chapter III in ND 118.

6 St Thomas Aquinas, *Summa Theologiae*, I–II, q. 56.

7 St Augustine, *Enarratio in Ps 118*, Sermon xviii, 3 in *PL* 37, 1552. The Latin texts reads: 'Proficit ergo noster intellectus ad intelligenda quae credat, et fides proficit ad credenda quae intelligat; et eadem ipsa ut magis magisque intelligantur, in ipso intellectu proficit mens. Sed hoc non fit propriis tanquam naturalibus viribus, sed Deo adjuvante atque donante; sicut medicina fit, non natura, ut vitiatus oculus vim cernendi recipiat.'

8 Vatican I, *Dei Filius* chapter III in ND 120.

9 Vatican I, *Dei Filius* chapter III in ND 119.

10 St Thomas Aquinas, *Summa Theologiae*, II–II, q. 1, a. 4.

11 See chapter 7, p. 210 above.

12 For some examples of the fulfilment of Old Testament prophecies in the New Testament, see chapter 7, pp. 217–218 endnote 56 above.

13 Vatican I, *Dei Filius* chapter III. Italics mine.

14 St Augustine, *Sermon* 242, chapter 8, n. 12 in *PL* 38, 1143. The Latin is 'Illi videbant caput, et credebant de corpore: nos videmus corpus, credamus de capite.'

15 St Thomas Aquinas, *De Veritate*, q. 14, a. 8.

16 Vatican I, *Dei Filius*, canon 5 on chapter 3 in DS 129.

17 See St Thomas Aquinas, *Commentary on Book 3 of the Sentences*, d. 24, q. 1, a. 2.

18 Pope Leo XIII, Encyclical *Aeterni Patris* 5.

19 R. H. Benson, *Paradoxes of Catholicism* (New York: Longmans, Green

and Co., 1913), pp. 86–87.

[20] Pope Leo XIII, Encyclical *Providentissus Deus* 23.

[21] Vatican II, *Gaudium et Spes* 36.

[22] Vatican II, *Gaudium et Spes* 34.

[23] See Vatican I, *Dei Filius*, chapter IV.

[24] St Ignatius of Loyola, *The Spiritual Exercises* (Trans. T. Corbishley) (Wheathamstead: Anthony Clarke, 1979) n. 365, p. 122. I am very grateful to Fr. J. M. McDermott, SJ, for his kind help regarding the interpretation of this passage. Personally, I feel it may be unwise to push St Ignatius' axiom too far, especially in matters of discipline, as voluntarism would ensue.

[25] See my work, *The Sacramental Mystery* (Leominster: Gracewing, 1999) pp. 84–85.

[26] See St Thomas Aquinas, *Summa Contra Gentiles*, Book 1, chapter 7: 'Ea igitur quae ex revelatione divina per fidem tenentur, non possunt naturali cognitioni esse contraria.'

[27] See CCC 37. See also Pope Pius XII, Encyclical *Humani Generis* 2.

[28] See Pope Pius XII, *Humani generis* 4. Actual grace denotes the special graces that come to us from God to enable us to perform specific 'acts', including coming to faith.

[29] Vatican I, *Dei Filius*, chapter II in ND 114.

[30] See St Thomas Aquinas, *Summa Theologiae*, I, q. 1, a. 8: 'cum enim gratia non tollat naturam sed perficiat.' See also pp. 90–91 above.

[31] Pope Pius XII, *Discourse to the Pontifical Academy of Sciences*, 3 December 1939 in *DP*, p. 37.

[32] Benson, *Paradoxes of Catholicism*, pp. 91–92.

[33] Pope Pius XII, *Discourse to University Youth*, 20 April 1941 in M. Chinigo (ed.), *The Teachings of Pope Pius XII* (London: Metheuen, 1958), p. 146.

[34] See St Thomas Aquinas, *De Veritate*, q. 14, a. 1; *Summa Theologiae*, II–II, q. 2, a. 1,; ibid., q. 4, a. 1.

[35] Vatican I, *Dei Filius* chapter III in DS 3008. See also H. Pope, 'Faith' in *The Catholic Encyclopaedia* 5 (New York: Robert Appleton Co., 1909) pp. 752–759.

[36] St Augustine, *Sermo* 247, 2 in *PL* 38, 1157. The Latin expression is: 'Ubi defecit ratio, ibi est fidei aedificatio.'

[37] H. Belloc, *Survivals and New Arrivals* (London: Sheed and Ward, 1939), pp. 283–284.

[38] See CCC 39.

[39] Cf. St Thomas, *Summa Theologiae*, I, q. 1, a. 9; q. 22, a. 1; *Commentary on Boethius' De Trinitate*, Part 1, q. 1, a. 1.

[40] See Vatican I, *Dei Filius*, chapter 4 in DS 3016.

[41] S. L. Jaki, *Cosmos and Creator* (Edinburgh: Scottish Academic Press, 1980) p. 56. Cardinal Ratzinger makes the same point when he states: 'It is not accidental that the Apostles' Creed begins with the

confession: «I believe in God the Father Almighty, Creator of heaven and earth.» This primordial faith in the Creator God (a God who really is God) forms the pivot, as it were, about which all the other Christian truths turn. If vacillation sets in here, all the rest comes tumbling down.' J. Card. Ratzinger and V. Messori, *The Ratzinger Report* (Leominster: Fowler Wright Books, 1985) p. 78.

42 Pope John Paul II, Apostolic Constitution *Sapientia Christiana* (1979) 67 §2. See Vatican I, Dogmatic Constitution *Dei Filius* Chapter IV 'Faith and Reason' in DS 3016 (English translation ND 132) which describes 'the connection of these mysteries with one another.'

43 See, for example, the discourse of Pope John Paul II to the American bishops, 15 October 1988 in OR 248/128 (16 October 1988), p. 4: 'Not every philosophy is capable of providing that solid and coherent understanding of the human person, of the world, and of God which is necessary for any theological system that strives to place its knowledge in continuity with knowledge of faith.'

44 See John Paul II, *Fides et Ratio* 50.

45 Congregation for the Doctrine of the Faith, *Instruction on the Ecclesial Vocation of the Theologian* (Vatican City: Libreria Editrice Vaticana, 1990), 10.4.

46 See John Paul II, *Fides et Ratio* 86.

47 Ibid., 87.

48 S. L. Jaki, *The Absolute Beneath the Relative and Other Essays* (Lanham, MD: University Press of America, 1988), p. 211, note 3.

49 See John Paul II, *Fides et Ratio* 88. See also pp. 14–15 above.

50 See Ibid.

51 See pp. 17–18, 139–140 above.

52 A good analysis of atheism is found in Vatican II, *Gaudium et Spes* 19: 'The word atheism is applied to phenomena which are quite distinct from one another. For while God is expressly denied by some, others believe that man can assert absolutely nothing about Him. Still others use such a method to scrutinize the question of God as to make it seem devoid of meaning. Many, unduly transgressing the limits of the positive sciences, contend that everything can be explained by this kind of scientific reasoning alone, or by contrast, they altogether disallow that there is any absolute truth. Some laud man so extravagantly that their faith in God lapses into a kind of anaemia, though they seem more inclined to affirm man than to deny God. Again some form for themselves such a fallacious idea of God that when they repudiate this figment they are by no means rejecting the God of the Gospel. Some never get to the point of raising questions about God, since they seem to experience no religious stirrings nor do they see why they should trouble themselves about religion. Moreover, atheism results not rarely from a violent protest against the evil in this world, or from the absolute

character with which certain human values are unduly invested, and which thereby already accords them the stature of God. Modern civilization itself often complicates the approach to God not for any essential reason but because it is so heavily engrossed in earthly affairs.'

53   Cf. Vatican II, *Gaudium et Spes* 21.

54   See Ibid. 36.

55   See Ibid. 57.

56   See *CCC* 309.

57   Cf. St Thomas Aquinas, *Summa Theologiae*, I, q. 25, a. 6. See also See my *Mystery of Creation* (Leominster: Gracewing, 1995), p. 57.

58   Cf. St Thomas Aquinas, *Summa Contra Gentiles* III, 71.

59   Cf. St Augustine, *De libero arbitrio*, Book 1, chapter 1, n. 1 in *PL* 32, 1221–1223; St Thomas Aquinas, *Summa Theologiae*, I–II, q. 79, a. 1.

60   See St Augustine, *Enchiridion*, chapter 11 in *PL* 40, 236.

61   See my *Mystery of Creation*, p. 191.

62   Council of Florence, *Decree for the Copts* in DS 1333. Se also St Thomas Aquinas, *Summa Theologiae*, I, q. 48, a. 1.

63   St Augustine, *Enchiridion*, chapter 11 in *PL* 40, 236.

64   See *CCC* 312.

65   J. Pieper, *Happiness and Contemplation* translated by R. & C. Winston (New York: Pantheon Books, 1958), p. 31.

66   See St Thomas Aquinas, *Summa Contra Gentiles*, Book 3, chapter 71: 'A certain philosopher ... asks: "If God exists, whence comes evil?" But it could be argued to the contrary: "If evil exists, God exists." For, there would be no evil if the order of good were taken away, since its privation is evil. But this order would not exist if there were no God.'

67   See *CCC* 309.

68   Cf. St Thomas Aquinas, *Summa Theologiae*, II–II, q. 92, a. 1.

69   St John Damascene, *De fide orthodoxa*, Book 2, Chapter 7 in *PG* 94, 891–894.

70   See Hebrews 9:27–28 and Romans 6:10.

CHAPTER 9

THE MIND AND THE HEART OF FAITH

Our mind is never so filled with pleasure as during such thoughts of the divinity .... This pleasure, this confidence that man's heart naturally has in God, assuredly comes from nowhere but the congruity existing between God's goodness and the soul. It is a great but secret congruity; a congruity that all men know but few understand, a congruity that can neither be denied nor easily penetrated. We are created to the image and likeness of God.

St Francis de Sales, *Treatise on the Love of God*

God keeps His holy mysteries
Just on the outside of man's dream;
In diapason slow, we think
To hear their pinions rise and sink,
While they float pure beneath His eyes,
Like swans adown a stream.

Abstractions, are they, from the forms
Of His great beauty? – exaltations
From His great glory? – strong previsions
Of what we shall be? – intuitions
Of what we are – in calms and storms,
Beyond our peace and passions?

Things nameless! which, in passing so,
Do stroke us with a subtle grace.

> *We say, 'Who passes?' – they are dumb.*
> *We cannot see them go or come:*
> *Their touches fall soft, cold, as snow*
> *Upon a blind man's face.*
>
> *Yet, touching so, they draw above*
> *Our common thoughts to Heaven's unknown,*
> *Our daily joy and pain advance*
> *To a divine significance,*
> *Our human love – O mortal love,*
> *That light is not its own!*
>
> Elizabeth Barrett Browning,
> 'Human Life's Mystery'

Love and Reason

In the Hebrew mentality of the Scriptures, the heart (*lēb*) does not represent, as one may think at first sight, the centre of love and emotions, but rather of the mind and the will together. The heart is thus the organ of thought rather than of feeling. The Semitic mentality considered the human being as a unity, an animated body, while the Greeks tended to the idea of an incarnate spirit.[1] Thus, in the biblical vision, the whole person responds to God who reveals Himself in creation, in history and in His incarnate Word. Earlier on, it has been observed that St Thomas often defines the act of faith as the assent of the intellect determined by the will.[2] Therefore, both the mind and the heart have a part to play in the adventure of faith. The genius of the medieval synthesis was that the mind and heart were sustained together in harmonious and organic unity, but in modern times they have been separated with disastrous results. For example, when love is exaggerated at the expense of reason, there develops a heady and inconsistent fundamentalism. On the other hand when reason is exaggerated at the expense of love, a dry and dusty rationalism is obtained. Reason alone is insufficient to accompany faith, which would remain dry and sterile without love; St James stresses this very clearly with his statement that faith without works is dead: 'You believe in the one God – that is creditable enough, but even the demons have the same belief, and they tremble with fear' (Jas 2:19). Now the motive for works or actions is love, therefore faith without love is dead. However at the same time, a faith based purely on the will without reason would be a faith without solid foundation.

According to Kant, the only object of theoretical reason is the world of phenomena; the validity of the principle of causality is restricted to what can be perceived through the senses. Thus Kant rejected all the proofs of God's existence, save the ontological argument. God's existence then became a postulate of practical reason. Kant's philosophy influenced Protestant theology of the nineteenth century, which also rejected natural theology and the rational foundation of religion. For F. Schleiermacher (1768–1834), in the German Romantic perspective, religious concepts in general and the idea of God in particular, are derived from sentiment. This idea fathered many themes in modern theology based on personal and individual religious experience, with a sharp separation of knowledge from faith. However, the experience of God without objective truth can become simply an experience of our own selves. To this day, the affective side of faith is perhaps overstressed at the expense of its rational basis.

This approach in which faith is based purely on sentiment was criticised by Pope Pius XII:

> Finally, they reproach this philosophy taught in our schools for regarding only the intellect in the process of cognition, while neglecting the function of the will and the emotions. This is simply not true. Never has Christian philosophy denied the usefulness and efficacy of good dispositions of soul for perceiving and embracing moral and religious truths. In fact, it has always taught that the lack of these dispositions of good will can be the reason why the intellect, influenced by the passions and evil inclinations, can be so obscured that it cannot see clearly.

Indeed, St Thomas holds that the intellect can in some way perceive higher goods of the moral order, whether natural or supernatural, inasmuch as it experiences a certain 'connaturality' with these goods, whether this 'connaturality' be purely natural, or the result of grace; and it is clear how much even this somewhat obscure perception can help the reason in its investigations. However it is one thing to admit the power of the dispositions of the will in helping reason to gain a more certain and firm knowledge of moral truths; it is quite another thing to say, as these innovators do, indiscriminately mingling cognition and act of will, that the appetitive and affective faculties have a certain power of understanding, and that man, since he cannot by using his reason decide with certainty what is true and is to be accepted, turns to his will, by which he freely chooses among opposite opinions.[3]

C. S. Lewis (1898–1963) also suggested that it was foolhardy to base religion on pure sentiment:

Doctrines are not God: they are only a kind of map. But the map is based on the experience of hundreds of people who really were in touch with God – experiences compared with which any thrills or pious feelings you or I are likely to get on our own way are very elementary and very confused. And secondly, if you want to get any further, you must use the map ... [This] is just why a vague religion – all about feeling God in nature, and so on – is so attractive. It is all thrills and no work; like watching the waves from the beach. But you will not get to Newfoundland by studying the Atlantic that way, and you will not get eternal life by simply feeling the presence of God in flowers or music. Neither will you get anywhere by looking at maps without going to sea. Nor will you be very safe if you go to sea without a map.[4]

In some ways, reason corresponds to the content aspect of faith, and love corresponds to the commitment aspect of faith. It is necessary to hold both aspects together in order that both faith and reason are healthy and balanced.

As regards the relation between knowledge and love,

St Thomas Aquinas, following on from St Augustine, suggested that nothing can be loved unless it has been known beforehand.[5] St Augustine allowed a nuance in his own formulation, and as regards the love of God admitted: 'Even He therefore who is not known, but yet is believed, can be loved.'[6] Moving on from here, interpersonal relationships and other areas of human experience indicate that the axiom 'nothing can be known unless it has been loved beforehand' can also be true.[7] Namely love is a great stimulus in knowing people. This is the Franciscan approach which tends to put the primacy on love. Augustine also lays this emphasis in his expression 'love is the weight by which I act. To whatever place I go, I am drawn to it by love.'[8] St Thomas Aquinas also stressed that love is a motivation to see the truth, in his adage 'where love is, there vision will be also.'[9] Therefore in the dynamic relationship between the mind and the heart, both reason and love have their own respective parts to play.

Faith has therefore a mind and a heart, because human persons, as distinct from the animals, possess two specific features, which are hallmarks of spiritual being. These are knowing, through the intellect, and love, especially through the power of the will. It is through these faculties that humans relate to being, to each other and ultimately to God. Wisdom, or the grasp of the ultimate principles of being, can be distinguished by a logical differentiation into *sophia* and *phronesis*. *Sophia* is the speculative understanding exercised by the intellect, linked with that which is true. *Phronesis* is the practical wisdom or judgement whereby the will orders life to its proper end; this aspect is connected with that which is good. *Sophia* and *phronesis* are united, and ultimately truth and goodness come together in wisdom. A person's relationship with being is based on truth, goodness, and wisdom. The relationship of the intellect to being, namely knowledge, seeks truth. The relationship of the will to being, namely love, seeks the good. Truth and goodness are essentially linked with being and are joined by wisdom. Therefore, love and knowledge must have a fundamental unity. Knowledge without love cannot act and love without knowledge cannot know what is truly good, just as *sophia* and *phronesis* can only function properly when joined. It follows that the intellect and the will are connected faculties. This corresponds to the attribute of unity, which denotes inner integrity or wholeness. This unity is dynamic and manifests itself in a wise, ordered life.

Ultimately, knowledge and love, *sophia* and *phronesis*, share the same Source and the same Destiny. Knowledge in its quest for truth will at last reach God as ultimate Truth. Love in its pursuit of good will finally arrive at God as infinite Good. God is the pure actualisation of truth and goodness, that is, Being Himself. From this conclusion, we can see that there must be a God; otherwise, there would be no ultimate end and life would be utterly meaningless. Love and knowledge are thus inextricably bound together in man's very nature and if we live according to our nature, they will guide us straight to our Source and Ultimate End. This union is achieved through a life lived in the cultivation of virtue on our part, and by God's perfect love for us that constantly draws us toward Him. If we do not follow this natural path of love and knowledge, we will only find emptiness and despair, since our nature will never be fulfilled.

However both reason and love are true gifts of God. St Augustine expresses it thus, 'What, then, is it to believe in God? It is to love Him by believing, to go to Him by believing, and to be incorporated in His members. This, then, is the faith which God demands of us; and He does not find what He may demand except where He has given what He may find.'[10] This is what is meant by 'living' faith, or faith which is 'informed' by charity, or love of God. If faith is seen only as an assent elicited by the intellect, then this bare faith has not the true character of a moral virtue and is not a source of merit. Only when it is inflamed by charity does this faith become fired with the habitual sanctifying grace of God which alone gives to the will that due tendency to God as man's supernatural end which is requisite for supernatural and meritorious acts.

Following St Augustine, William of St Thierry saw the mind and heart of the human person as a reflection and image of the mystery of the Most Holy Trinity. This image was imprinted upon man and woman at the creation. William envisaged three faculties which reflect the Holy Trinity, the memory, the intellect and the will. In particular, the memory is important since through this faculty, the human being can always remember the power and the goodness of his Creator. The memory generates reason from itself, and then memory and reason by themselves produce the will. These three faculties make up a unity, even if they exercise a threefold action, just as in the Holy Trinity, there are three Persons and one substance. For William, just as the Father generates, the Son is generated and the Holy Spirit proceeds from the Father and the Son, so for the human being, reason is generated from memory, and from memory and reason proceeds the will. Thus the Father is associated with the memory, the Son with reason and the Holy Spirit with the will.[11] For William, the two eyes for seeing God are love and reason, which are constantly palpitating in a kind of natural tension. If one of these eyes tries to operate without the other, it does not make much progress. Instead, if both work together, they become very powerful and in a sense become one single eye. The process is, however, not easy, because one of the eyes, namely reason, can only see God in what He is not, while love only rests in what God is. William thus traces a perceptive connection of reason with the negative way to God and love with the positive way to God.[12] The basis for this affirmation is that reason requires secure paths upon which to travel; on the other hand, love journeys onward despite its inadequacy, and understands better through its ignorance. Thus reason seems to proceed through that which is not towards that which is, while love, leaving aside that which is not is content to immerse itself in that which is. Reason enjoys a greater degree of sobriety, while love possesses a greater degree of happiness. When these two faculties co-operate with one another, reason teaches love and love enlightens reason. In this happy collaboration, reason leaves room for the sentiment of love, and love is happy to be contained within the limits of reason.[13]

In his mystical theology, St Bonaventure pointed out the limitations of reason in a discourse about God, at the same time indicating Christ as the source of wisdom, and the Holy Spirit as the source of love:

> Christ is both the way and the door. Christ is the staircase and the vehicle, like the throne of mercy over the Ark of the Covenant, and the mystery hidden from the ages. A man should turn his full attention to this throne of mercy, and should gaze at Him hanging on the cross, full of faith, hope and charity, devoted, full of wonder and joy, marked by gratitude, and open to praise and jubilation. Then such a man will make with Christ a pasch, that is, a passing-over. Through the branches of the cross he will pass over the Red Sea, leaving Egypt and entering the desert. There he will taste the hidden manna, and rest with Christ in the sepulchre, as if he were dead to things outside. He will experience, as much as is possible for one who is still living, what was promised to the thief who hung beside Christ: Today you will be with me in paradise... For this passover to be perfect, we must suspend all the operations of the mind and we must transform the peak of our affections, directing them to God alone. This is a sacred mystical experience. It cannot be comprehended by anyone unless he surrenders himself to it; nor can he surrender himself to it unless he longs for it; nor can he long for it unless the Holy Spirit, whom Christ sent into the world, should come and inflame his innermost soul....If you ask how such things can occur, seek the answer in God's grace, not in doctrine; in the longing of the will, not in the understanding; in the sighs of prayer, not in research; seek the bridegroom not the teacher; God and not man; darkness not daylight; and look not to the light but rather to the raging fire that carries the soul to God with intense fervour

and glowing love. The fire is God, and the furnace is in Jerusalem, fired by Christ in the ardour of his loving passion.[14]

A further issue is whether there is a natural love or desire for God, just as there exists a natural knowledge of God. St Francis de Sales (1567–1622) discussed this issue in detail. He proposed that we do indeed have a natural inclination to love God above all things:

> The divine heavenly Author and Master of nature works with fire and lends His mighty hand to it so that it leaps upward, with water so that it flows downward to the sea, with earth so that it sinks lower and remains there when it finds its place. So too He has planted in man's heart a special natural inclination not only to love good in general but to love in particular and above all things His divine goodness, which is better and more loving than all things. Hence the sweetness of His supreme providence required that He would contribute to those fortunate men of whom we speak such help as would be necessary to put into practice and to effectuate that inclination.[15]

God bestowed upon man both natural and supernatural aids for loving Him. The natural aid, being consonant with nature, tends to the love of God as Author and sovereign Master of nature, and the supernatural help corresponds not just to the simple nature of man, but to nature adorned, enriched and honoured by original justice, which is a supernatural quality proceeding from a very special free gift of God. In particular, as regards the love above all things which such help would enable people to practise, it would be called natural, because virtuous actions take their names from their objects and motives, and this love of which we speak would only tend to God as acknowledged to be Author, Lord and Sovereign of every creature by natural light only, and consequently to be amiable and estimable above all things by natural inclination and tendency. If man and woman had not fallen through original sin, not only would they have possessed this natural inclination to love God but even naturally would be able to carry out this inclination. Human nature is no longer endowed with that original soundness and righteousness which the first man had in his creation, but on the contrary is greatly depraved by sin. Nevertheless, 'that holy inclination to love God above all things remains with us, as does the natural light by which we know that His supreme goodness is loveable above all things.' Thus St Francis de Sales points to a natural love of God alongside the natural light of reason, and actually affirms that 'it is impossible for a man who thinks attentively about God even by natural reason alone, not to feel a certain glow of love.'[16] A natural love immediately follows on from the first knowledge of God that the human being acquires.[17]

Despite the fact that human beings have a natural inclination to love God above all things, after the Fall they do not possess the power to carry through this inclination. St Francis de Sales applies an analogy to illustrate his point. Eagles are very strong in flight, yet they have incomparably more sight than flight, and extend their vision much quicker and further than their wings. So our souls, animated with a holy natural inclination towards God, possess far more light in the understanding to see how loveable God is, than power in the will to love Him. Sin has caused a greater weakening in man's will than the darkening which it has effected in his intellect, and the rebellion of the sensual appetite, which we call concupiscence, does indeed disturb the understanding, but still it is against the will that it principally stirs up sedition and revolt. Hence 'the poor will, already very weak, is shaken by the continual assaults which concupiscence launches against it and it cannot make as much progress in divine love as reason and natural inclination indicate it should.'[18] Various philosophers can be marshalled as testimonies not only of a great knowledge of God, but also of a strong inclination towards him. These great philosophers include Socrates, Plato, Aristotle, Hippocrates, and Seneca.

Socrates, the most highly praised amongst them, came to the clear knowledge of the unity of God, and felt in himself such an inclination to love Him, that many were of the opinion that he never had any other aim in teaching moral philosophy than to purify minds that they might better contemplate the sovereign good, which is the simple unity of the Divinity. Plato declared in his definition of philosophy and of the philosopher, that to be a philosopher is nothing else but to love God, and that a philosopher is none other than a lover of God. Aristotle tried to prove the unity of God and spoke honourably of this in many places. Nevertheless, these ancient thinkers who experienced a strong inclination to love God were all lacking in strength and courage to love Him well. They glorified Him in some ways, attributing to Him titles of honour, yet they did not glorify Him as they ought, that is, they did not glorify Him above all things. They lacked the courage to destroy idolatry, but compromising with idolaters, they held the truth prisoner in their hearts, and preferred the honour and comfort of their lives above the honour due to God. An example of this lack is seen in Socrates who, as Plato reports, spoke upon his deathbed concerning the gods as though there had been many, yet he knew so well that there was but One only. Also, Plato who understood so clearly the truth of the divine unity ordained that sacrifice should be offered to many gods.

St Francis de Sales also compares the wounded and wretched human nature with the palm-tree growing in a colder climate. This tree attains some imperfect progress and produces some immature and deformed fruits, but in order to bear entire, ripe and seasoned dates, a hotter climate is needed. In like manner, the human heart naturally produces certain beginnings of God's love. However, 'to advance as far as loving Him above all things, which is the true ripeness of the love owed to such supreme goodness, belongs only to hearts animated and assisted by heavenly grace, and in the state of holy charity.'[19] This little imperfect love of which nature by itself feels the stirrings, is but a will without will, a will that would but wills not, a sterile will, which does not produce true effects, 'a paralytic will which sees the healthful pond of holy love, but does not have the strength to throw itself into that pool.'[20]

While this natural inclination to love God is partial and incomplete, it is not useless. When man and woman fell through original sin, God was very merciful and did not take away all the resemblance to the Creator which the human being naturally possesses. God left the natural light of reason in our minds so we could seek and find Him and imparted to our hearts the natural inclination to love Him. For though by this mere natural inclination we cannot be so happy as to love God as we ought, yet if we employed it faithfully, the sweetness of the divine piety would afford us some assistance, by which we might make progress. If we co-operated with this first assistance, the paternal goodness of God would bestow upon us another greater gift, and lead us from good to better in all sweetness, till He brought us to the sovereign love, to which our natural inclination impels us: since it is certain that to him who is faithful in a little, and who does what is in his power, the divine goodness never denies its assistance to advance him more and more.

This natural inclination in the human heart to love God above all things has a purpose. On God's part it is a handle by which He can hold us and draw us to Himself; and the divine goodness seems in some way to keep our hearts tied as little birds on a string, by which He can draw us when it pleases His mercy to take pity upon us. On our part it is a mark and memorial of our first principle and Creator, to Whose love it moves us, giving us a secret intimation that we belong to His divine goodness.

The beautiful inclination which God has left impressed in our hearts testifies that we have a natural sense of belonging to our Creator, and furthermore, though He has let us go at the mercy of our free will, that we still belong to Him, and that He has reserved the right of taking us again to Himself, to save us, according as His holy and gracious providence shall require. Hence this inclination is not only a light, in that it makes us see where we are to go, but also a joy and gladness, for it comforts us when we stray, giving us a hope that He who engraved and left in us this clear sign of our origin intends also and desires to bring us back to it, if we be so happy as to let ourselves be taken back by His divine goodness.[21]

A further figure who attempted to balance the mind and the heart of religion was Blaise Pascal, when he delineated the respective rôles played by reason and love in the search for truth. For Pascal, truth is known not only by the mind, but also by the heart, and it is through the heart that we know first principles. Reason tries in vain to challenge these first principles. The sceptics, whose aim is to make this challenge, labour to no purpose. We know that we do not dream, and, however impossible it is for us to prove it by reason, this inability demonstrates only the weakness of our reason, but not, as they affirm, the uncertainty of all our knowledge. For the knowledge of first principles, such as space, time, motion, number, is as sure as any of those items which we obtain from reasoning. Reason must therefore trust these intuitions of the heart, and must base every argument upon them. Pascal claimed that we have intuitive knowledge of the three-dimensional nature of space and of the infinity of number, while reason shows that there are no two square numbers one of which is double the other. For him, principles are intuited, propositions are inferred, all with certainty, though in different ways. Hence for Pascal 'it is as useless and absurd for reason to demand from the heart proofs of her first principles, before admitting them, as it would be for the heart to demand from reason an intuition of all demonstrated propositions before accepting them.'[22]

St John of the Cross discussed the purification which the mind and the heart must undergo in order to arrive at a deeper union with God. According to him, faith radically purifies the understanding, charity purifies the will, and, interestingly, it is the virtue of hope which purifies the memory:

> This, then, is the disguise which the soul says that it wears in the night of faith, upon this secret ladder, and these are its three colours. They constitute a most fit preparation for the union of the soul with God, according to its three faculties, which are understanding, memory and will. For faith voids and darkens the understanding as to all its natural intelligence, and herein prepares it for union with Divine Wisdom. Hope voids and withdraws the memory from all creature possessions; for, as Saint Paul says, hope is for that which is not possessed; and thus it withdraws the memory from that which it is capable of possessing, and sets it on that for which it hopes. And for this cause hope in God alone prepares the memory purely for union with God. Charity, in the same way, voids and annihilates the affections and desires of the will for whatever is not God, and sets them upon Him alone; and thus this virtue prepares this faculty and unites it with God through love. And thus, since the function of these virtues is the withdrawal of the soul from all that is less than God, their function is consequently that of joining it with God.[23]

Love enables reason to be humble in its search for God, but at the same time does not humiliate it. There is thus a world of difference between the purification which God's love offers to the mind and heart in its search for God, and the annihilation of the human faculties proposed by Eastern religions like Buddhism. Divine love provides a conversion and healing of human reason. Love also needs to be guided by reason, lest it be blind.

Divine Rationality

The overall framework of our considerations on the mystery of reason and its healing by divine love must centre on Christ. He is the divine Physician who heals all the ills of the mind and the heart. He it is who refocuses the unity between the mind and heart which was lost through the Fall, and which is damaged through personal sins. At one particular stage in the Church's history, there developed the devotion to the Sacred Heart of Jesus. Worship is rightly paid to His Heart of flesh, inasmuch as it symbolises and recalls the love of Jesus. Thus, although rightly directed to the material Heart, adoration does not stop there: it also includes love, that love which is its principal object, but which it reaches only in and through the Heart of flesh, the sign and symbol of this love. Devotion to the Sacred Heart already existed in the eleventh and twelfth centuries, where the wound in the Heart of Christ symbolised the wound of love. St Bonaventure was one of the medieval writers who dealt with the theology of the Sacred Heart.[24] However, it was during the period when Jansenism had turned cold the sense of God's love, that the devotion really developed as an antidote to this heresy and its effects, proposing the Heart of Jesus as the universal symbol of love. Devotion to the Heart of Jesus is a recognition of that love which is central to the Christian faith: 'The Sacred Heart is ... quite rightly considered the chief sign and symbol of that love with which the divine Redeemer continually loves the eternal Father and all human beings without exception.'[25]

Now it could well be asked whether the human mind needs a similar healing from the coldness of rationalism by means of the parallel devotion to the Sacred Head of Jesus, which could be seen as a complement to devotion to the Sacred Heart. Devotion to Our Lord's Sacred Head already existed in the medieval hymn, attributed to St Bernard:

> O sacred Head ill-uséd,
> by reed and bramble scarred,
> that idle blows have bruiséd,
> and mocking lips have marred,
> how dimmed that eye so tender,
> how wan those cheeks appear,
> how overcast the splendour,
> that angel hosts revere.[26]

In possibly the earliest text which forges this link, St Bridget of Sweden (1303–1373) closely associated a devotion to the Sacred Heart of Jesus with a veneration of His Sacred Head. She prayed to Christ as Head of all men and angels, and universal King, whose Head was crowned with thorns, and whose Heart is praised by all creatures in heaven and on earth.[27]

The devotion was present in one part of Austria in the nineteenth and twentieth centuries.[28] It was also spread in England around the same time by the Venerable Teresa Higginson (1844–1905), a Catholic school-teacher. She received a private revelation from Christ to make known that His Sacred Head be worshipped as the Seat of Divine Wisdom, to atone for a period of extraordinary intellectual pride and apostasy, and at the same time to be the healing antidote for that intellectual pride.[29] The essential content of this devotion can be summed up in Teresa's own words:

> I was considering the excessive love of the Sacred Heart and offering to my Divine Spouse this same love to make amends for our coldness, and His constancy and infinite riches to make up for our poverty and misery, when our divine Lord suddenly represented to me the Divinity as a very large bright crystal stone in which all things are reflected or are, past, present and to come, in such a manner that all things are present to Him. This immense precious stone sent forth streams of richly coloured lights brighter beyond comparison than ten thousand suns, which I understood represented the infinite attributes of God. This great jewel also seemed to be covered with innumerable eyes which I understood represented the Wisdom and Knowledge of God .... Our Blessed Lord showed me this Divine Wisdom as the guiding power which regulated the motions and affections of the Sacred Heart, showing me that it had the same effect and power over its least action, and raising it, as the sun draws up the vapour from the ocean. He gave me to understand that an especial devotion and veneration should be paid to the Sacred Head of Our Lord as the Seat of divine Wisdom and guiding

power of the Sacred Heart, and so complete this heavenly devotion.[30]

Teresa clarified how this devotion would be the completion of devotion to the Sacred Heart. Devotion to the Sacred Head of Christ is an expression of adoration towards the Wisdom of the Father and of the Love of God revealed in the Light which shines in the darkness and enlightens every person coming into this world. Specifically the adoration of the Sacred Head of Our Lord is directed to the Seat of Divine Wisdom, for the Head of Christ is the sanctuary of the powers of His Soul and the faculties of His Mind and in these the Wisdom which guided every affection of the Sacred Heart and the motions of the whole Being of Jesus our Lord and God. This devotion does not separate the attributes of His Soul or Mind, or of the divine Wisdom which guided, governed and directed all in Christ, true God and true Man, but gathers them all together to be specially honoured, with His sacred Head adored as their Temple. Just as the head is also the centre of all the senses of the body, and so also this devotion is the completion, not only of the devotion of the Sacred Heart, but the crowning and perfection of all devotions.[31]

Furthermore devotion to the Sacred Head of Jesus would constitute the atonement for and the antidote to man's intellectual pride in this modern era. Man outrages the divine Wisdom by the abuse of the powers of his mind and by his sins, thus tending to erase the image of the triune God in himself. Also by wild folly, man tries also to rob creation of its God. If the sun be taken away we cannot have light or heat. If faith, the light of the soul, is taken away, then humanity suffers decay and desolation. Purely worldly wisdom which is in fact folly has, since the Enlightenment, drawn people into an abyss of darkness which is Hell. In the past, when the heart of man set his affections against God, the Sacred Heart of Jesus really human yet divine, because united to the Person of God the

Son was the atoning object and Jesus revealed the burning love of His Sacred Heart and complained of man's coldness and demanded a reparation, and souls were warmed in that furnace of divine love and souls burned again with charity towards the God of Love. In this period of history, when infidelity, pride of intellect and open rebellion against God and His revealed law, are filling the minds of people and drawing them away from the sweet yoke of Jesus and binding them with the cold heavy chains of self-seeking private judgement, they abandon all desire to be governed and wish to govern themselves in disobedience to God and to His holy Church. In the face of this need for spiritual healing, Jesus the incarnate Word, the Wisdom of the Father who became obedient even unto death on the Cross, again offers an antidote, an object which can and does, and will in every way make up and repay a hundredfold the debt that is contracted to the infinite justice of God.[32]

Christ gives an organic, harmonious and synthetic meaning to all the syllables, words and works of creation and history, for in the Incarnation He sums up in Himself the entire history of salvation, humanity and all creation.[33] He is the eternal and universal King who recapitulates all things in Himself, all things in heaven and on earth.[34] It is through Christ that the mystery of reason finds its true meaning and deeper purpose because He took man into Himself and in Him the invisible 'became visible, the incomprehensible became comprehensible, the impassible became passible, the Word became man. He recapitulated all things in Himself, so that, just as the Word of God has primacy over heavenly, spiritual and invisible beings, so He does over visible and corporeal beings. Assuming this primacy in Himself and giving Himself as Head to the Church, He draws all things to Himself.'[35] This coming together of all being in Christ, the centre of time and space, gradually takes place in history, as the obstacles, the resistance of sin and the Evil One, are overcome.[36] Christ revealed God to man, and presents man to God. At the same time, He preserved the invisibility of the Father, lest man should despise God through over-familiarity, and so that he should always possess something and yet have to work towards it. On the other hand, Christ really manifested God to men, lest man, falling away from God altogether, should cease to exist. For the glory of God is the living person; and the life of man and woman consists in beholding God. For if the manifestation of God which is made by means of the creation, gives life to all those living on the earth, much more does that revelation of the Father which comes through the Word, give life to those who see God.[37] Thus, in Christ, any fragmentation between faith and reason is overcome, and any opposition between knowing and loving is healed and transfigured. In this earthly life, the healing of mind and heart is given to us through Christ in the Eucharist,[38] in the gift of His Body and Blood, which recreates us until we see Father, Son and Holy Spirit face to face in the fullness of the Beatific Vision, which perfects all natural and supernatural knowledge and love which we have as pilgrims in this present passing world.

Notes

1 See J. L. McKenzie, 'Aspects of Old Testament Thought' in R. E. Brown, J. A. Fitzmeyer, R. E. Murphy (eds.) *The New Jerome Biblical Commentary* (London: Geoffrey Chapman, 2000), p. 1295.

2 See St Thomas Aquinas, *De Veritate*, q. 14, a. 1; *Summa Theologiae*, II–II, q. 2, a. 1; ibid., q. 4, a. 1. See pp. 95–97, 232–234 above.

3 Pius XII, Encyclical *Humani Generis* 33.

4 C. S. Lewis, *Mere Christianity* (New York: MacMillan, 1958), p. 120.

5 See St Thomas Aquinas, *Summa Theologiae* I, q. 60, a. 1: 'nihil amatur nisi cognitum.' See St Augustine, *De Trinitate*, Book 8, chapter 4 in *PL* 42, 951; Book 10, chapter 1 in *PL* 42, 971–974; Book 10, chapter 2 in *PL* 42, 974–975. See especially Book 10, chapter 2, 4 where St Augustine wrote: 'No studious person, then, no inquisitive person, loves things he does not know, even while he is urgent with the most vehement desire to know what he does not know. For he either knows already generically what he loves, and longs to know it also in some individual or individuals, which perhaps are

praised, but not yet known to him; and he pictures in his mind an imaginary form by which he may be stirred to love. And whence does he picture this, except from those things which he has already known? And yet perhaps he will not love it, if he find that form which was praised to be unlike that other form which was figured and in thought most fully known to his mind. And if he has loved it, he will begin to love it from that time when he learned it; since a little before, that form which was loved was other than that which the mind that formed it had been wont to exhibit to itself. But if he shall find it similar to that form which report had proclaimed, and to be such that he could truly say I was already loving thee; yet certainly not even then did he love a form he did not know, since he had known it in that likeness. Or else we see somewhat in the species of the eternal reason, and therein love it; and when this is manifested in some image of a temporal thing, and we believe the praises of those who have made trial of it, and so love it, then we do not love anything unknown, according to that which we have already sufficiently discussed above. Or else, again, we love something known, and on account of it seek something unknown; and so it is by no means the love of the thing unknown that possesses us, but the love of the thing known, to which we know the unknown thing belongs, so that we know that too which we seek still as unknown; as a little before I said of an unknown word. Or else, again, everyone loves the very knowing itself, as no one can fail to know who desires to know anything. For these reasons they seem to love things unknown who wish to know anything which they do not know, and who, on account of their vehement desire of inquiry, cannot be said to be without love. But how different the case really is, and that nothing at all can be loved which is not known, I think I must have persuaded everyone who carefully looks upon truth. But since the examples which we have given belong to those who desire to know something which they themselves are not, we must take thought lest perchance some new notion appear, when the mind desires to know itself.'

The formulation later became *Nihil volitum nisi precognitum.* See G. O'Collins, *Fundamental Theology* (London: Darton, Longman and Todd, 1981) p. 148.

6   St Augustine, *De Trinitate*, Book 8, chapter 4, n. 6 in *PL* 42, 951.
7   See O'Collins, *Fundamental Theology*, p. 148. The Latin formulation became *Nihil cognitum nisi prevolitum.*
8   St Augustine, *Confessions*, Book 13, chapter 9 in *PL* 32, 849. The Latin phrase is 'Pondus meum, amor meus; eo feror, quocumque feror.'
9   St Thomas Aquinas, *Commentary on Book 3 of the Sentences*, d. 35, q. 1, a. 2. The Latin expression is 'Ubi amor, ibi oculus.'
10   St Augustine, *Tractatus xxix in Joannem*, 6 in *PL* 35, 1631: 'Quid est

ergo credere in eum? Credendo amare, credendo diligere, credendo in eum ire, et ejus membris incorporari. Ipsa est ergo fides quam de nobis exigit Deus: et non invenit quod exigat, nisi donaverit quod inveniat.'

11   See William of St Thierry, *De natura et dignitate amoris*, 5 in Guglielmo di Saint-Thierry, *Opere* 3 (Rome: Città Nuova, 1998), pp. 69–70. See St Augustine, *De Trinitate* Book X, chapter 2, 17–19 in *PL* 42, 982–984.

12   See William of St Thierry, *De natura et dignitate amoris*, 25 in Guglielmo di Saint-Thierry, *Opere* 3, pp. 90. The concepts of the positive way and the negative way have been dealt with in chapter 1, pp. 21–22 above.

13   See William of St Thierry, *De natura et dignitate amoris*, 25 in Guglielmo di Saint-Thierry, *Opere* 3, pp. 90–91.

14   St Bonaventure, *The Journey of the Mind to God*, chapter 7, nn. 1, 2, 4, 6 in St Bonaventure, *Opera Omnia*, vol. 5 (Quaracchi: Collegio San Bonaventura, 1891), pp. 312–313.

15   St Francis de Sales, *Treatise on the Love of God*, Book 1, chapter 16. Translated with notes by J. K. Ryan, (Rockford: Tan, 1974) p. 93.

16   Ibid., p. 94.

17   See ibid., pp. 94–95, where St Francis de Sales uses a pretty image from nature to illustrate his point: 'Among partridges it often happens that certain of them steal the eggs of others so that they may hatch them out, being moved either by their avidity to become mothers or by a stupidity that causes them to be mistaken as to their own eggs. Then follows a strange but well-established fact. As soon as the partridge that was hatched out and nourished under the wings of the strange hen hears the first call of its true mother, which had laid the egg from which it came, it leaves the thieving partridge, returns to the first mother, and joins itself to her brood. This is because of the correspondence it had with its first origin, although this correspondence did not show openly but remained hidden, shut up and asleep as it were at the bottom of its nature until it met with its object. Then, immediately aroused and as if awakened, it does its work and impels the young partridge's appetite to its first duty. It is the same with our heart. Although it may be fashioned, nourished and brought up among corporeal, base and transitory things, and so to speak under nature's wings, yet at the first glance it casts on God, at the first knowledge that it gets of Him, that natural and initial inclination to love God, which was as though drowsy and imperceptible, awakens in an instant. Suddenly it appears like a spark from among the ashes. It touches our will and gives to it a glow of that supreme love owed to the sovereign and first principle of all things.'

18   Ibid., Book 1, chapter 17, p. 95.

19   Ibid., p. 97.

20   Ibid.

21   Ibid., Book 1, chapter 18, p. 97–99.

22   B. Pascal, *Pensées* translated by W. F. Trotter (New York: E. P. Dutton, 1958), # 282.

23   St John of the Cross, *Dark Night of the Soul*, Book II, chapter 21, 11.

24   See St Bonaventure, *Lignum vitae*, 29–30, 47 in St Bonaventure, *Opera Omnia* vol. 8 (Quaracchi: Collegio San Bonaventura, 1898), pp. 79–80, 85.

25   CCC 478.

26   The translation is by Ronald Knox. The original Latin runs:
    Salve, caput cruentatum,
    Totum spinis coronatum,
    Conquassatum, vulneratum,
    Arundine verberatum,
    Facie sputis illita.

    Salve, cuius dulcis vultus,
    Immutatus et incultus,
    Immutavit suum florem,
    Totus versus in pallorem
    Quem coeli tremit curia.

27   See the following texts in a prayer attributed to St Bridget, in Bridget of Sweden, *Revelaciones* ed. B. Bergh and S. Eklund (Uppsala: Almqvist and Wiksells, 1977–1992) Book 12, 'Four Prayers', Prayer 3, line 66: 'Domine mi Ihesu Christe, tu vere es caput omnium hominum et angelorum et dignus rex regum et dominus dominancium, qui omnia opera facis ex vera et ineffabili caritate. Et quia caput tuum benedictum corona spinea coronari humiliter permisisti, idcirco caput et capilli tui benedicti sint et honorentur gloriose dyademate imperiali celumque et terra et mare et omnia, que creata sunt, in eternum tue subiaceant et obediant potestati. Amen.' Also *ibid.*, line 77: 'Domine mi Ihesu Christe, quia benedictum cor tuum regale et magnificum numquam tormentis nec terroribus seu blandiciis flecti potuit a defensione regni tui veritatis et iusticie nec tuo sanguini dignissimo in aliquo pepercisti sed magnifico corde pro iusticia et lege fideliter decertasti legisque precepta et perfeccionis consilia amicis et inimicis tuis intrepide predicasti et pro defensione ipsorum cum tuis sanctis sequacibus moriendo in prelio victoriam obtinuisti, idcirco dignum est, vt inuictum cor tuum in celo et in terra semper magnificetur et a cunctis creaturis et militibus triumphali honore incessanter laudetur. Amen.'

28   In particular, the devotion existed in Klagenfurt, Austria, where an

image of the Sacred Head of Christ was venerated after a miracle. See J. Maier, *Des heiliges Hauptes Mahnung und Trost* (Klagenfurt: Konrad Walcher, 1917) and G. Baumann, 'Iconographische Betrachtung zum «Heiligen Haupt zu Klagenfurt». Ein volksbarockes Andachtsbild als Erbe alter europäischer Bildtraditionen.' In *Unvergängliches Kärnten. Beitrage zur Heitmatkundige Kärntens. Die Kärntner Landsmannschaft* (10/1976) pp. 57–71.

29   It should be pointed out that the devotion to the Sacred Head of Our Lord does not yet enjoy the full approval of Church authorities. Nevertheless, at least one Archbishop of Liverpool had placed the imprimatur on the litany of the Sacred Head. The cause for the Beatification of the Venerable Teresa Higginson was sent to Rome in 1935, but the case was shelved in 1938, apparently because of her promotion of a devotion not authorised by the Church.

30   C. Kerr, *Teresa Helena Higginson* (London: Sands and Company, 1927) p. 104.

31   Cf. Ibid., pp. 105–106.

32   Cf. Ibid., pp. 131–132. The theology of the devotion is expressed also in the Litany which we reproduce here:

Litany to the Sacred Head of Jesus

Lord have mercy on us

Christ have mercy on us

Lord have mercy on us

Christ hear us

God the Father of heaven

God the Son, Redeemer of the world

God the Holy Spirit

Holy Trinity, One God

Lord have mercy on us

Christ have mercy on us

Lord have mercy on us

Christ graciously hear us

have mercy on us

have mercy on us

have mercy on us

have mercy on us

Sacred Head of Jesus **Formed by the Holy Spirit in the womb of the Blessed Virgin Mary,**
Guide us in all our ways

Sacred Head of Jesus **Substantially united to the Word of God**
Guide us in all our ways

Sacred Head of Jesus **Temple of Divine Wisdom**
Guide us in all our ways

Sacred Head of Jesus **Hearth of eternal clarities**
Guide us in all our ways

Sacred Head of Jesus **Sanctuary of infinite intelligence**
Guide us in all our ways

Sacred Head of Jesus **Providence against error**
Guide us in all our ways

Sacred Head of Jesus **Sun of heaven and earth**
Guide us in all our ways

Sacred Head of Jesus **Treasure of science and pledge of faith**
Guide us in all our ways

Sacred Head of Jesus **Beaming with beauty, justice and love**
Guide us in all our ways

Sacred Head of Jesus **Full of grace and truth**
Guide us in all our ways

Sacred Head of Jesus **Living lesson of humility**
Guide us in all our ways

Sacred Head of Jesus **Reflection of God's infinite majesty**
Guide us in all our ways

Sacred Head of Jesus **Object of the delights of the heavenly Father**
Guide us in all our ways

Sacred Head of Jesus **Who received the caresses of the Blessed Virgin Mary**
Guide us in all our ways

Sacred Head of Jesus **On whom the Holy Spirit reposed**
Guide us in all our ways

Sacred Head of Jesus **Who allowed a reflection of Thy Glory to shine on Tabor**
Guide us in all our ways

Sacred Head of Jesus **Who had no place on earth to lay**
Guide us in all our ways

Sacred Head of Jesus **To whom the perfumed ointment of Magdalen was pleasing**
Guide us in all our ways

Sacred Head of Jesus **Who deigned to tell Simon that he did not anoint Thy Head when Thou entered his house**
Guide us in all our ways

Sacred Head of Jesus **Bathed in a sweat of blood in Gethsemane**
Guide us in all our ways

Sacred Head of Jesus **Who wept over our sins**
Guide us in all our ways

Sacred Head of Jesus **Crowned with thorns**
Guide us in all our ways

Sacred Head of Jesus **Disgracefully outraged during the passion**
Guide us in all our ways

Sacred Head of Jesus **Consoled by the loving gesture of Veronica**
Guide us in all our ways

Sacred Head of Jesus **Which thou inclined towards the earth at the moment Thou saved us by the separation of Thy Soul from Thy Body on the cross**
Guide us in all our ways

Sacred Head of Jesus **Light of every man coming into this world**
> Guide us in all our ways

Sacred Head of Jesus **Our Guide and our Hope**
> Guide us in all our ways

Sacred Head of Jesus **Who knows all our needs**
> Guide us in all our ways

Sacred Head of Jesus **Who dispenses all graces**
> Guide us in all our ways

Sacred Head of Jesus **Who directs the movements of the Divine Heart**
> Guide us in all our ways

Sacred Head of Jesus **Who governs the world**
> Guide us in all our ways

Sacred Head of Jesus **Who will judge all our actions**
> Guide us in all our ways

Sacred Head of Jesus **Who knows the secrets of our hearts**
> Guide us in all our ways

Sacred Head of Jesus **That we want to make known and adored by the whole world**
> Guide us in all our ways

Sacred Head of Jesus **Who ravishes the angels and the saints**
> Guide us in all our ways

Sacred Head of Jesus **That we hope to contemplate one day, unveiled**
> Guide us in all our ways

V. We adore Thy Sacred Head , O Jesus,
R. And we submit ourselves to all the decrees of Thine infinite Wisdom.

[33] See Pope John Paul II, *Discourse at General Audience* 1, 14 February 2001.

[34] See Eph 1: 10 and St Irenaeus, *Adversus haereses*, Book III, chapter 21, n. 9 in *PG* 7, 954.

[35] St Irenaeus, *Adversus haereses*, Book III, chapter 16, n. 6 in *PG* 7, 925–926.

[36] See Pope John Paul II, *Discourse at General Audience* 2, 14 February 2001.

[37] See St Irenaeus, *Adversus haereses*, Book IV, chapter 20, n. 7 in *PG* 7, 1037.

[38] One of the earliest descriptions of this effect of the Eucharist is found in St Irenaeus, *Adversus haereses*, Book V, Chapter 2, nn. 2–3 in *PG* 7, 1125–1128: 'And as we are His members, we are also nourished by means of the creation, and He Himself grants the creation to us, for He causes His sun to rise, and sends rain when He wills. He has acknowledged the cup which is a part of the creation as His

own blood, from which He bedews our blood; and the bread (also a part of the creation) He has established as His own body, from which He gives increase to our bodies. When, therefore, the mingled cup and the manufactured bread receives the Word of God, and the Eucharist of the blood and the body of Christ is made, from which the substance of our flesh is increased and supported, how can they [i.e. the Gnostics] affirm that the flesh is incapable of receiving the gift of God, which is life eternal.... Just as a cutting from the vine planted in the ground fructifies in its season, or as a grain of wheat falling into the earth and becoming decomposed, rises with manifold increase by the Spirit of God, who contains all things, and then, through the wisdom of God, serves for the use of men, and having received the Word of God, becomes the Eucharist, which is the body and blood of Christ; so also our bodies, being nourished by it, and deposited in the earth, and suffering decomposition there, shall rise at their appointed time, the Word of God granting them resurrection to the glory of God, even the Father, who freely gives to this mortal immortality, and to this corruptible being incorruption. The strength of God is made perfect in weakness, in order that we may never become proud, as if we had life from ourselves, and exalted against God, our minds becoming ungrateful; but learning by experience that we possess eternal duration from the excelling power of this Being, not from our own nature, we may neither undervalue that glory which surrounds God as He is, nor be ignorant of our own nature, but that we may know what God can bring about, and what benefits man receives, and thus never wander from the true comprehension of things as they are, that is, both with regard to God and with regard to man.'

SELECT BIBLIOGRAPHY

POPE JOHN PAUL II, Encyclical Letter *Fides et ratio*. (Vatican City: Libreria Editrice Vaticana, 1998).

ARTIGAS, M., *The Mind of the Universe. Understanding Science and Religion*. (Philadelphia and London: Templeton Foundation Press, 2000).

BEHE, M. J., *Darwin's Black Box. The Biochemical Challenge to Evolution*. (New York: The Free Press, 1996).

BEHE, M. J., DEMBSKI, W. A. AND MEYER, S. C., *Science and Evidence for Design in the Universe*. (San Francisco: Ignatius Press, 2000).

CARREL, A., *The Voyage to Lourdes*. With an Introduction by Stanley L. Jaki. (USA: Real-View-Books, 1994).

D'ARCY, M. C., *The Mind and Heart of Love*. (London: Faber and Faber, 1946).

GILSON, E., *Methodical Realism*. Translated by P. Trower. (Front Royal, VA: Christendom Press, 1990).

HAFFNER, P., *Creation and Scientific Creativity. A Study in the Thought of S.L. Jaki* (Front Royal, VA: Christendom Press, 1991).

HAFFNER, P., *Mystery of Creation* (Leominster: Gracewing, 1995).

MCINERNY, R. M., *Aquinas and Analogy* (Washington, D.C.: The Catholic University of America Press, 1996).

JAKI, S. L., *The Road of Science and The Ways to God* (Edinburgh: Scottish Academic Press, 1978).

JAKI, S. L., *Science and Creation: From Eternal Cycles to an Oscillating Universe* (Edinburgh: Scottish Academic Press, [2]1986).

JAKI, S. L., *Means to Message. A Treatise on Truth* (Grand Rapids: Eerdmans, 1999).

PLANTINGA, A., *Faith and philosophy. Philosophical studies in religion and ethics* (Grand Rapids: Eerdmans, 1964).

PLANTINGA, A., *God and Other Minds. A study of the rational justification of belief in God* (Ithaca: Cornell University Press, 1969).

SWINBURNE, R., *The coherence of Theism* (Oxford: Clarendon Press, 1977).

SWINBURNE, R., *The existence of God* (Oxford: Clarendon Press, 1979).

SWINBURNE, R., *Faith and Reason* (Oxford: Clarendon Press, 1981).

SWINBURNE, R., *Is there a God?* (Oxford: Oxford University Press, 1996).

STANNARD, R., *The God Experiment: Can Science Prove the Existence of God?* (Mahweh, NJ: Hidden-Spring, 1999).

INDEX